# FESTIVAL ESSAYS FOR PAULINE ALDERMAN

Pauline Alderman, 1975

# FESTIVAL ESSAYS FOR PAULINE ALDERMAN

## A Musicological Tribute

*Editor*

Burton L. Karson

*Associate Editors*

Joan Meggett, Eleanor Russell, and Halsey Stevens

Brigham Young University Press

Library of Congress Cataloging in Publication Data
Main entry under title:

Festival essays for Pauline Alderman.

CONTENTS: Mathiesen, T. J.   Problems of terminology
in ancient Greek theory:  APMONIA.—Wingell, R. J.
Hucbald of St. Amans and Carolingian music theory—
Hultberg, W. E.   Diego Pisador's Libro de musica de
vihuela (1552). [etc.]
    1. Alderman, Pauline, 1893-     2. Music—
Addresses, essays, lectures.  I. Karson, Burton L.
ML55.A4  1976          780          75-35963
ISBN 0-8425-0101-0

Library of Congress Catalog Card Number: 75-35963
International Standard Book Number: 0-8425-0101-0
© 1976 by Brigham Young University Press. All rights reserved
Brigham Young University Press, Provo, Utah 84602
Printed in the United States of America

76    1.5M    7050

# Contents

# Foreword

If a scholar and teacher can be measured by the products of her students and the honors proffered by her colleagues, then the present volume may serve as a testament to the success of Pauline Alderman.

The daughter of Henry H. and Edith Kelty Alderman, Pauline Alderman was born in LaFayette, Oregon, 16 January 1893. She attended public schools and graduated from Washington High School in Portland in 1911. After intermittent piano lessons, she studied seriously with Als Klingenberg and then extensively with Abby Whiteside in Portland and New York.

She took her baccalaureate at Reed College (1916) where she composed music for campus dramatic productions and at the same time studied pipe organ privately with Max Cushing. She later studied harmony with Carolyn Alchin at the University of Washington and the University of California at Berkeley. During 1923-1924 she attended the Institute of Musical Art in New York City where she worked at counterpoint and composition under Percy Goetschius. Her studies in composition continued with George McKay at the University of Washington where in 1931 she received a Master of Arts degree with a thesis titled *"Bombastes Furioso,* a study of 18th century musical style."

During 1934 to 1935 she organized and participated in a private class taught by Arnold Schoenberg in Los Angeles. In 1936 she researched the history of ballad opera at the British Museum in London, and in 1938 she was admitted to the University of Edinburgh for work toward the Doctor of Philosophy. While in Edinburgh, she studied composition with Donald Francis Tovey until continued illness terminated his active teaching. She then transferred to the University of Strasbourg for doctoral studies under the guidance of Yvonne Rokseth. There she began research on the *air de cour* and worked on musical bibliography, notation, and the history of French Renaissance music with Guillaume de Van.

The approaching war forced her return to America, a journey punctuated by several exciting adventures in northern France while she was trying to obtain passage home. Her doctorate in musicology was finally completed at the University of Southern California in 1946 with a dissertation titled "Antoine Boësset and the *Air de Cour.*" Further work in composition directed by Ernst Toch plus readings in comparative literature were included in her doctoral studies. In spring and summer of 1948 she undertook postdoctoral research at the Paris Bibliothèque Nationale, once again under the direction of Yvonne Rokseth.

Dr. Alderman's teaching career began in 1916 in McMinnville, Oregon, where she taught English literature and music in the junior high school. In 1918 she moved to Lincoln High School in Portland, and from 1920 to 1923 she taught music history and theory at Ellison White Conservatory. She instructed in piano and theory at Pomona College near Los Angeles from 1924 to 1928 and then returned north to teach music history and theory at the University of Washington.

In 1930 she was appointed Assistant Professor of Theory in the College of Music at the University of Southern California, beginning an unbroken affiliation of forty-five years. She served as Professor of Music and Chairman of the Department of Music History from 1952 until her retirement in 1960, after which she has continued to teach as Professor Emeritus. During the years 1961 to 1973, when not occupied at USC, Dr. Alderman taught at Boston University and at the University of California at Santa Barbara. She also has been visiting professor at the University of British Columbia, the University of Manitoba, Catholic University in Washington, D.C., California State University, Los Angeles, and Brigham Young University.

Numerous awards have been conferred on Dr. Alderman. In 1940 she won an ASCAP prize for her operetta, *Come on Over,* with libretto by Evelyn West. In 1950 the Society for Education by Radio pronounced NBC's "Pioneers of Music" the best educational radio program of the year; program scripts and pamphlets for use by students across the country were written by Pauline Alderman. The University of Southern California Music Alumni Association gave her its Distinguished Alumnus of the Year citation in 1961 and a Special Alumni Award in 1972. In 1973 she was honored by her USC colleagues with the Ramo Music Faculty Award, and in 1974 the Southern California Chapter of the American Musicological Society awarded her Life Membership.

Dr. Alderman was president of the Southern California Chapter of the AMS in 1954 and a member of its national council from 1954 to 1960. Other memberships include the Music Library Association,

Mu Phi Epsilon, Phi Beta Kappa, Pi Kappa Lambda, Pi Kappa Phi, the Dolmetsch Foundation, and the American Recorder Society.

Although teaching has been her primary interest, Dr. Alderman has published *Introduction to Concert Music* (1942); *Theme and Variations* (1943-1945), weekly scripts for the radio programs of the USC School of Music faculty; *Pioneers of Music* (1950); and *A Survey of Vocal Literature* (1952). She has also read papers at national and local meetings of AMS, MLA, and MENC, and has produced articles and reviews for various periodicals. She now has two new books in preparation: *A Short History of Art Song* and *We Build a School of Music,* a colorful history of USC's School of Music.

Beyond her own professional accomplishments, Dr. Alderman's most profound influence has been through her extraordinary and vital teaching. A class of musical historians at USC last year enjoyed a stalwart eighty-one-year-old as she taught a new course in Art Song of the Early Nineteenth Century. During her long career she has guided theses and dissertations to completion with the same keen and friendly advice that she continues to impart to her many graduates who occupy major teaching and research positions throughout the country.

As Dr. Alderman approached her eightieth birthday in 1973, her friends and colleagues searched for an appropriate honor and gift. A *Festschrift* by some of her former students and distinguished colleagues was enthusiastically endorsed and support was assured by the USC Music Alumni. Contributions were solicited, collected, and edited by Joan Meggett (longtime music librarian at USC), Eleanor Russell, Halsey Stevens, and myself.

She has given us more than we can ever return, but at long last, with admiration and affection, we offer these festival essays to Pauline Alderman.

Burton L. Karson<br>May 1975

# Contributors

Clifford R. Barnes—Ph.D., University of Southern California; Visiting Professor of the Performing Arts, Xavier University.

Alice Ray Catalyne—Ph.D., University of Southern California; Professor Emeritus, Los Angeles Valley College.

Martin Chusid—Ph.D., University of California, Berkeley; Professor of Music, New York University; formerly Professor of Music, University of Southern California.

Henry Leland Clarke—Ph.D., Harvard University; Professor of Music, University of Washington.

John Gillespie—Ph.D., University of Southern California; Professor of Music, University of California, Santa Barbara.

George Truett Hollis—Ph.D., University of Southern California; Professor of Music, East Los Angeles College.

Warren Earle Hultberg—Ph.D., University of Southern California; Professor of Music, State University of New York, Potsdam.

Dolores M. Hsu—Ph.D., University of Southern California; Professor of Music, University of California, Santa Barbara.

Burton L. Karson—D.M.A., University of Southern California; Professor of Music, California State University, Fullerton.

Siegmund Levarie—Ph.D., University of Vienna; Professor of Music, Brooklyn College, City University of New York; formerly Visiting Professor, University of Southern California.

Ernst Levy—Studied in his native Basel and Paris; formerly Professor of Music, Massachusetts Institute of Technology.

Thomas J. Mathiesen—D.M.A., University of Southern California; Assistant Professor of Music, Brigham Young University.

Joan Milliman—M.A., University of Southern California (Doctoral Candidate); American Association of University Women Research Scholar, Cambridge.

Paul A. Pisk—Ph.D., University of Vienna; Professor of Music (retired), University of Texas; formerly Visiting Professor, University of Southern California.

Johannes Riedel—Ph.D., University of Southern California; Professor of Music, University of Minnesota.

Eleanor Russell—Ph.D., University of Southern California; Associate Professor of Music, California State University, Northridge.

Halsey Stevens—M.M., Litt.D. (*honoris causa*), Syracuse University; Andrew W. Mellon Professor in the Humanities and Professor of Music, University of Southern California.

Pierre M. Tagmann—Ph.D., University of Bern; Associate Professor of Music, University of Southern California.

Olga Termini—Ph.D., University of Southern California; Assistant Professor of Music, California State University, Los Angeles.

Ruth Watanabe—M.M., University of Southern California; Ph.D., University of Rochester; Associate Professor of Music and Librarian of Sibley Music Library, Eastman School of Music, University of Rochester.

Sir Jack Westrup (d. 1975)—M.A., Honorary D. Mus., University of Oxford; Late Heather Professor of Music, University of Oxford; formerly Visiting Professor, University of Southern California.

Glenn C. Wilcox—Ph.D., University of Southern California; Associate Professor of Communications, Murray State University, Kentucky.

Richard J. Wingell—Ph.D., University of Southern California; Assistant Professor of Music, University of Southern California.

# PART I

# Problems of Terminology in Ancient Greek Theory: ΑΡΜΟΝΙΑ

Since the seventeenth century when interest in the musical theory of the ancient Greeks began to make itself felt among the ranks of the musicians and the philologists, confusion has existed over the meaning of certain key technical terms. Translators both of earlier times and of the present day have not directed enough attention towards establishing consistent definitions of these terms. Instead, we find many important and highly exclusive Greek terms translated by general words such as "music," or "melody," or "harmony." These translators have been joined by an enormous mass of writers working from these secondary sources and attempting to project entirely unlikely hypotheses onto the Greek theorists. Although some of these well-known hypotheses are convincing taken as isolated documents separate from the theoretical texts themselves, they mostly avoid a truly viable manipulation of the Greeks' subtle grammatical distinctions. Indeed, primary consideration has been given by students of Greek theory to discovering some overriding practical concept along the lines of the Medieval theorist's use of the Gamut, rather than to following the direction set by the important Hellenic writers themselves: namely, a treating of the phenomenon of musical sound according to the established conventions of philosophic argument and according to the new Aristotelian method of scientific investigation.

The interest in presenting purely practical manuals is a later intellectual manifestation and is *not* a part of the thinking of Plato, Aristotle, Aristoxenus, and Ps. Plutarch. Yet, the Greek theorists have always been treated as a group by scholars, and always as if they were in some way Hellenic Medievalists. Within the body of Greek theorists from Aristoxenus to Alypius there is, however, a change of approach: the early theorists are principally philosophic Pythagoreans and Aristotelians; the later theorists are principally technical practitioners.

Philosopher and practitioner alike use technical words with some degree of care, and the key to understanding their work must be a

3

knowledge of their terminology. As even the cursory examination will show, however, there has been neither any attempt to treat technical terms consistently, nor any attempt to treat the theorists within their respective schools of thought and their consequent linguistic milieu. Furthermore, and of equal gravity is the fact that the extant translations have been made from the most heavily emended texts.

So the problem is difficult but may be reduced to this: if the treatment of certain key words has been inconsistent or ungrammatical in the translations, and if the translations have been based on corrupt texts, our concept of Greek musical theory may be wholly or partly in error.

In fact, I propose that our approach to Greek music (at least of the Hellenic period) through scale systems, modes, pitch-keys, and the like, has led us along a path that neither the technical terms nor the fashion of thinking of the time will support, and that misinterprets the subtleties of the theorists. We must therefore discard at the outset our idea that Greek music (of the Hellenic period) had some modal system, that it used ten specific and different terms interchangeably, and that the major theorists such as Aristoxenus were mere authors of "Methods" rather than philosophers. Most of all, we must keep distinctly separate the theorists of the Hellenic tradition and those of the Greco-Roman tradition because, in some ways, there is a shifting of point of view. So we depart from the assumption that ἁρμονία, τρόπος, τόνος, μουσικός, μουσική, and μέλος are all vague and indistinct terms that may be used in any convenient way. In fact, each term has a distinctive meaning determined by a contextual study, and these meanings go much beyond mere musical technique. Table 1, by way of illustration, contains a few of the commonly misinterpreted words with explanations of their meanings.

## Table 1

| | |
|---|---|
| ἁρμονία | Harmonia. The divine ordering of the Universe. The goal of the musician, through which he affects the soul of the listener. Also used in the sense of "the perfect example," hence the phrase "a Dorian harmonia." |
| ἁρμονική | The Science of Harmonia. That system of principles and procedures through which harmonia is codified, and through which the abstract concept may be discussed. |
| ἁρμονικός | A Harmonicist. One who has mastered and practices the principles of ἁρμονική. Sometimes used in a derogatory fashion by the theorists to refer to one knowing all the rules and minutiae and still failing to correctly observe or imitate |

the phenomena. The term is occasionally used by the theorists in an adjectival sense where it means "embodying harmonia."

ἐναρμόνιον    Enharmonic. A purely technical term that refers to one of the three genera. Sometimes used in conjunction with μέλος , in which case it refers to the character of the noun—an enharmonic melos.

μέλος    Melos. Music* as Being, including both the production of sound and the sensing of it. An ontological term, it does not have the purely practical sense of "music," but is, like harmonia, an abstract.

μουσική    The Science of Music. One of the branches of Athenian education, it is a system of procedures and principles through which melos is treated and obtained. Melos may also be obtained without regard to the science, but this kind of melos is condemned as "lacking propriety." ἁρμονική and μουσική are similar in concept, μουσική being the more practical, ἁρμονική being the more ethical.

μουσικός    A musician. This term implies to the Greek one who has mastered and practices the principles of μουσική. The Greek "musician" is a poet as well, and to some extent every well-educated Athenian is μουσικός.

*(Music = words, melody, rhythm, gesture)

Table 2 illustrates in graphic form the hierarchical functions of these same terms.

Table 2

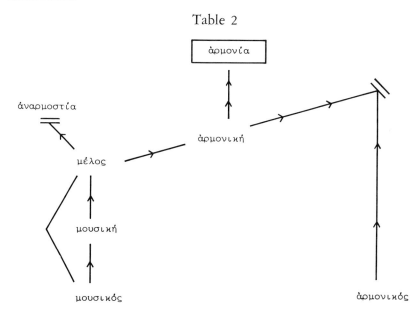

Referring to table 1, note that μέλος has the broad meaning of music as Being. It necessitates not only production of sound but also the sensing of it. Aristoxenus in Book I, section 14, speaking of motions of the voice says: "It is necessary to define each of these according to two references of production, according to the production of sound, and the discrimination of it; this is the voice and the hearing."[1] The combination of these two separate parts is μέλος. It is thus an ontological term, not a practical one. μουσική on the other hand is adjectival and implies the noun τέχνη or ἐπιστήμη. This same implication is found elsewhere in the grammarians and especially in Aristotle, Aristoxenus's teacher. So μουσική has the meaning of the Science of Music and is also understood as one of the three branches of Athenian education: μουσική, γράμματα, γυμναστική.[2] μουσικός, also adjectival, is used either in the sense "musical," that is, pertaining to the practice of μουσική, or as a substantive, "musicians," those who produce μέλος, perhaps according to μουσική. Adjectival forms built on ἁρμονία will work in the same way: ἁρμονική—the Science of Harmonia.

Referring to table 2, note the hierarchical arrangement of the terms. Thus the μουσικός plays and sings according to μουσική and the result is μέλος. If the regulation of the μουσική that produces μέλος has been managed according to ἁρμονική, the result may be ἁρμονία

This brings us to a discussion of ἁρμονία, a word of tremendous importance to every writer from Homer to Bacchius, and a word around which there has been much confusion.[3] Some circles regard it as a synonym for enharmonic genus and some as a synonym for mode; most regard it as a practical word. Yet this is a word of elemental importance to Greek theory. An examination of ἁρμονία provides an example of the contextual study of terms applied and illustrates the abstract quality of the word. In so illustrating, we will have moved some in the reevaluation of technical terms.

---

[1] Unless otherwise indicated, all translations are those of the author. There are a great many text editions and translations of the Greek theorists. For a list, see my *Bibliography of Sources for the Study of Ancient Greek Music* (Hackensack, N.J., 1974).

[2] Cf. Plato *Republic* 403C.

[3] Some interesting texts relative to ἁρμονία may be found at the following places (a selective listing): Plato *Timaeus* 34C-37, 47D, 80B, 90D; Plato *Cleitophon* 407D; Aristotle *Problems* XIX 918b 13-23; Aristoxenus *Harmonics* 1. 1, 2, 4, 5, 7, 8, 16, 17, 18, 19, 24, 25, 26, and 28; Plutarch *That Epicurus actually makes a pleasurable life impossible* 1096a; Plutarch *Concerning Music* 1133B, 1133E, 1135A-B, 1136B-C, 1136E, 1137A, 1137E, 1138A, 1138C-D, 1139B, 1139E, 1139F, 1140A, 1141B, 1141F, 1142A, 1142D, 1142F, 1143A-E, 1145A, 1145F, 1147; Sextus Empiricus *Against the Musicians* 13, 36, 37, 50, 51.

For a fundamental treatment of the question of ἁρμονία, see Bonaventura Meyer, ΑΡΜΟΝΙΑ. *Bedeutungsgeschichte des Wortes von Homer bis Aristoteles* (Zürich, 1932).

In Plato's *Timaeus* 34C-37, the so-called Timaeus scale is presented. This "scale" is significant in its illustration of the great union between the order of the Universe and the order of musical proportions.[4] Plato writes:

And he began to divide as follows:

> first he took one part from the whole;
> next he took the double of this;
> then a third part half as much again as
>    the second part and the triple of the first;
> then a fourth part twice as much as the second;
> then a fifth part three times as much as the third;
> then a sixth part the octuple of the first;
> then a seventh part the twenty-seventh multiple of the first.

This order gives the multiples of two and three, or 1, 2, 4, 8, and 1, 3, 9, 27. Next Plato shows how these large spaces are to be filled up: by the insertion of means, one of which exceeds and is exceeded by the same proportional part, and one which exceeds and is exceeded by the same integer. Here he speaks of the so-called harmonic and arithmetic mean. The harmonic mean is based on exceeding and being exceeded by the same proportion of each extreme, or 8 is to 6 as 12 is to 8; the arithmetic mean is based on exceeding and being exceeded by the same number, or 9 is to 6 as 12 is to 9. If 12 and 6 represent the higher and lower notes of an octave $(2:1)$, we can see at once that the harmonic and arithmetic means are the sesquialteran and sesquitertian ratios—3:2 and 4:3—or the fifth and the fourth. In addition, the above excerpt tacitly shows that music is sublime because it alone, through its proportional makeup, is a physical manifestation of that order of the Universe. This correct and satisfying organization is referred to at the end of the section as ἁρμονία.

Excerpt 1

Plato—*Timaeus* 36E-37

| | |
|---|---|
| ἡ δ' ἐκ μέσου πρὸς τὸν ἔσχατον οὐρανὸν πάντη διαπλακεῖσα κύκλῳ τε αὐτὸν ἔξωθεν περικαλύψασα, αὐτή τε ἐν αὐτῇ στρεφομένη, θείαν ἀρχὴν | And the soul, being entirely woven from the middle to the outermost heaven, and being surrounded by a circle from without, and herself revolving within herself, began a divine beginning of never-ending and sen- |

[4]For a provocative discussion of this work, see F. M. Cornford, *Plato's Cosmology. The Timaeus* of Plato translated with running commentary (London, 1937; reprint 1971). Additional points of interest may be found in Jacques Handschin, "The Timaeus Scale," *Musica disciplina* 4 (1950): 3-42.

ἤρξατο ἀπαύστου καὶ ἔμφρονος βίου       sible life through all time. And
πρὸς τὸν ξύμπαντα χρόνον. καὶ τὸ        whereas the body of heaven is visible,
                                        so is the soul invisible, but partakes
μὲν δὴ σῶμα ὁρατὸν οὐρανοῦ γέγονεν,     of reasoning and *harmonia* . . . .
αὐτὴ δὲ ἀόρατος μέν, λογισμοῦ δὲ
μετέχουσα καὶ ἁρμονίας ψυχή, . . .

In Plato's *Timaeus* 47C-E, there is further definition of the term, specifically in relation to music.

### Excerpt 2
### Plato—*Timaeus* 47C-E

Φωνῆς τε δὴ καὶ ἀκοῆς πέρι πάλιν       Concerning sound and hearing, [we
ὁ αὐτὸς λόγος, ἐπὶ ταὐτὰ τῶν αὐτῶν     say] the same thing again, they were
                                       given by the gods for the same rea-
ἕνεκα παρὰ θεῶν δεδωρῆσθαι. λόγος      sons. For these purposes speech was
τε γὰρ ἐπ' αὐτὰ ταῦτα τέτακται,        arranged and makes a great contri-
                                       bution to them; also the *Science of*
μεγίστην ξυμβαλλόμενος εἰς αὐτὰ         *Music,* as it uses audible sound, is
μοῖραν, ὅσον τ'αὖ μουσικῆς φωνῇ        given for *harmonia.* And *harmonia,*
χρηστικὸν πρὸς ἀκοὴν ἕνεκα ἁρμονίας    which has motions like the turning of
                                       the soul within us, was given by the
ἐστὶ δοθέν· ἡ δὲ ἁρμονία, ξυγγενεῖς    Muses to him who uses the Muses
ἔχουσα φορὰς ταῖς ἐν ἡμῖν τῆς ψυχῆς    with intelligence, not for non-rational
περιόδοις, τῷ μετὰ νοῦ προσχρωμένῳ     pleasure, as is done now, but as an
                                       aid to bring the *anharmonious* revo-
Μούσαις οὐκ ἐφ' ἡδονὴν ἄλογον,         lution of the soul within us into order
καθάπερ νῦν, εἶναι δοκεῖ χρήσιμος,     and concord with itself; and rhythm
                                       also, because of the lack of measure
ἀλλ' ἐπὶ τὴν γεγονυῖαν ἐν ἡμῖν ἀνάρ-   and deficiency of grace in most of us,
μοστον ψυχῆς περίοδον εἰς κατακόσμη-   was given as a helper by the same
                                       gods for the same purposes.
σιν καὶ συμφωνίαν ἑαυτῇ ξύμμαχος ὑπὸ
Μουσῶν δέδοται· καὶ ῥυθμὸς αὖ διὰ
τὴν ἄμετρον ἐν ἡμῖν καὶ χαρίτων ἐπι-
δεᾶ γιγνομένην ἐν τοῖς πλείστοις ἕξ-
ιν ἐπίκουρος ἐπὶ ταῦτα ὑπὸ τῶν αὐτῶν
ἐδόθη.

Here illustrated is the importance of the combination of sound and hearing, implying μέλος. Plato states that μουσική, when applied audibly, may produce ἁρμονία and further notes that ἁρμονία in music reestablishes in the soul the unvariable revolutions (or propor-

tions) of the Universe. This implies purely proportional and satisfying qualities in music. Plato, of course, condemns the thought that
music is an irrational pleasure and makes a double entendre. The
sense is both ethical and practical.[5] Aristoxenus also discusses this
practical aspect of using intervals that are not in keeping with ἁρμονία
because they are not an outgrowth of the unvarying proportions of the
Universe.[6] They are therefore not able to restore the variable proportions within our own soul.

In *Timaeus* 80B a verbalization of the tacit implication of *Timaeus*
34C-37 is made: namely that music is the physical manifestation of
divine order.

### Excerpt 3
### Plato—*Timaeus* 80B

. . . ἀπoληγoύσης δὲ ὁμοιότητα
πρoσάψαντες μίαν ἐξ ὀξείας καὶ βα-
ρείας ξυνεκεράσαντο πάθην, ὅθεν
ἡδoνὴν μὲν τoῖς ἄφρoσιν, εὐφρoσύνην
δὲ τoῖς ἔμφρoσι διὰ τὴν τῆς θείας
ἁρμoνίας μίμησιν ἐν θνηταῖς γενoμέ-
νην φoραῖς παρέσχoν.

And so they blend and run together
as one single sensation from high and
low pitches, giving pleasure to the
unintelligent, and to the intelligent a
delight through the imitation of divine *harmonia* by mortal motions.

The interesting point is made here that ἁρμονία has the power to
furnish pleasure even though the hearer may not be able to sense its
presence. To the intelligent, the perfect "harmonic" quality gives delight and proportion. If ἁρμονία were merely a proportional abstract, it could not be assumed that the unintelligent would be affected. Perhaps ἁρμονία is something more than a physical manifestation of universal order. One last excerpt will serve to further
clarify Plato's concept of this term.

In *Timaeus* 90D is found a further illustration that ἁρμονία re-
stores the proportional order within ourselves.

### Excerpt 4
### Plato—*Timaeus* 90D

τῷ δ'ἐν ἡμῖν θείῳ ξυγγενεῖς εἰσι
κινήσεις αἱ τoῦ παντὸς διανoήσεις
καὶ περιφoραί. ταύταις δὴ ξυνεπό-

For the divine part within us, the
favorable motions are the thoughts
and revolutions of the Universe. It is
necessary that each follow these, recti-

---

[5]For an examination of the Greeks and irrationality, see E. R. Dodds, *The Greeks
and the Irrational* (Berkeley, California, 1951).
[6]Aristoxenus *Harmonics* 1. 16.

μενον ἕκαστον δεῖ, τὰς περὶ τὴν γέ-
νεσιν ἐν τῇ κεφαλῇ διεφθαρμένας
ἡμῶν περιόδους ἐξορθοῦντα διὰ τὸ
καταμανθάνειν τὰς τοῦ παντὸς ἀρμο-
νίας τε καὶ περιφοράς, τῷ κατανοου-
μένῳ τὸ κατανοοῦν ἐξομοιῶσαι κατὰ
τὴν ἀρχαίαν φύσιν, ὁμοιώσαντα δὲ
τέλος ἔχειν τοῦ προτεθέντος ἀνθρώ-
ποις ὑπὸ θεῶν ἀρίστου βίου πρός τε
τὸν παρόντα καὶ τὸν ἔπειτα χρόνον.

fying the corrupted revolutions in our head, there since birth, by learning the *harmonia* and revolutions of the Universe, making the part that thinks like the object of the thought according to its old nature, and having achieved the likeness, gain the end of life set before men by the gods as good for the present and for the future.

It seems clear that to Plato this is the primary meaning of the term. Yet when Aristoxenus applies this concept to music, its scope is somewhat enlarged. Plato was not a musician, but his influence on Aristoxenus is very marked.

Before reaching Aristoxenus, one example from Aristotle bears consideration. In *Problem* XIX 918b (Although probably a later compilation, the *Problems* undoubtedly contain Aristotelian material.) is a discussion of many things musical, but of special interest is this one sentence.

### Excerpt 5
### Aristotle—*Problem XIX* 918b

αἴτιον δὲ ὅτι τὸ παλαιὸν οἱ ἐλεύ-
θεροι ἐχόρευον αὐτοί· πολλοὺς οὖν
ἀγωνιστικῶς ᾄδειν χαλεπὸν ἦν, ὥστε
ἐναρμόνια μέλη ἐνῇδον.

The reason is that in old times the free citizens made up the chorus; now it was hard for many to sing [together] dramatically, so they sang in the *enharmonic melos.*

Here a variant word is discovered, based on the same root, but with a slightly different meaning. The word, ἐναρμόνια is joined with μέλη. ἐναρμόνιον is a term normally used to denote a particular genus of tetrachord, the enharmonic. It is frequently substantive, implying γένος. Here, however, it agrees with μέλη and specifically indicates a μέλος that has an enharmonic *character* because of its organization. Yet in one standard edition the sentence is translated: "The reason is that in the old days free citizens acted in the choruses; hence it was difficult for a number to sing together like professional artists, so that they performed their songs in the enharmonic scale."[7]

---

[7]Aristotle *Problems* I-XXI, translated by W. S. Hett, Loeb Classical Library, 316 (Cambridge, Mass., 1970), p. 387.

μέλος is much more than a scale. The larger implication of the combination is missed and the technical terms are misinterpreted.

In any discussion of the musical theorists themselves, Aristoxenus is paramount. The fragments from what appears to be the first book of his musical treatise contain a wealth of speculative information relative to the nature of μέλος, to what sort of μέλος exhibits ἁρμονία, and to range and character of singing.

Harmonics 1. 2. 8-17 shows Aristoxenus's characteristic use of terms. ἁρμονία is used in conjunction with σύστημα (a scale) emphasizing that the two words are by no means interchangeable. ἁρμονικός appears here as a substantive, in the same way as μουσικός appears in table 1. The meaning in this case is "A Harmonicist," or one who practices the proportional sciences.

Excerpt 6

Aristoxenus—*Harmonics* 1. 2. 8-17

τοὺς μὲν οὖν ἔμπροσθεν ἁρμονικοὺς
εἶναι βούλεσθαι μόνον, αὐτῆς γὰρ
τῆς ἁρμονίας ἥπτοντο μόνον, τῶν δ'
ἄλλων γενῶν οὐδεμίαν πώποτ' ἔννοιαν
5 εἶχον. σημεῖον δέ· τὰ γὰρ διαγράμματα αὐτοῖς τῶν ἁρμονιῶν ἔκκειται
μόνον συστημάτων, διατόνων δ' ἢ χρωματικῶν οὐδεὶς πωποθ' ἐώρακεν. καί
τοι τὰ διαγράμματά γ' αὐτῶν ἐδήλου
10 τὴν πᾶσαν τῆς μελῳδίας τάξιν, ἐν
οἷς περὶ συστημάτων ὀκταχόρδων ἁρμονιῶν μόνον ἔλεγον.

5 ἔχων Ma. corr. εἶχον Mb. ‖ 6 αὐ-
τοὺς in αὐτοῖς corr. A. ‖ 12 ἔλεγεν
R. ‖

The men of early times wished only to be Harmonicists, for only the *Harmonia* did they take up. They never had any concept for the other genera. This is evident because the diagrams are derived solely by means of the *Harmonia* scales; of the diatonic or chromatic, nobody shows anything. And so, the diagrams of these scales show the whole order of melody in which they only speak in terms of the scales of the *Harmonia* octochords.

This paragraph is rather well known, but only in the heavily emended version. Indeed, all of the published Greek texts of Aristoxenus are very heavily emended. The following excerpt shows the text as emended by Paul Marquard[8] (and followed in large part by all subsequent editors), and the text as I would propose it with most of the emendations deleted.

---

[8]Paul Marquard, *Die harmonischen Fragmente des Aristoxenus* (Berlin, 1868), p. 2.

## Excerpt 7
### Aristoxenus—*Harmonics* 1. 2. 8-17

| Marquard's text and apparatus | New text and apparatus |
|---|---|

15 τοὺς μὲν οὖν ἔμπροσθεν [ἡμμένους     τοὺς μὲν οὖν ἔμπροσθεν ἁρμονικοὺς

τῆς ἁρμονικῆς πραγματείας συμβέβη-     εἶναι βούλεσθαι μόνον, αὐτῆς γὰρ

κεν ὡς ἀληθῶς] ἁρμονικοὺς εἶναι     τῆς ἁρμονίας ἥπτοντο μόνον, τῶν

βούλεσθαι|μόνον, αὐτῆς γὰρ τῆς ἁρ-     δ' ἄλλων γενῶν οὐδεμίαν πωποτ'

μονίας ἥπτοντο μόνον, τῶν δ'ἄλλων|     ἔννοιαν εἶχον. σημεῖον δὲ· τὰ γὰρ    5

γενῶν οὐδεμίαν πώποτ' ἔννοιαν εἶχον.     διαγράμματα αὐτοῖς τῶν <u>ἁρμονιῶν</u>

σημεῖον δὲ· τὰ γὰρ|διαγράμματα αὐ-     ἔκκειται μόνον συστημάτων, διατό-

τοῖς τῶν <u>ἐναρμονίων</u> ἔκκειται μόνον     νον δ'ἢ χρωματικῶν οὐδεὶς πωποθ'

20 συστημά|των, διατόνων δ'ἢ χρωματικῶν     ἑώπακεν. καί τοι τὰ διαγράμματά

οὐδεὶς πώποθ' ἑώρακεν.|καί τοι τὰ     γ' αὐτῶν ἐδήλου τὴν πᾶσαν τῆς με-    10

διαγράμματά γ' αὐτῶν ἐδήλου τὴν πᾶ-     λῳδίας τάξιν, ἐν οἷς περὶ συστημά-

σαν τῆς με|λῳδίας τάξιν, ἐν οἷς περὶ     των ὀκταχόρδων <u>ἁρμονιῶν</u> μόνον ἔλεγον.

συστημάτων ὀκταχόρδων <u>ἐναρμονίων</u>|     _____

μόνον ἔλεγον.                       5 ἔχων Ma. corr. εἶχον Mb. || 6 αὐ-

_____             τοὺς in αὐτοῖς corr. A. || 12 ἔλεγεν

15-16 ἡμμένους-ἀληθῶς verba restitui         R. ||

ex Procli ad Plat. Tim. pag. 192 A

(Schneider) ||18 ἔχων Ma. εἶχον Mb.||

19 ἁρμονιῶν libb. || 20 διάτονον δὲ ἢ

χρωματικὸν S. ||22 ἁρμονιῶν libb. ||

23 ἔλεγεν R. ||

A comparison of the standard English translation of this section by
Henry S. Macran,[9] based on emended texts, and a translation of the
text with emendations deleted defines the marked shift in meaning.

## Excerpt 8

| Macran | Mathiesen |
|---|---|

The early students of Harmonic con-     The men of early times wished only
tented themselves, as a matter of fact,     to be Harmonicists, for only the *Har-*
with being students of *Harmonic* in     *monia* did they take up. They never
the literal sense of the term; for they     had any concept for the other genera.
investigated the *enharmonic* scale     This is evident because the diagrams
alone, without devoting any considera-     are derived solely by means of the
tion to the other genera. This may     *Harmonia* scales; of the diatonic or
be inferred from the fact that the     chromatic, nobody shows anything.
tables of scales presented by them are     And so, the diagrams of these scales
always of enharmonic scales, never     show the whole order of melody in

_____

[9]Henry S. Macran, *The Harmonics of Aristoxenus,* edited with translation, notes,
introduction, and index of words (Oxford, 1902), pp. 165-66.

in one solitary instance of diatonic or chromatic; and that too, although these very tables in which they confined themselves to the enumeration of enharmonic octave scales nevertheless exhibited the complete system of musical intervals.

which they only speak in terms of the scales of the *Harmonia* octochords.

Without the emendations, Aristoxenus is chiding the Pythagorean Harmonicists. He is completely consistent here and speaks entirely in terms of ἁρμονία scales, quite a different thing from genera. He also speaks of the "Harmonia octochord," a scientific device mentioned by Ptolemy and tacitly implied by Euclid, not of "enharmonic octave scales." In all this, he is dealing with the important Pythagorean background. Marquard, Westphal, Macran, and other editors were anxious for Aristoxenus to be specific; they considered he was writing a "Method." So, as excerpt 7 illustrates, they emended two of the ἁρμονία to ἐναρμόνιον and added an entirely unnecessary phrase pulled out of a commentary to Plato's *Timaeus* and written around seven hundred years after Aristoxenus. A momentary comparison of excerpts 7 and 8 will show how much the sense is changed.

Later in the same book (1. 4. 9-12) the verbal form ἁρμόζω appears and is used in an important context.

### Excerpt 9
#### Aristoxenus—*Harmonics* 1. 4. 9-12

Εἶτα περὶ μέλους ὑποδηλωτέον καὶ τυπωτέον οἵαν ἔχει φύσιν τὸ κατὰ μουσικήν, ἐπειδὴ πλείους εἰσὶ φύσεις μέλους, μία δ' ἐστί τις ἐκ πασῶν αὐτοῦ ἡ τοῦ ἡρμοσμένου καὶ μελῳδουμένου.

Then concerning *Melos*, it is necessary to show and outline in how far it has a nature according to the *Science of Music*, since there are many natures of *Melos*, and only a certain one of all of these is organized through *Harmonia* and is suitable for melody construction.

Here it is made clear that ἁρμονία has some relationship to the suitable setting of μέλος. Later Aristoxenus and Ps. Plutarch will use the term as a basis for judging the propriety of certain melodies. It is important also to note the use of μουσική signifying the Science of Music and used in contrast to the broader term μέλος, or music as Being. Implied here is the axiom that the Science of Music is only one way of organizing music as Being (intimating that it is the best), since music has many natures, not all of which would have ἁρμονία.

By way of a brief tangent, Aristoxenus's *Harmonics* 1. 16. 30-31 illustrates a fifth manner for codifying intervals, specifically in the terms of rational-nonrational as used in *Timaeus* (excerpt 2).

## Excerpt 10
### Aristoxenus—*Harmonics* 1. 16. 30-31

πέμπτη δὲ καθ' ἣν διαφέρει τὰ ῥητὰ τῶν ἀλόγων.

fifth, according to which the rational differs from the non-rational.

The sense implied is mathematical. A surd will not contain ἁρμονία; a rational interval may, and thus Aristoxenus sets up this contrast as a way of defining and codifying intervals.

In *Harmonics* 1. 26. 30-33, ἁρμονία and ἐναρμόνιος are used in close proximity. This is a particular spot where "enharmonic" is often read for ἁρμονία. Yet this is not necessary and is a misinterpretation. ἐναρμόνιος refers to a particular parhypate of a particular genus, a genus that is the outgrowth of the principles of ἁρμονία, and we assume that Aristoxenus chose different terms for some purpose. An examination of the context reveals a discussion of the position of the parhypate. One is common to the colors and the diatonic genus. These genera *may* exhibit ἁρμονία, but they may also exhibit other natures of music. The enharmonic genus (which we know from Aristoxenus was almost out of use during his time because of its great subtlety) *can only* exhibit ἁρμονία because ἁρμονία is the very essence of it. So consequently Aristoxenus is careful to make clear that one parhypate is peculiar to ἁρμονία, and this is *represented* in the enharmonic genus—a veiled distinction, but an important one. It is evident that Aristoxenus is aware of a major difference between the two terms. This distinction is lost if both terms are translated "enharmonic." So the passage must read:

## Excerpt 11
### Aristoxenus—*Harmonics* 1. 26. 30-33

παρυπάτης δὲ δύο εἰσὶ τόποι--ὁ μὲν κοινὸς τοῦ τε διατόνου καὶ τοῦ χρώματος, ὁ δ' ἕτερος ἴδιος τῆς ἁρμονίας--· κοινωνεῖ γὰρ δύο γένη τῶν παρυπατῶν. ἐναρμόνιος μὲν οὖν ἐστι παρυπάτη πᾶσα ἡ βαρυτέρα τῆς βαρυτάτης χρωματικῆς, . . .

There are two positions for the parhypate, the one common to the diatonic and *color*, the other unique to the *Harmonia*, for the two genera share the parhypate. For every parhypate is *enharmonic* which is lower than the lowest *chromatic* [parhypate], . . .

And yet, both terms are often read "enharmonic":

We find but two *loci* for the parhypate, one common to the diatonic and the chromatic genus and one peculiar to the enharmonic. For two of the genera have the Parhypate in common. Every Parhypate lower than the lowest chromatic is enharmonic.[10]

The important distinction is lost here.

This section has also been subjected to some misleading emendation and careless treatment of other technical words. The following excerpt shows the text as Marquard and Westphal give it, where comparison with excerpt 11 will reveal that an entire phrase has been shunted to a different spot. Furthermore, the word χρώματος, from χρῶμα has been universally translated in the theorists as "chromatic genus." But there is another term, χρωματικός, seen just at the end of the excerpt, used in this sense.

Excerpt 12

Marquard's text for

Aristoxenus—*Harmonics* 1. 26. 30-33[11]

παρυπάτης δὲ δύο εἰσὶ τόποι, ὁ μὲν
κοινὸς|τοῦ τε διατόνου καὶ τοῦ χρώ-
ματος, --κοινωνεῖ γὰρ τὰ δύο|γένη
30 τῶν παρυπατῶν, --ὁ δ' ἕτερος ἴδιος
τῆς ἁρμονίας. ἐναρμόνιος μὲν οὖν
ἐστὶ παρυπάτη πᾶσα ἡ βαρυτέρα τῆς
βαρυτάτης|χρωματικῆς, . . .

29 τα add. Mx.

When the theorists use χρῶμα as in the excerpt, they mean the "colors" obtained from the movable notes of the tetrachord and found within the diatonic *and* chromatic genus. So the sense here is general; the parhypate is common from the diatonic through all the colors. In his use of terminology, Aristoxenus is clearly distinguishing between the chromatic genus and color in general, between ἁρμονία and the enharmonic genus, but this distinction is lost in the standard translations.

Although there is an abundance of examples from Ps. Plutarch's dialogue on music, περὶ μουσικῆς (mostly gleaned from Aristoxenus), there is one spot in particular worthy of note. 1143E (34)

---

[10]Macran, p. 184.
[11]Marquard, pp. 36 & 38.

shows precisely the same contrasting of terms seen in Aristoxenus. It illustrates not only that the terms are *not* interchangeable, but also that the subtlety of Aristoxenus was not lost on whomever assembled this dialogue.

### Excerpt 13
#### Plutarch—*Concerning Music* 1143E (34)

Τριῶν δ' ὄντων γενῶν εἰς ἃ διαιρεῖται τὸ ἡρμοσμένον, ἴσων τοῖς τε τῶν συστημάτων μεγέθεσι καὶ ταῖς τῶν φθόγγων δυνάμεσιν, ὁμοίως δὲ καὶ ταῖς τῶν τετραχόρδων, περὶ ἑνὸς μόνου οἱ παλαιοὶ ἐπραγματεύσαντο, ἐπειδήπερ οὔτε περὶ χρώματος οὔτε περὶ διατόνου οἱ πρὸ ἡμῶν ἐπεσκόπουν, ἀλλὰ περὶ μόνου τοῦ ἐναρμονίου, καὶ αὖ τούτου περὶ ἕν τι μέγεθος συστήματος, τοῦ καλουμένου διὰ πασῶν, περὶ μὲν γὰρ τῆς χρόας διεφέροντο, περὶ δὲ τοῦ μίαν εἶναι μόνην αὐτὴν τὴν ἁρμονίαν σχεδὸν πάντες συνεφώνουν.

οὐκ ἂν οὖν ποτε συνίδοι τὰ περὶ τὴν ἁρμονικὴν πραγματείαν ὁ μέχρι αὐτῆς τῆς γνώσεως ταύτης προεληλυθώς, ἀλλὰ δηλονότι ὁ παρακολουθῶν ταῖς τε κατὰ μέρος ἐπιστήμαις καὶ τῷ συνόλῳ σώματι τῆς μουσικῆς, καὶ ταῖς τῶν μερῶν μίξεσί τε καὶ συνθέσεσιν. ὁ γὰρ μόνον ἁρμονικὸς περιγέγραπται τρόπῳ τινί.

Of the three genera into which organization according to Harmonia is divided, being equal in the magnitudes of scales and functions of notes and likewise of tetrachords, concerning only one the ancients studied; *never* the *color* nor the diatonic did those before us consider, but only the *enharmonic,* and of this, one certain magnitude of scale, the so-called octave. Concerning the *shading,* they differed; but concerning this, however, that one thing only was *Harmonia* itself, nearly everyone agreed.

Not ever could one understand what concerns the *study of Harmonia* who had [only] advanced as far as this inquiry, but clearly only one who follows the sciences—according to [each] part and as a body of the *Science of Music* taken altogether—, and the mixtures and syntheses of the parts. Only the *Harmonicist* is defined in this manner.

In the course of one short section ἐναρμόνιος, ἁρμονία, ἁρμονική, and ἁρμονικός appear. Furthermore, we find χρῶμα (color), and χρόα (shade), two distinct words, generally mistranslated as "chromatic." The meanings of all these technical words are consistent with what was seen in Aristoxenus. In fact, this passage may be recognized as a copy of Aristoxenus's material (note, for example, excerpts 8 and 9). ἐναρμόνιον refers to a genus, and is clearly contrasted with "color" and "diatonic." ἁρμονία is used in its philosophic role and in direct contrast to a mere genus. ἁρμονική is linked to πραγματεία, a substitute for ἐπιστήμη, in this case carrying the specific meaning of the "study" of the organizational principles behind structuring μέλος according to ἁρμονία. Lastly, ἁρμονικός is used substantively as noted earlier. Once again, χρῶμα has the meaning of color obtained from the movable notes. It is a general term as opposed to the specific χρωματικός. The term χρόα is also found in Aristoxenus and refers to the slight shading that may vary the pitch and quality of *any* note in μέλος. Reading "chromatic" for these two words distorts the meaning of the excerpt, as is readily apparent.

So it is demonstrable that the Greeks took immense care to select precisely the right word, and that they assumed very subtle distinctions between words built on the same root. Should we have imagined that it would be otherwise? Yet students of Greek music have shown inconsistency in their approach to technical terms, with resulting divergences of theory and many untenable hypotheses. ἁρμονία is by no means the only such problematic term.[12]

At least this much can now be said: ἁρμονία as a term in the Hellenic stylists, Plato, Aristotle, Aristoxenus, and Ps. Plutarch, has a significance all its own. It signifies that perfect ordering of all the elements of music—music, which is the sole physical manifestation of the order of the Universe. It has the power to order the variable proportions in man's own soul and is the only musical order accepted by the philosophers as noble and good. Greek musical theorists are not separate from their philosophic foundation, and their labyrinthine treatises must be approached from this standpoint for a full yield.

Thomas J. Mathiesen

---

[12]The problem is compounded by the gradual change in meaning of many of the words, especially from early theorists like Aristoxenus to later theorists like Cleonides.

# Hucbald of St. Amans and Carolingian Music Theory

To denote the intellectual revival of the period from 800 to 1000 as the "Carolingian Renaissance" is perhaps to create a false impression. The term "Renaissance" immediately calls to mind sixteenth-century Italy; the term is also borrowed to describe the intellectual ferment of the twelfth century. In comparison with those better-known periods, the Carolingian Renaissance shrinks to such proportions that the term itself seems pretentious.[1] Charlemagne's reform of clerical education led to a revival of learning at his court and in the monasteries of the Empire, but even that revival is often dismissed as a return to old authors, rather than the development of new learning, so that it seems difficult to single out specific contributions with the exception of some renewed interest in Classical authors and the invention of the famous Carolingian miniscule style of writing.

In one area, however, the contributions of the Carolingian period are particularly significant, and that field is music theory. Unfortunately, a combination of circumstances has relegated this school of theory to relative obscurity. The arrogant claims of Guido of Arezzo effectively hide the fact that he built on Carolingian foundations.[2] Some scholars dismiss all Carolingian theorists as mere collators of earlier ideas.[3] Others, like Hugo Riemann, let their own framework and historical point of view color their perceptions of history. Riemann felt strongly that only those treatises that deal with contrapuntal theory are significant; hence, the history of Medieval theory really begins for him with the *Musica enchiriadis*, which was ascribed to Hucbald until Hans Müller demonstrated in 1884 that Hucbald was

---

[1]Cf. Charles Homer Haskins, *The Renaissance of the Twelfth Century* (Cambridge, Mass., 1928), pp. 16-20; Carl Stephenson, *Mediaeval History,* 4th ed., rev. Bryce Lyon (New York, 1962), pp. 163-68; and R. R. Bolgar, *The Classical Heritage and Its Beneficiaries* (London, 1954; reprint ed., New York, 1964), pp. 91-129.

[2]Joseph Smits van Waesberghe, ed., *Guidonis Aretini Micrologus,* Corpus scriptorum de musica, 4 (Rome, 1955), pp. 85-87.

[3]Gustave Reese, *Music of the Middle Ages* (New York, 1940), pp. 125-26.

not the author.[4] Faced with the conclusion—if Müller were correct—that Hucbald ceased to have any importance, Riemann stubbornly insisted that Hucbald was in fact the author of the *Musica enchiriadis,* and hence an important theorist.[5] He also neglected the one work now ascribed to Hucbald, the *De musica,*[6] since it did not fit into his views.

The purpose of this article is to suggest that an objective look at Carolingian theorists, particularly Hucbald of St. Amans and his *De musica,* creates an entirely different picture. Carolingian theoretical works do seem somewhat conservative, next to Guido or John of Afflighem. But compared to the early Medieval source works on music—Boethius, Martianus Capella, Isidore of Seville, and Cassiodorus—the Carolingian treatises are progressive and innovative, closer to Guido than to Boethius or Capella. Although there is reliance on previous authority and a certain conservatism, there is in this school of theory a new approach, a practical purpose, and a willingness to grapple with practical problems. Guido, whether or not he acknowledged the fact, built his theory and his fame on solid Carolingian foundations.

We should point out that to study Hucbald's work, one needs to go beyond Gerbert's edition of the *De musica,* which is unreliable, particularly in the case of diagrams, musical examples, and titles of chant selections.[7] Fortunately, we can now base discussion on the pioneer work of Rembert Weakland,[8] and use as a text the excellent Brussels manuscript of the *De musica* that he discovered.[9]

Before we single out progressive, proto-Guidonian elements in Hucbald's treatise, it would be well to look at his use of previous authorities. There is certainly evidence of conservative holdovers from the earlier Greek theories, or at least the Medieval understanding of Greek ideas.

Two previous authorities are cited by name. The first is Boethius, the standard Latin source of Greek musical theory. Hucbald does not quote Boethius directly; he does refer to him, always deferentially;

---

[4]Hans Müller, *Hucbalds echte und unechte Schriften über Musik* (Leipzig, 1884).

[5]Hugo Riemann, *History of Music Theory,* trans. and with commentary by Raymond Haggh (Lincoln, Nebraska, 1962), pp. 11 passim; and 345, n. 1.

[6]The work is sometimes referred to as *De harmonica institutione,* after Gerbert's title; the rubric in the Brussels manuscript reads simply "Incipit Musica Hubaldi"; in any case, only one treatise is now ascribed to Hucbald.

[7]Martin Gerbert, *Scriptores ecclesiastici de musica* (St. Blasien, 1784; reprint ed., Hildesheim, 1963), 1:104-21.

[8]Rembert Weakland, O.S.B., "Hucbald," *Die Musik in Geschichte und Gegenwart* 6(1957):822-27; idem, "Hucbald as Musician and Theorist," *Musical Quarterly* 42 (1956): 66-84.

[9]Brussels, Bibliothèque Royale, Ms. 10078/95. The *De musica* appears on ff. 84v-92r.

in one place he calls him "doctor mirabilis, omnium prudentissimus artium liberalium perquisitor."[10]

Hucbald makes one casual reference to Martianus Capella, crediting him with providing Latin translations of the Greek string names.[11] It seems clear, however, that the influence of Martianus Capella on the *De musica* and on Carolingian theory in general may be far more significant than the one reference would indicate. First of all, studies of Medieval literature indicate that Capella's work, *De nuptiis philologiae et Mercurii,* was a work of immense importance for the Carolingian era, when it functioned as the most important source concerning the definition and content of the seven liberal arts.[12] Second, Remi of Auxerre, a friend and academic colleague of Hucbald, wrote a word-by-word commentary on the *De nuptiis.*[13] Although the commentary is not especially helpful and constitutes another example of the strange Medieval penchant for such unenlightening works, the existence of the commentary does indicate the importance of Capella to the Carolingians; one may assume that Hucbald knew both the original and his friend's commentary. Third, the text of the *De nuptiis* indicates that it could well have served as a starting point for Hucbald's treatise. Although Capella is more famous for his extravagantly allegorical writing and in the field of music for his contribution to the idea of music of the spheres, Book IX, *De harmonia,* is actually a treatise on music. The first third of the book is allegorical plot; the final third deals with metrics and prosody, customarily a part of the topic of music in the early Middle Ages. The middle third of the Book IX[14] is a short, businesslike treatise on music theory, treating the notes of the scale, consonance, modes, tetrachords, and intervals. One idea Capella states is borrowed directly by Hucbald and others: in distinguishing musical sounds from cries or noises, Capella says that musical sounds are analogous to *phthongoi,* vowels, in speech.[15]

Whether or not the hypothesis of the influence of Martianus Capella can be proven, there is direct evidence in the *De musica* of Hucbald's use of previous authorities. Although there are often discrepan-

---

[10]ff. 86r-86v.

[11]f. 90r.

[12]Ernst Curtius, *European Literature and the Latin Middle Ages,* trans. Willard R. Trask (New York, 1953), pp. 36-39; Bolgar, pp. 35-37; and Kathi Meyer-Baer, *Music of the Spheres and the Dance of Death* (Princeton, N.J., 1970), pp. 33-35. *De nuptiis* is available in a modern edition by Adolph Dick (Leipzig, 1925).

[13]Besides Gerbert's version (1:63-94), there is a modern edition: Cora Lutz, ed., *Remigii Autissiodorensis commentum in Martianum Capellam* (Leiden, 1965).

[14]Dick, ed., pp. 494-516.

[15]Ibid., p. 500; Hucbald's version appears on f. 86r.

cies between the old theories and the way he uses them, still the late Greek ideas appear.

Some of Hucbald's terminology is Greek, either transliterated or written in Greek characters. He consistently names the notes of the scale by their Greek names, from *proslambanomenos* to *nete hyperboleon*.[16] Although, as we shall see, he suggests more convenient ways of naming the notes, his basic system is still to use the Greek string names. All the tetrachords from which his scale is constructed have unwieldly Greek names,[17] which in their constant repetition must have been as tiresome for the scribe as they are for the reader.

The use of tetrachords to construct the scale is another Greek concept that persisted in all theorists until Guido and his hexachord system. The Carolingian tetrachord, however, was not the Greek one; the latter is a descending four-note unit, of which the two outer notes are fixed and the two inner notes are movable, whereas the Carolingian scale is built of ascending conjunct and disjunct tetrachords, of which all the notes are invariably fixed in a tone-semitone-tone pattern.[18]

Perhaps the clearest example of what must have been a conscious discrepancy between old and new theories is Hucbald's explanation of the two types of semitone, the *semitonium minus* and the *semitonium maius*.[19] This distinction was a Greek idea; it is perhaps significant that Hucbald uses these simple Latin terms, rather than the Greek names, and never explains the mathematical difference between the semitones other than to state that they are unequal in size and together equal a tone. The striking thing is that after the explanation of the two semitones he never again alludes to them. From that point on, "semitone" is used in our sense of a single entity: half a tone; the minor third, for example, he constructs from a tone and an unspecified semitone; tetrachords follow the tone-semitone-tone pattern; and so forth. Still, he felt constrained to repeat the old theory, whether he used it or not.

Further evidence of the persistence of Greek ideas is the *sonus-phthongus* analogy borrowed from Capella, which we have already cited, and the fact that the only musical instruments alluded to in the entire treatise are the *kithara*[20] and the *ydraulia* or hydraulic organ.[21]

---

[16]The Greek names are first listed on ff. 89r and 89v and are used consistently thereafter.

[17]The tetrachord names are explained on ff. 88v-89r.

[18]f. 88r.

[19]f. 86v.

[20]e.g., f. 87r.

[21]e.g., f. 86v.

But awareness of the strong Greek current in Hucbald's work should not lead one to the conclusion that he and the other Carolingians were mere repeaters of old information. Greek ideas persist in music theory long after the Middle Ages, and that persistence is not the last indication in the history of Western music that theory changes slowly. Further, even Guido, for all his claims to a new approach, includes in his *Micrologus* Greek ideas that were omitted by Hucbald, such as the chapter on metrics,[22] and the legend of Pythagoras and his felicitous chance discovery of harmonic proportions.[23]

But what is much more important are Hucbald's new ideas, either departures from the specific earlier information that he knew or else entirely new concepts and approaches. Hucbald's treatment of the semitone, already mentioned, is one clear example of a departure from previous information. An even clearer example is Hucbald's treatment of *toni* or modes; a comparison of both authors on this point is illustrative. Capella describes a late Greek version of the modes.[24] There are five finals, each governing one basic scale and two subsidiary scales, one below and one above the basic scale, for a total of fifteen modes. The five basic modes are Lydian, Iastian, Aeolian, Phrygian, and Dorian, each with its hyper- and hypo- subsidiaries. Hucbald never mentions the previous modal systems and has a very clear explanation of the basic Carolingian understanding of the eight ecclesiastical modes.[25] There are four modes, called *protus, deuterus, tritus,* and *tetrardus,* each having an authentic and plagal form; he refers to the *primus, secundus* way of numbering the modes, calling them one through eight, as an alternate option. This way of explaining the modes persists for some time, although the one through eight numbering becomes the basic one and *protus autentus* and *plagalis* becomes the alternate system.

It is interesting that Carolingian theorists use transliterated Greek ordinals rather than Latin numbers in naming the modes. One is tempted to construe this borrowing as another example of the Medieval tendency to equate "learned" with "Greek," a tendency that seems to be a recurring theme in Western culture. The significant point about these Greek terms, as well as the Dorian, Phrygian terminology, is that Greek terms are used to describe an entirely new system; the Greek modal system is never discussed.

Even more significant than Hucbald's departures from what earlier theorists say about specific topics are the entirely new areas of

[22]Smits van Waesberghe, ed., pp. 158-77.
[23]Ibid., pp. 228-33.
[24]Dick, ed., pp. 497-99.
[25]ff. 91r-92r.

practical concern he introduces into his treatise. It is this concern for practical and pedagogical matters that most distinguishes Carolingian theory from earlier theory and most closely foreshadows the work of Guido.

The clearest example of Hucbald's practical approach is his concern for the problem of exact notation. Like Guido, he was anxious to make available some way of notating the huge chant repertoire; like Guido, his concern was teaching music in cathedral schools, not monasteries where the *in campo aperto* notation of his time was not a problem for singers who had a lifetime to learn the chant by rote. The fact that Guido, not Hucbald, developed the staff may be a result of the century that separates them; the staff seems a short logical step from the later, carefully heightened notation styles. In any case, Hucbald certainly grappled with the problem of accurate pitch notation.

Hucbald suggests two notational systems that have the advantage of denoting definite pitch. The more widely cited system is intriguing because of a superficial resemblance to the staff, but is mentioned by him somewhat in passing as an example in the course of discussing semitones.[26] It consists in writing the syllables of a chant text on lines so that each line represents a note of the scale and the spaces represent intervals between them, which are marked at the left edge as *T* for tone or *S* for semitone. This system appears in other treatises, notably the *Musica enchiriadis;* its appearance in both places may have been one of the reasons for ascribing the *Musica enchiriadis* to Hucbald. But in the *Musica enchiriadis,* this system is used for several examples in early organum styles;[27] Hucbald gives one short example, illustrating tones and semitones in the scale. Nowhere does he suggest this system as a practical system of chant notation.

Later in his treatise, Hucbald does propose a practical way of notating pitch, which he recommends using in conjunction with chant notation.[28] The system is similar to the daseian notation of the *Musica enchiriadis* and the *Alia musica;*[29] but in this case, letters and symbols are assigned to specific notes, and these letters and symbols are written over the neumes of the chant notation so that the singer knows the exact pitches and intervals. Immediately after he explains the system, he includes a list of all the notes of the scale and the symbol for each. In the Brussels manuscript, there is a third column, listing the letters

[26]Folio 87r; a facsimile of the passage appears in Weakland's article, "Hucbald," pp. 825-26.
[27]Cf. Gerbert, 1:156 passim.
[28]ff. 90v-91r.
[29]A facsimile of daseian notation appears in Carl Parrish, *The Notation of Medieval Music* (New York, 1957), Plate XI.

A-G in capitals for the bottom octave and lowercase letters for the upper octave, a variant of the system used by Guido and all after him. We must recall, however, that the Brussels manuscript dates from the late eleventh or early twelfth century,[30] and the A-G system must be a scribal addition; it is unlikely that Hucbald would include the system without comment since it is such an obvious improvement over his system of letters and symbols.

It is important to emphasize that Hucbald recommends using these symbols in conjunction with *in campo aperto* neumatic notation. He is concerned about notation of definite pitch, but wants to retain neume notation for the subtleties of performance practice it indicates. The section is worth quoting for its testimony to the tenth-century understanding of chant notation:

> Hae tamen consuetudinariae notae non omnino habentur non necessariae, quippe cum et ad tarditatem seu celeritatem cantilenae, et ubi tremulam sonus contineat vocem, vel qualiter ipsi soni iungantur in unum vel distinguantur ab invicem, ubi quoque claudantur inferius vel superius pro ratione quarumdam litterarum, quorum nil omnino hae artificales notae valent ostendere, admodum censentur proficuae.[31]

This early testimony to the sophistication of chant notation—and especially the phrase "tarditatem seu celeritatem cantilenae," which seems to indicate different rhythmic values—deserves comment. As much as Hucbald wants a definite pitch notation, he does not want it at the cost of abandoning neumatic notation. Within a century after his death, both desires were accommodated by neume notation on a staff; even heightened neumatic notation would have satisfied him.

Another indication of the practical side of Hucbald's work is his use of musical examples. Sixty-one chant selections are supplied in a relatively short treatise; he always cites actual chant for illustration rather than *cantiunculae,* or theoretically constructed typical melodies. Four examples are unidentifiable because the reference is too brief to be specific, but all the rest can be located in standard chant

---

[30]Joseph Smits van Waesberghe, et al., eds., *The Theory of Music from the Carolingian Era up to 1400*, Répertoire international des sources musicales, B III 1 (Munich, 1961), pp. 55-57.

[31]f. 90v.

The customary neumes should not be considered altogether useless; for they serve to indicate the slowing or speeding up of the melody, where the singing contains a *tremula vocis* [the *quilisma*], how notes should be joined together or sung distinctly [the *pressus*], and where the tones should be closed higher or lower, because of certain letters [liquescents]; the theoretical signs [letters or symbols] can indicate none of these things, but still they are advantageous.

sources.[32] Only sixteen are from sanctoral liturgies; of those, several are from the liturgies of saints associated with Christmas, such as Stephen and the Holy Innocents. Of the forty-one selections from the temporal cycle, four examples are from the Pentecost season, ten from the Easter cycle, and twenty-seven from the Christmas cycle—Advent, Christmas, and Epiphany. In other words, half the examples he cites are from the opening sections of readily available liturgical books. He makes reference easy for his student readers and uses saints' liturgies only when he must; once, for example, he cites the *Benedictus* antiphon from the feast of St. Symphorian, a rare local liturgy, to illustrate an ascending minor sixth, a difficult interval to find in the standard chant repertoire.[33]

In summary, although it is easy to find evidence of reliance on previous authorities in Hucbald's treatise, it is not enough to dismiss his work as a summary of earlier ideas. He departs from earlier authority on several major questions, and his treatise deals with practical, pedagogical problems that were entirely foreign to earlier theory.

Guido claimed originality for his ideas and achieved much greater fame and circulation than his predecessors; his fame outshines the Carolingians even today. But he was not the first to recognize a discrepancy between traditional theory and the practice of Gregorian chant;[34] although he may indeed have been the first to build a simple theoretical system based on practice, he relied on the insights of the Carolingians and constructed his system as the final extension of their efforts to preserve what was valid of traditional theory and to develop answers to entirely new practical questions.

Richard J. Wingell

---

[32]René-Jean Hesbert, *Antiphonale missarum sextuplex* (Brussels, 1935); and *Corpus antiphonalium officii* (Rome, 1963).
[33]Cf. Weakland, "Hucbald as Musician," pp. 72-73.
[34]Joseph Smits van Waesberghe, *De musico-paedigogico et theoretico Guidone Aretino eiusque vita et moribus* (Florence, 1953), pp. 146-50.

# PART II

# Diego Pisador's
# *Libro de Musica de Vihuela* (1552)

Diego Pisador, first son and eldest of three children of Isabel and Alonso Pisador, was born ca. 1508 at Salamanca. In 1526 Diego took minor ecclesiastical orders but went no further in this endeavor. Most of the information concerning the vihuelist is obtained from records of lawsuits between Diego and his father: one (1553) in which Diego obtained a decision regarding his portion of his mother's estate, another (1557) involving payment by Diego to his father of sums collected for rentals. Further records of Diego after this apparently are not available.

Published at Salamanca in 1552, the *Libro* contains seven books, 99 folios instead of the 112 usually cited. Included are works for solo vihuela (in Italian lute tablature) or for voice and vihuela (the voice part in mensural notation or indicated by red numbers in the tablature). The copy held by the University of California at Berkeley has, on the title page, the price of the volume given in manuscript as 629 maravedis.

Briefly, the organization of the *Libro* is as follows:

Title Page, Dedications, Prologue, Table of Contents

Book I: *Diferencias* on "Conde Claros" (romance) and "Guardame las Vacas" (villancico); pavana; five additional romances; sonetos; fantasias

Book II: Villancicos (including four by Juan Vasquez); Pange Lingua; Sacris Solemnis; Dixit dominus domino (2); In exitu Israel

Book III: Fantasias in all (8) modes

Book IV: Four masses (mostly complete) by Josquin des Pres; Benedictus from Josquin's *Missa de Fortuna Desperata*

Book V: Four masses (mostly complete) by Josquin des Pres; Pleni sunt coeli from Josquin's *Missa de Fortuna Desperata*

Book VI: Motets *a* 4, *a* 5, *a* 6 (by Josquin, Gombert, Willaert, Basurto, Monton, Morales)

29

Book VII: Villanescas; chansons; madrigal (Arcadelt)

For the present study, the copies of the *Libro* held by the Sibley Music Library, Eastman School of Music, Rochester, New York, and the University of California, Berkeley, have been primarily considered. Other known extant copies include those held by the following libraries:

Spain: Biblioteca de San Lorenzo del Escorial; Madrid, Biblioteca Nacional (2 copies, one imperfect)

France: Paris, Bibliothèque Nationale

Great Britain: London, British Museum

Netherlands: The Hague, Gemeentemuseum

With the exception of the latter, all of these have been examined, either actually or on microfilm. Only minor differences exist among them—most of the differences being concerned with the alignment of red figures in the tablature and varying degrees of clarity (or nonclarity) of certain other figures. Pagination and other problems are similar in all of the copies examined.

Howard Brown notes that the coat of arms on the title page of the *Libro* is that of the royal family of Spain and the coat of arms on f. 98v (actually 93v) is that of Guillermo Millis, a printer and bookseller active in Spain between ca. 1540 and 1555, citing the 1872 *Cátalogo de la Biblioteca de Salvá* (page 350) by Pedro Salvá y Mallen as his source of information.[1] The colophon on f. 93v, however, reads *Hecho por Diego Pisador vezino de Salamanca y impresso en su casa.* Thus it is at least possible that Pisador himself may have had something to do with publishing the volume.

Pisador dedicates the volume to Prince Philip, stating that he hopes the Prince may find in it relief from the efforts of conversation and that this volume is the most beneficial that has been compiled until now. Although Pisador mentions that the volume contains six books, it actually contains seven as listed above; perhaps the last was added shortly before publication.

## PRACTICAL CONSIDERATIONS

In his *Libro,* Pisador offers a variety of works, mostly well known at the time, arranged for solo vihuela or voice and vihuela. With the possible exception of the fantasias in Book III and a few other similar examples that may be actual compositions by Pisador, the *Libro*

---

[1]Howard M. Brown, *Instrumental Music Printed before 1600: A Bibliography* (Cambridge, Mass., 1965), pp. 139 and 141.

essentially consists of vihuela settings, presumably by Pisador, of works by established composers. The designations *de fuera* or *cantada por defuera* are reserved for those selections in which the voice part is provided in mensural notation; those in which the voice part appears in red figures in the tablature either carry no mention of this fact or it is stated clearly that the voice to be sung is indicated in red. Bal y Gay thoroughly discusses the matter of performance practice as related to the red figures (i.e., whether they are to be sung as well as played) with the general conclusion that in the case of Fuenllana at least, mensural notation is used for voice parts that definitely are not doubled by the instrument, inferring that the red figures *are* doubled (if desired) by the voice, but are *always* played by the instrument.[2] Such red figures are typical of vihuela intabulations, beginning with Milan (1536) and continuing with Narvaez (1538), Mudarra (1546), Valderrabano (1547), Pisador (1552), Fuenllana (1554), Daza (1576).

Pisador's specifications on this matter bear out the above position: e.g., in Book III, the first twelve fantasias have red figures, with the designation that the voice to be sung is in red; the remaining twelve fantasias are to be played only. In Book IV, the first two Josquin masses have red figures; for the balance of Book IV and all of Book V Pisador specifies that the pieces are to be played without singing. Of the eleven villanescas in Book VII, six are for solo vihuela, five have voice parts in mensural notation. All of the selections with either red figures or voice parts in mensural notation have texts; no texts are provided for the selections intended for solo performance. The "texts" for the first twelve fantasias of Book III are simply the syllables *ut, re, mi, fa, sol, la,* and appear in different ranges. Pisador explains in the prologue that one of the reasons for the inclusion of the fantasias is that they may help the performer to understand the modes; his directions, however, do not clarify whether the pitches indicated by the syllables refer only to voice entries in the polyphonic texture or are intended for singing.

The *Descendit Angelus* by Cristóbal Morales, included in Book VI, is apparently known only through its appearance in this volume. Two works, also in Book VI, *Dom Complerentur* and *Angelus Domini,* are by the little-known composer García de Basurto, active as *maestro de capilla* from ca. 1518 to 1548. The piece *Alta* (an ancient German dance) included by Felipe Pedrell in the *Cancionero musical popular español* as a work by Pisador does not appear in the *Libro.* Brown

---

[2] J. Bal y Gay, "Fuenllana and the Transcription of Spanish Lute Music," *Acta musicologica* 11 (1940): 16-27.

notes that the dance is a polyphonic arrangement of the tenor *La Spagna* by Francisco de la Torre.[3]

## PEDAGOGICAL CONSIDERATIONS

Although Pisador has included pieces of various degrees of difficulty, he does not specify "D" (*dificil*) or "F" (*facil*) in the manner of Fuenllana. He does state, however (e.g., at the beginning of Book III), that the *"villanescas a tres" son para principiantes.* In the introductory material he discusses the *compas* (*el mismo que el del canto*), the placement of frets and strings on the vihuela, a method for tuning the instrument (which results in the usual 4-4-3-4-4), the figures of mensural notation (*las figuras del canto de organo*) including the tie and dot of augmentation, duple meter, and triple proportion (*ternario*). He plainly states that he has avoided excessive glossing to avoid confusion. Pisador's tablature is entirely for the six-course vihuela, with the first string shown as the "lowest" course.

From the pedagogical point of view, Pisador does not present his material in order from simple to difficult. Indeed, some of the more demanding works (e.g., the *diferencias*) appear in Book I; easier examples appear later on. In the prologue Pisador states that he has included simple, moderate, and difficult works, music of few and many voices, both discant and counterpoint, with *mucha variedad en todo para que el animo del que deprende se pueda recrear y espaciar por ella* (much variety in all so that the spirit of him who understands can recreate and amuse himself by it). His implication is that the study of music is possible without a teacher (*otro maestro*) and should be a pleasant occupation for those who pursue it.

## THEORETICAL CONSIDERATIONS

### TUNINGS AND CLEFS

In the *Declaracion de instrumentos musicales* (1555) on f. 104ff Juan Bermudo explains vihuela tunings and presents diagrams showing pitches available in each tuning according to fret placement. Thus tuning implies not only pitch but also different types of fret placement as determined by comma measurements, arranged in order to make available the diatonic pitches; F, C, G sharps; B and E flats. None of Bermudo's diagrams indicate the availability of the enharmonics G, D, or A flats, or A and D sharps.

Statements such as *Es la clave de cesolfaut la tercera en tercero traste* (the C clef is on the third string on the third fret) are provided

---

[3]Brown, p. 141.

by Pisador for selections having the voice part in red figures. Tunings for selections having mensural notation are indicated by statements such as *Entónase la boz la segunda en tercero traste* (Intone the voice on the second string on the third fret), thus relating the tuning to the starting note in the voice part. This results, for example, in the E tuning for *Gentil Cavallero* (f. 13) and the A tuning for *Si te vas a bañar Juanica* (f. 14v). Tunings are not specified for the works for solo vihuela; presumably these utilize the more usual G tuning. Scordatura involving the lowering of the sixth string one tone is sometimes indicated, as for example in the Sanctus of the *Missa La Sol Fa Re Mi* by Josquin (f. 56v). Unfortunately, Pisador seems to forget occasionally the scordatura he has indicated and designates frets that would be used in the regular tuning—thus causing a few difficulties for performers and scholars.

Although Bermudo explains (f. 101ff) that clefs are to be placed on the strings where they are appropriate and specifies that both C and F clefs are to be designated, Pisador is not very careful about clef placement. His clefs appear about half of the time on the correct strings; frequently, however, they appear on incorrect strings. In all but two cases, he specifies the C clef appearing on the

| | |
|---|---|
| Third string, first fret | (A tuning) |
| Third string, third fret | (G tuning) |
| Second string, first fret | (E tuning) |
| Second string, open | (F tuning) |
| Second string, third fret | (D tuning) |

For one example (f. 10v), a villancico by Juan Vasquez, Pisador designates the G clef on the third fret, second string (A tuning); for another (f. 79v), *Qui seminant in lachrymis* by Gombert, he states *la clave de cesolfaut la tercera en segundo traste* (the C clef is on the third string on the second fret), which results in a virtually impossible A-flat tuning. Thus the statement undoubtedly is in error. Pisador nowhere specifies the F clef.

For the voice parts in mensural notation, Pisador uses the C clef or the G clef—placed and changed as necessary to keep the pitches on the staff.

CHROMATICISM

Gustave Reese,[4] Charles Warren Fox,[5] and others have pointed out the importance of considering the intabulations of sixteenth-century

[4]Gustave Reese, *Music in the Renaissance*, rev. ed. (New York, 1959), p. 623.
[5]Charles Warren Fox, "Accidentals in Vihuela Tablatures," *Bulletin of the American Musicological Society* 4 (1940): 22-24.

vihuelists in view of contemporaneous attitudes toward chromaticism. Although it may be said that much of this attitude is *quantitative* (i.e., more sharps and perhaps more flats appear in the tablatures than in twentieth-century editions of the vocal works in question), examination of representative tablatures indicates also a different *qualitative* attitude towards chromaticism than is generally recognized. Comparisons of Pisador's intabulations of Josquin's masses with editions such as those by Smijers indicate not only the use of more chromaticism in the sixteenth century but also a different concept of chromaticism than that generally accepted today. Also, different attitudes toward uses of perfect and imperfect consonances and dissonance treatment become apparent.

### Voice Leading and Rhythmic Aspects

In setting polyphonic works for the vihuela, Pisador attempts to maintain insofar as is possible the lines indicated in the original. Because of the nature of the instrument, it is impossible at times to provide all of the notes in the polyphonic texture in their full duration; Pisador almost always manages, however, to retain the contrapuntal and/or harmonic sense of a given passage. The transcribing of tablature to standard notation involves enormous problems of determining voice leading, particularly in a polyphonic texture. Since parts frequently cross and move from string to string, it is exceedingly difficult to accurately determine the original voice leading from the tablature alone. Cadence structures, especially those provided within works for specific purposes (entries of new voices, for example), sometimes assist in the determination of proper voice leading. Cadences also help the transcriber to determine ties, syncopations, and other rhythmic aspects.

Because of the nature of the instrument, a note that is relatively long in the original must sometimes be released in order that another voice may be played on the same string. A comparison with the vocal original is informative in this regard.

Pisador uses bar lines to delineate the measurement of the *compas* (i.e., beat, measure, or tactus). He states in the prologue that the *compas* is determined by the raising and lowering of the foot. Examination of the repertoire, however, demonstrates that there apparently is no one satisfactory approach to the problem of note values: for some examples, a reduction of 4:1 is acceptable; for others, 2:1 seems best; for still others, an exact correspondence seems preferable.

Above the tablature, Pisador provides mensural notation figures to indicate basic rhythmic values and the movement of the most active voice (or voices) as they occur and change. Dots in the tablature serve to align the figures of mensural notation with particular numbers in the tablature. As usual, the general flow of the music and the smallest note values indicated furnish the basic criteria for determining the tempo and hence the tactus and ratio of reduction in note values appropriate for any given selection. Obviously, there is much room for disagreement among scholars and performers in this and other matters.

The emerging idiomatic instrumental music of the sixteenth century has its roots in and is based on the vocal repertoire of its own and earlier periods. Examination of intabulations of the repertoire offered by Pisador and his contemporaries offers opportunities for further insight into performance practices and theoretical attitudes of the time. Although for decades researchers have been reminded of these facts, seldom are comparative studies of vocal and instrumental versions of works presented. The following transcription of Pisador's setting of a *Pater Noster* by Adrian Willaert (ff. 77-78) and the accompanying analysis comparing Pisador's intabulation with Hermann Zenck's edition[6] of the same work may serve to clarify and document many of the points discussed earlier. Continued preparation and availability of similar studies will deepen understanding of sixteenth-century performance practices and attitudes toward theoretical concepts.

## TRANSCRIPTION AND COMPARATIVE ANALYSIS OF A *PATER NOSTER* BY WILLAERT

### TRANSCRIPTION

The format for presentation of the *Pater Noster* includes a transcription to standard notation placed below a representation of Pisador's intabulation of the same work. The G tuning is specified by Pisador by the statement *Es la clave de cesolfaut la tercera en tercero traste* (the C clef is on the third string on the third fret); thus the clef that appears at the beginning of the original tablature, and that is retained in the representation, is erroneously placed on the fourth string. In the transcription the soprano part is written in the treble clef, stems up; the alto part is in the treble clef, stems down. The tenor part is in the bass clef, stems up; the bass part is in the bass clef, stems down. Notes in the tenor part marked "+" in the transcription appear in red in the original tablature, a method used by Pisador and other vihuelistas to designate notes to be sung. The signature is justified by Pisador's

[6]Adrian Willaert, "Pater Noster," *Adrian Willaert: Opera omnia, 2,* ed. Hermann Zenck, Corpus mensurabilis musicae, 3 (Rome, 1950), pp. 11-14.

consistent use of B-flat. Duple meter is determined by the general flow of the music and by Pisador's mensural indications above the tablature.

Bar line and measure numbers in the transcription correspond to those in the Zenck edition of the same work. Rhythmic values indicated by Pisador in mensural notation above the tablature have been halved in order to correspond to the Zenck edition.

Adrian Willaert:  PATER NOSTER

(from Diego Pisador:  LIBRO. . . , Folios 77, 77 verso, 78)
Transcription:  W. E. Hultberg

& in        te ra        rra    //

pa

nē nos tru        //        pa

sicut    &    nos      si

cut &    nos dimi      ti   mus     ij

de bi to   ri     bus   no   stris/   et

ne nos indu    cas  in   ten taci    o    nē    //◦

et   ne nos  in   du cas in ten ta  tionē  sed      li  be

ra  nos      a    ma    lo    sed  li   be   ra

nos  a  ma  lo.

## COMPARATIVE ANALYSIS

The analysis is based on a comparison of Pisador's intabulation of Willaert's *Pater Noster* with Zenck's edition of the same work. Organization of the analysis is as follows:
Column

- A  Measure number
- B  Accidentals in the tablature; not in the Zenck edition
- C  Accidentals in the Zenck edition; not in the tablature
- D  Musica ficta in the Zenck edition; also in the tablature
- E  Musica ficta in the Zenck edition; not in the tablature
- F  Musica ficta recommended in the Zenck edition; in the tablature
- G  Musica ficta recommended in the Zenck edition; not in the tablature

- H  Comments

Primarily considered here are notational differences other than those involving chromaticism, variations in voice leading, embellished passages, chord structures of particular interest, and other important aspects of the music not covered by the other categories.

Two notational divergences that appear frequently and are fairly obvious are not mentioned in the commentary: (1) rests in the transcription that indicate where a string must be released to allow another voice to be played on the same string and (2) notes not repeated in the vocal original that are repeated in the tablature. (Continued on page 51.)

Table 1: Comparative Analysis

| A | B | C | D | E | F | G | H |
|---|---|---|---|---|---|---|---|
| Measure Number | Accidentals in Tab.; not in Z | Accidentals in Z; not in Tab. | Musica Ficta in Z; also in Tab. | Musica Ficta in Z; not in Tab. | Musica Ficta recommended in Z; in Tab. | Musica Ficta recommended in Z; not in Tab. | Comments |
| 4 | | | | | | | Two beats lacking in Tab. |
| 7 | | | | | | | Error in Tab.: the 2 on the second string should be on the first string. |
| 11 | S: b natural | | | | | | |
| 13 | | | | | | | Z has d and e as eighth notes in A on first beat; the d is omitted in Tab. Z has quarter rest in S on first beat. |
| 15 | B: e♭ | | | | | | S:g that appears in Z is omitted in Tab. |
| 16 | T: f♯<br>A: e♭ | | | | | | |
| 17 | | | | | | | A has e natural in Z, e♭ in Tab. |
| 18 | A: e♭ | | | | | | In Z, A (second beat) has d and c as eighth notes; Tab. has two d's. |

19 S: f#

20 B:g in Tab. does not appear in Z.

21 A: f# T:b♭ in Tab. appears in A in Z.
T:a in Tab. (second half of second beat) appears in A in Z.

28 Error in Tab.: the 3 on the first string should be on the second string.
A:g (first beat in Tab.) does not appear in Z; instead the a from previous measure is tied over.
B:d (first beat in Z) does not appear in Tab.

31 Tab. has both a and f (first beat in A).
In Tab., S is embellished (third and fourth beats); S is not embellished in Z.

33 In Tab. B is embellished (third and fourth beats);

| A | B | C | D | E | F | G | H |
|---|---|---|---|---|---|---|---|
| 34 | | | | | | | B is not embellished in Z. In Tab., S is embellished (first and second beats); S is not embellished in Z. T has b♭ and a as eighth notes in Tab.; Z has the a only. |
| 35 | | | | | | | In Tab., S is embellished (third and fourth beats); S is not embellished in Z. |
| 36 | | | | S: f# (f natural in Tab.) | | | |
| 37 | | | | | | | T: a in Tab. does not appear in Z; Z has half rest at this point. |
| 45 | | | A: e♭ | | | | |
| 46 | | | A: e♭<br>T: f# | | | | |
| 47 | S: f# | | | | | | A: b♭ in Z does not appear in Tab. |
| 48 | | | A: e♭ | | | | |
| 49 | S: f#<br>T: c# | | | | | | |
| 50 | | | | T: e♭ | S: f# | | |

| | | | | | |
|---|---|---|---|---|---|
| 51 | S: b natural | | B: eᵇ | T: eᵇ | |
| 52 | T: c# | | B: eᵇ | | Note French Aug. sixth implication in Tab.; it is not apparent in Z. |
| 54 | | S: f natural | | | S is embellished (third and fourth beats in Tab.); S is not embellished in Z. |
| 56 | | A: eᵇ (third and fourth beats) | | | |
| 57 | A: c# | | | | |
| 58 | S: f# | | B: eᵇ | | |
| 59 | A: b natural (second and third beats) | A: b natural (fourth beat) | | | In Tab., A is embellished (third and fourth beats); A is not embellished in Z. |
| 61 | A:b natural | | | | |
| 63 | T: f# | | | | B:d on first beat in Z is omitted in Tab. S:a on fourth beat in Z is omitted in Tab. |

| A | B | C | D | E | F | G | H |
|---|---|---|---|---|---|---|---|
| 64 | | | | | | | A:e^b (musica ficta) in Z appears as d in Tab. |
| 65 | | | | | | | |
| 66 | T: b natural | S: f# | | | | | |
| 67 | | A: e^b | | | | | A:d (third beat in Tab.) does not appear in Z (the e^b receives three beats instead). S:g in Z is omitted in Tab. |
| 68 | S: f#<br>T: b natural (third beat) | | | | | | T in Z has two a quarter notes and two b^b quarter notes. |
| 71 | T: f#<br>B: f# | | | | | | |
| 72 | | | | | | | T and B in Tab. are exchanged as compared with Z. |
| 73 | A: c# | | | | | | |
| 75 | T: f# | | | | | | |
| 76 | S: f# | | | | | | |
| 77 | B: f# (followed later by f natural) | | | | | | |

| | | | |
|---|---|---|---|
| 78 | | | |
| 80 | | B: e♭ | B in Z has d (last half of second beat); Tab has c. On last half of fourth beat, T has both a and b♭ in Tab.; Z has b♭ in A only. |
| 82 | | S: f# | |
| 83 | B: b natural | | |
| 84 | A: f#<br>B: b natural | | |
| 86 | T: c#<br>A: b natural | A: f# | B:c (second beat in Z) does not appear in Tab. |
| 87 | | | |
| 89 | | S: c# | |
| 91 | T: f# | | In Tab., T is embellished (third and fourth beats); T is not embellished in Z. In Tab., B is embellished (first and second beats); B is not embellished in Z. |
| 92 | A: b natural | | |
| 93 | S: f# | | |
| 95 | | S: f# | |
| 96 | | A: e♭ | |

| A | B | C | D | E | F | G | H |
|---|---|---|---|---|---|---|---|
| 97 | | | A: b natural | | | | |
| 100 | A: b natural | | | | | | |
| 101 | S: f# | | | | | | |
| 102 | | | S: f# | | | | |
| 103 | | T: b natural | | | | | |
| 104 | | | | T: b natural | | | |
| 105 | | | | | | | Error in Tab.: 5 instead of 3 should be on third string. |
| 106 | | | S: f# | | | | |
| 107 | | T: b natural | | | | | |
| 108 | | | | T: b natural | | | |
| 110 | A: c# | B: e♭ | | | | | |
| 112 | | | A: b natural | | | | |
| 114 | | | | | | | Entire chord on first beat of Z is missing in Tab. |
| 116 | | | | S: e♭ | | | |

Accidentals that are clearly marked and that appear in both the tablature and the Zenck edition are not mentioned in the commentary.

Explanations

Abbreviations:

S = Soprano
A = Alto
T = Tenor
B = Bass
Z = Zenck, Hermann, ed. *Adrian Willaert: Opera Omnia* 2. Rome, 1950.

Tab. = Tablature (refers to Pisador's intabulation of the same *Pater Noster* and/or the accompanying transcription).

Lower case letters are used to refer to particular notes.
Range is not designated because S, A, T, B are specified.
*Beat* refers to quarter-note motion in either Tab. or Z.

Warren Earle Hultberg

# The Palace Church of Santa Barbara in Mantua, and Monteverdi's Relationship to Its Liturgy*

Church music practice in Mantua, as elsewhere in the first part of the sixteenth century, was marked by its close relationship to and dependence upon liturgical needs. For ecclesiastical Mantua, the papal Sistine Chapel and the Julia Chapel of St. Peter's in Rome remained the determining model, and the a cappella vocal style developed there was strictly observed. The music life of the court followed a different pattern of development: its characteristics were determined by the new type of musician whose creative talents were directed first and foremost toward the aristocratic chamber. He is the established minstrel, whom we meet now, cloaked in a new garb: accustomed to serving, faithful to his master in all things, he has become the *familiaris* of the noble patron. Armed with a plucked or bowed stringed instrument, his singing is heard in the circles of the highest society—*dilettanti* and even, in the entourage of his lord, in the church. Thus begins the victorious advance of the instrumentalist, who in the course of the century will match his art against the previously unquestioned supremacy of vocal music.

The rapid social rise of the instrumental musician gave impetus at the Gonzaga Court to a new musical practice independent of the church. The first stage of independence was reached with the cultivation of chamber music forms; names such as Marchetto Cara, Bartolomeo Tromboncino, Giovanni Angelo Testagrossa, and Francesco da Milano are proof enough of this. Nevertheless, there was at this time no church belonging directly to the Court; therefore, the larger musical functions of sacred nature always took place in the Cathedral

*This paper was presented, in somewhat different form, to the California Chapter Meeting of the AMS at the University of Southern California in Los Angeles, Spring 1971.

of San Pietro. It was not until the construction of the palace church of Santa Barbara that the court itself could be involved in the cultivation of an autonomous church music. Henceforth, the House of the Gonzagas had a church of its own, thus relieving the Cathedral and the old burial church of San Paola of their former ceremonial functions.

The musical life of Mantua now existed on three levels: (a) the traditional church music practice, with its strong orientation toward Rome (the center for this remained the Cathedral of San Pietro); (b) the *courtly* church music at Santa Barbara, with its special characteristics; and (*c*) the secular courtly music in the chambers of the Gonzaga residences in and around Mantua.

The construction of the Basilica Palatina di Santa Barbara dates back to Duke Guglielmo, the ruler of Mantua from approximately 1550 to 1587. Few of his predecessors—and none who came after him—could equal him as a ruler. He was a nearly perfect sovereign who seemed to embody Petrarch's admonition: "You must not only be the lord of your people, but also the father of your country; and you must love each subject as if he were your own child." Generous by nature and a lover of pomp, though never lavish or wasteful, by temperament irascible, energetic and impetuous, as well as stubborn and moody, Guglielmo possessed nevertheless the genial, never ceasing patience of his famous grandmother, Isabella d'Este, and like her, never lost sight of his goals. In matters of intellect, too, he was highly gifted, with many faceted interests encompassing art and, above all, music.

While Guglielmo was still in his youth the idea of building a church to Santa Barbara, the patron saint of his family, had already taken form. He entrusted the plan of the church to the Mantovan architect, Giovan Battista Bertani. Under Bertani's direction, the palace church of Santa Barbara was constructed between 1563 and 1565. The structure was single naved, in the style of a Basilica, with three chapels on either side; the presbytery and chancel stood several feet above the level of the rest of the church. Above the entrance porch Bertani designed a second choir loft where "the musicians may be placed to sing the solemn high festival masses."[1] Thus, the conditions were created that would enable Mantua to develop the double-choir style of Venice. A twelve-register organ, built by Graziadio and Costanzo Antegnati, was placed in the foremost chapel on the right side.

In every respect the church bespoke the taste and grandeur of its founder. The Duke, through connections in Rome, was able to ar-

---

[1] See Ippolito Donesmondi, *Dell 'istoria ecclesiastica di Mantova* (Mantua, 1613-16), 2:212.

range a special administrative position for his church that remained in effect until the Concordancy between Italy and the Vatican in 1929. But even this extremely exceptional arrangement for the Basilica did not completely satisfy the Duke; he wanted his independence from Rome to be even more apparent and for this reason devoted his efforts toward the introduction of his own special liturgy. For he had not only interested himself in liturgical questions, but had become quite learned in them. Founded on this knowledge, the prototype for a Missal as well as for a Breviary, which he drafted, derived from more than pure presumptuousness on his part. He sent these in 1568 to Rome with the intent of receiving papal approbation of them. Such extravagances met with great opposition in the Vatican. Nevertheless, his almost limitless perserverance and his ambition were finally rewarded with success: on 10 November 1583, Guglielmo's liturgy was approved by Pope Gregory XIII. In connection with this, the Pope is supposed to have said that he would rather abdicate than to wrestle a second time with such a stubborn and unyielding supplicant as this. Now the Duke had—with official blessings—his own liturgy. Even this, however, was not sufficient; now he had to have his own music! To this end Guglielmo had a considerable number of large choir books made that are preserved to this day in the Archivio Storico Diocesano in Mantua. These contain the cantus firmi of the special liturgy of the Santa Barbara church.

Knud Jeppesen has shown that, in accordance with prevailing polyphonic practice of the time, the unity of tonality was recognized in this liturgy as the foremost musical principle. Thus, all five parts of the ordinary of the mass are in the same key. To this end the chronological order of the Kyriale sections were changed, and sometimes whole sections were ·rewritten. Jeppesen offers the comment that the responsibility for these Mantuan revisions cannot totally be laid at the doorsteps of the Mantuan musicians; quite possibly such "improvements" were of an older origin that has not yet been traced. At any rate, Mantua was not alone in such misunderstandings of the character of Medieval melody, for this was a general tendency of the sixteenth century, the "Golden Age of Choral Reform." "Under the circumstances," Jeppesen writes, "one can't help but be amazed at encountering a considerable number of melodies in the Santa Barbara Kyriales which are of high artistic merit and exhibit a fine sense of style."[2] In general, one can say that while Guglielmo's striving for his

[2]Knud Jeppesen, "The Recently Discovered Mantova Masses of Palestrina," *Acta musicologica* 22 (1950): 36; idem, "Monteverdi, Kapellmeister an S.ta Barbara?" in *Claudio Monteverdi e il suo tempo,* ed. R. Monterosso (Venice-Mantua-Cremona, 1968), p. 313.

own liturgy was, on the one hand, founded in his own personal ambition, yet on the other hand, it demonstrates the courtly attitude toward the single-voiced liturgy.

From the very beginning—and continuing until the decline of the Gonzaga line—the musical practices of the church of Santa Barbara were the responsibility of the court musicians, and the dukes reserved for themselves the right to engage all musicians for the palace church. Initially, the money had to come from the pocket of Guglielmo: in a letter of 27 August 1578, he complains that due to insufficient funds from the church he must donate his own private cappella for the church's needs. By the end of the 1580s, however, the church's financial status was so secure that it was able to establish its own choir, entirely independent of the court. From this time onward, the church was able to have at its service its own maestro di cappella, its own cantus firmus teacher for the clerics, an organist, and an ensemble of six to eight professional singers, all paid from the coffers of the church.[3]

This was the situation at the church and court when, in 1590/91, the young Monteverdi became a member of the chamber ensemble. Existing virtually under the same roof was the emancipating practice of the chamber and the new music making of the church that was beginning, in its own right, to free itself from the bonds of conservative, Roman orientation. What was Monteverdi's position vis-à-vis the Palace Church of Santa Barbara; was he a member of the singers-collegium there that was responsible for the musical liturgy?; or was he there in another capacity, perhaps as maestro di cappella; and which of his compositions were intended for sacred events in Mantua?[4] Monteverdi first appeared in the Mantuan court records as a viola player, and then in 1594, also as a singer. As a composer he made his mark with the publications of his Madrigal Books in 1592, 1603, and 1605, his Scherzi Musicali in 1607, and of course, his dramatic works: the epoch-making Orfeo in 1607, and in 1608, Arianna—of which we have only a fragment—and Ballo delle Ingrate. There is no evidence that he wrote any church music in Mantua before 1610; the fact of the matter is, it was not until two years before his departure from Mantua in 1612 that he published his In illo tempore Mass and the famous Vespro della Beata Vergine—a work that was as great a landmark for church music as Orfeo was for the beginning of musical drama. The quantitatively modest portions of church music from this

---

[3]See P. M. Tagmann, "La capella dei maestri cantori della Basilica Palatina di Santa Barbara a Mantova (1565-1630)," in Civiltà Mantovana, Anno IV, no. 24 (1971).
[4]Ibid.

period already attest to a somewhat less than intensive relationship between Monteverdi and the palace church. Nonetheless, Leo Schrade writes in his *Monteverdi: Creator of Modern Music* that from 1602 onward, Monteverdi was responsible for all musical productions at the Court of Mantua, and says in regard to Monteverdi's conjectural musical activity at Santa Barbara, "he had to supervise and also to provide the music for the services or for special occasions of a religious character."[5] However, we have already established the fact that—aside from the works published in 1610—there are no church music compositions of Monteverdi from the Mantuan period. Bassano Casola, a court musician, states in a letter that the Vespers were printed in July 1610 and provided with a dedication to Pope Paul V in September of the same year.[6] It appears that with this work Monteverdi hoped—unfortunately in vain—to secure a place in the Seminario Romano for his son, Francesco. Thus we see that Monteverdi's sacred works of 1610 were composed with an eye to his forthcoming visit to the Pope in Rome. The text used in the Vespers strengthens this point of view.

In the central core of the Vesper composition, namely the five Psalms, Monteverdi did not take his texts from the Santa Barbara Breviary, but rather from the Roman Antiphonal. In the Santa Barbara Breviary only the first Psalm, *Dixit Dominus* (No. 112), appears, though here as the fourth Psalm. Thus we see that with exception of the Psalms No. 109 and 112, none of the others—neither the *Laetatus sum* (No. 121), nor the *Nisi Dominus* (No. 126), nor the closing *Lauda Jerusalem* (No. 147)—is found in the Mantuan Breviary; in place of these are lines from other Psalms: *Confitebor, Beatus vir,* and *Laudate Dominum.* Regarding the antiphons, we find no relationship at all between the Breviary of Santa Barbara and the Roman Antiphonal. And here Monteverdi follows neither the Roman nor the Santa Barbara model, with perhaps the single exception of the text preceding the second Psalm that coincides to a certain extent with the Roman antiphon text *Nigra sum.* At this point, we must ask ourselves where Monteverdi got the other texts for his chain of antiphon-substitutes, for they belong neither to the Antiphonale Romanum, nor to the Breviary of Santa Barbara: in neither is there a feast of Mary with which Monteverdi's texts would correspond. These compositions appear to be outside the traditional liturgical order.[7]

---

[5]Leo Schrade, *Monteverdi: Creator of Modern Music* (New York, 1950), p. 247.

[6]See Stefano Davari, *Notizie biografiche del distinto maestro di musica Claudio Monteverdi* (Mantua, 1885), pp. 23-24.

[7]If we assume, with Schrade, that the compositions were liturgical "in the strictest sense" and were "related to specific services which could never take place in profane

In order to answer the question of Monteverdi's participation in the services of Santa Barbara we must delineate the different areas of musical activity between the palace church and the court. Until the 1580s, the music of *both* was under the exclusive direction of Jaches Wert, one of the most representative musical figures of the generation directly preceding Monteverdi; under him was an imposing number of singers and instrumentalists: the documents of that time attest to around twenty musicians who performed at all chamber functions. That they were often required to sing and play in the church—without special remuneration!—is shown in a letter of a court official from the year 1579: "[il Duca] sin hora ha mandato il suo maestro di capella, organista, et suoi cantori continovamente a S.ta Barbara senza punto di spesa."[8] Giovanni Giacomo Gastoldi, the church musician who, some years later, also did very well for himself in court circles, substituted for his sick teacher, Jaches Wert, with increasing frequency in the years following 1582. It was under him that the church choir attained complete independence from the chamber. Around the year 1590 he had, as has already been mentioned, some six to eight singers at his disposal. From the beginning of the uninterrupted account entries,[9] December 1592 onward, Gastoldi is no longer referred to as *praefectus* (a title he was still using in his publication of 1588), but as the all-responsible and single-ruling maestro di capella of Santa Barbara, and he remained in this position until his death, which occurred on 4 January 1609.

From a letter of Baltasar Monteverdi, Claudio's father, we learn that his son was to be given this position after Gastoldi's death. Duke Vincenzo's final decision, however, was quite different. Perhaps he could not bear to part with the successful young chamber composer; or perhaps he felt that Monteverdi was not qualified enough for such

---

surroundings," then the question regarding the intended purpose of these compositions becomes even more obscure. Compare with Stephen Bonta, "Liturgical Problems in Monteverdi's Marian Vespers," *Journal of the American Musicological Society* 20 (Spring 1967): 87-106.

  [8]See the letter of Fed. Cattaneo (12 May 1579) in Arch. Gonzaga Mantua, Busta 2208, mentioned in Jeppesen, "Monteverdi," p. 316.

  [9]Regarding the extant archival material, I found—as have many other researchers there—that the musical source material at the palace church of Santa Barbara was strewn asunder in the middle of the nineteenth century thanks to an overly industrious clergyman by the name of Don Giuseppi Greggiati, who at that time abruptly appropriated nearly all of the collected musical documents and other sources of information relating to the Basilica Palatina di Santa Barbara. The works that Greggiati retained in his possession were left by him at his death to the local government of Ostiglia in the vicinity of Mantua. There they remain to this day, well ordered in the main, but not easily accessible in the Biblioteca Greggiati. The great majority of the musical documents (early prints, manuscripts) of the sixteenth and seventeenth centuries, however, were sold by Greggiati to the Milan Conservatory (see *Catalogo della Biblioteca del Conservatorio di musica 'G. Verdi', Fondi speciali I, Musiche della Cappella di Santa Barbara*, ed. Guglielmo Barblan, Biblioteca di Bibliografia italiana 68 [Florence, 1972]).

a position in church music. Whatever the case, the fact is that not Claudio Monteverdi, but rather the little-known Stefano Nascimbeni took the post as Gastoldi's successor. When Claudio's brother, Giulio Cesare, alleged that his brother was responsible for both church *and* chamber music—"tiene il carico de la musica tanto da chiesa quanto da camera"[10]—something appears to be not quite in order. Baldassare's letter shows that Claudio could not have held the position of which Giulio Cesare speaks; at the very most he might have, from time to time, just as a substitute taken over Gastoldi's duties at the palace church. The name of Monteverdi is not to be found in the ledgers of the account books of Santa Barbara, neither among the choir teachers nor the singers.[11] This much is now fact: Claudio Monteverdi during his twenty-three years at the Gonzaga Court was at no time directly connected with the palace church as *praefectus musices* or as maestro di capella.[12]

Nevertheless, one important question still remains unanswered: for what purpose, or for what occasion, might Monteverdi have composed the *Vespro?* As has already been mentioned, it was dedicated to Pope Paul V, together with the Mass *In illo tempore,* written in the conservative style of the old Flemish masters, based on eight, or according to Denis Stevens, even ten themes from Gombert's motet.[13] We saw also that Monteverdi did not wish to bind his expansive vesper composition to any particular liturgy. Rather, he attempted to utilize the new achievements of the courtly music—as they are discussed in the *Dichiarazione* of 1607—as an example of church music. We can establish that the Mass follows exactly the requirements of the *Prima Prattica* and that Monteverdi, in his second work, exemplified all of the advantages of the *Seconda Prattica;* he appears to have had two goals in mind in writing the *Vespro;* on the one hand he intended to introduce the Pope to the musical innovations of his

[10]O. Strunk, *Source Readings in Music History* (New York, 1950), p. 406.

[11]In Mantua, in rooms adjoining the palace church, several dozen volumes of account books have been preserved (now at the Archivo Storico Diocesano di Mantova, Fondo Basilica Palatina di S. Barbara); the lists of musicians from the years 1565 to 1627, that is to say, from the founding of the palace church to the death of the last of the Mantuan Gonzagas, have by error found their way into the fascicles of later centuries. I found the relevant documents in the account books of the seventeenth, eighteenth, and, partially, even of the nineteenth centuries (see my article "La cappella dei maestri cantori della Basilica Palatina di Santa Barbara a Mantova [1565-1630]" in *Civiltà Mantovana,* Anno IV, n. 24 [1971]).

[12]Schrade, who leans heavily on the Monteverdi biography of Domenico de'Paoli, builds his chapter on "Sacred Music in Mantua" on false premises insofar as he, following Monteverdi's election to director of court music in the chamber, ascribes to him the leadership of the chapel choir as well, and then ventures to assume his active participation in the music-making of the church. The facts, however, do not support this contention.

[13]See Denis Stevens's forthcoming publication on C. Monteverdi to be published by Oxford University Press (chapter on religious music).

*Seconda Prattica* and at the same time he wanted to use the opportunity to show the high artistic *niveau* of his court ensemble that, like other courtly chamber groups, was far above the performance level of the church musicians. It was with this in mind that he gave the two works their common title. Monteverdi is very specific in indicating that the Mass is "ad ecclesiarum choros" and the *Vespro* "ad sacella sive Principum cubicula," that is to say, for the private chambers of the Duke. It is also particularly instructive to note that the Mass text is printed in large uppercase letters, while the text of the *Vespro* is printed in the smallest possible type. This was undoubtedly done intentionally in order to avoid offending the conservative Roman Curia; the crucial innovations were intended to a certain extent to be slipped in to the traditional framework through the back door, as it were. Should, however, the composition gain the applause and approval of papal circles, then last but not least, the tiresome polemicist Artusi would have been dealt a solid rebuke. The *Vespro* must thus be judged as a musical-artistic *exemplum;* in it the musical innovations of the *Seconda Prattica* were brought to bear on the realm of sacred music. The title shows quite clearly Monteverdi's intention of fitting secular musical practice to sacred forms. It is a first and powerful manifestation of sacred chamber music!

Concerning the occasion for which the *Vespro* was composed, we have to remember that in 1608 Duke Vincenzo offered magnificent ceremonials for the wedding of his son Francesco to Margherita of Savoy. On 29 July 1609, a daughter was born to the princely couple and was baptized Maria. We therefore may assume that this event gave birth to the composer's intent to write a work dedicated to the Blessed Virgin, including perhaps some compositions of an earlier date as antiphon substitutes. As the Marian feasts of 5 August—the anniversary of the Dedication of the Santa Maria Maggiore Basilica in Rome, universally celebrated since 432—were too close to Maria's birthday, some parts of the *Vespro* may have been premiered on 15 August, the Assumption, or on 8 September 1609, the feast day of the Nativity of Our Lady. As we have no reason to doubt the word of Bassano Casola, we may further conclude that the *Vespro* reached its final stage sometime between Maria's birth and her name day, 25 March (Annunciation) 1610 and could have been performed *in toto* preceding Monteverdi's trip to Rome, on 8 September 1610, perhaps even in the same *sala* in which, some two and a half years earlier, *Orfeo* was presented to a large crowd.[14]

Pierre M. Tagmann

[14]The obvious parallelism of the opening measures in both works may indicate that they were performed in the same location.

# The Villancicos in Pedro Rimonte's *Parnaso Español* (1614)

Spain became an international power when Charles V was elected Holy Roman Emperor in 1519 and was, at least in appearance, the supreme state in Europe by the turn of the seventeenth century. She exported gold, soldiers, and the "Spanish etiquette"; she also exported musicians and music to Brussels, Vienna, Italy, and the New World. The Aragonese composer, Pedro Rimonte (1565-1627), was one of the Spaniards who found patronage abroad, becoming *maestro de capilla* (ca. 1603), then *maestro de la música de camara* to the Archdukes Albert and Isabella, governors of the rebellious Low Countries.[1]

Three imprints of Rimonte's work[2] were published in Antwerp by Pierre Phalèse during the relatively peaceful decades between the Peace of London (1604) and the expiration of the truce between the Spanish Netherlands and the states of Holland in 1621. They form part of the picture of a conscious effort to revive culture in the war-torn cities of Flanders and Brabant.[3] The last print, *Parnaso Español de madrigales y villancicos* (1614), is Rimonte's only secular collection and was published in the year in which he returned to the Aragonese city of Zaragoza. The *Parnaso* contains nine madrigals (four *a* 4, two *a* 5, and three *a* 6) and twelve villancicos (six *a* 5 and six *a* 6) and thus pairs two important polyphonic song forms inherited from the sixteenth century—the cosmopolitan Italianate madrigal and the traditional Spanish villancico.

---

[1]A short biographical summary and list of Rimonte's works are given in Miguel Querol's article for *Die Musik in Geschichte und Gegenwart* 11 (1963): 527. For further documentation concerning Rimonte's activities at the court in Brussels, see Eleanor Russell, "Pedro Rimonte in Brussels," *Anuario musical* 28 (1973): (forthcoming). Dates for Rimonte (=Ruymonte) are kindly supplied by Pedro Calahorra Martinez, who will soon publish a complete biography.

[2]Pedro Rimonte, *Missae sex iv. v. et vi vocum* (Antwerp, 1604); *Cantiones sacrae . . . et Hieremiae Prophetae Lamentationes sex vocum* (Antwerp, 1607); and *Parnaso Español de madrigales y villancicos a quatro, cinco, et seys* (Antwerp, 1614).

[3]P. Geyl, *The Revolt of the Netherlands* (London, 1932), contains an account of the military and political events leading to the governorship of Albert and Isabella and of the subsequent cultural revival in Flemish cities.

Phalèse gave the *Parnaso* an elegant format. The only complete exemplar[4] probably retains the original binding: six part-books, 14.5 x 18.5 cm. (4°), with paper covers and boxed in cardboard. The music is printed from a single impression; the text is in roman typeface with three sizes of capitals set in abstract floral patterns. Each part-book has a title page, dedication, and table of contents. The superius holds twenty-four folios (A1 to F4), but in addition has a beautifully engraved frontispiece showing cherubs holding a coat of arms and a figure conducting the Muses on Mount Parnassus, who play the organ, lyre, viols, cornetto, and sing from part-books. Apollo sits on the crest of Parnassus at the left, Pegasus leaps toward him from the right side of the print, and Athena sheds her wisdom on the assembled musicians and dancers from the center. The title page that follows shows that Rimonte was still maestro of chamber music for the Archduke and Archduchess in 1614,[5] and bears the favorite printer's mark of Pierre Phalèse.[6] The volume is dedicated, however, to "the most excellent Sr. Don Francisco Gómez de Sandoval," the powerful Duke of Lerma in Spain, whose coat of arms[7] appears on the frontispiece.

Rimonte's dedication, flattering a court favorite instead of the royal ruler proper, is a clear indication of the new turn Spanish politics took in the century following Philip III's accession in 1598. *Validos*—trusted courtiers such as Lerma—would make administrative decisions and would control royal patronage in the seventeenth century, in marked contrast to the close personal supervision typical both of the Catholic kings and Philip II.[8] And if Rimonte's dedication

---

[4]Paris, Bibliothèque Nationale, Res Vm7 45. Incomplete copies exist in Brussels, Barcelona, and Oxford. See Jean Peeters-Fontainas, *Bibliographie des impressions espagnoles des Pays-Bas meridionaux* (Nieukoop, 1965), no. 1128.

[5]F.1: *"Parnaso Español / de madrigales, y villancicos / a quatro, cinco et seys. / Compuestos por Pedro Rimonte, Maestro de Musica de la / Camera de los Ser^mos Principes / Alberto y Doña Isabel Clara Eugenia / Archiduques de Austria. / En Amberes / En Casa de Pedro Phalesio al Rey David / M.DCXIV."*

[6]Alphonse J. Goovaerts, *Histoire et bibliographie de la typographie musicale dans les Pays-Bas* (Antwerp, 1880), 1:61. The mark Phalèse used most frequently was probably a copy of the insignia above his door. It shows King David in his royal robes and crown playing a harp.

[7]Alberto and Arturo García Caraffa, *Enciclopedia heráldica y genealógica hispanoamericana* (Madrid, 1959), 82: figs. 232 and 405.

[8]Philip II's concern for even minute details is documented by innumerable marginal notes in his handwriting among the state papers in the archives of Simancas. On the other hand, his son, Philip III, avoided the affairs of state by turning over power and decisions to his favorite courtier, the Duke of Lerma, who became an untitled prime minister. Diplomats noted the shift; in 1602 the Venetian ambassador remarked that Lerma's favor was even more important than the King's. John Lynch, *Spain under the Hapsburgs* (New York, 1969), 2:14-29, discusses Lerma's career as *valido* and indicts both King and favorite: "If Philip III was the laziest ruler Spain has had, Lerma was incomparably the greediest."

shows an astute awareness of the shift in government policies, his villancicos in particular demonstrate an equally acute understanding of the shift to new musical techniques. This article examines those villancicos as works that best exemplify the forward-looking aspects of his style.

*    *    *

The traditional court villancico of the sixteenth century was a secular polyphonic composition shaped by a poetic-musical refrain. Its text involved courtly or pastoral love or popular folk themes. A few had religious subjects, associating bucolic settings with the scenes of Bethlehem. By the time of Rimonte's chapelmastership, however, settings of villancicos with spiritualized texts had become necessary equipment for any cathedral maestro. The competitions for the post of maestro de capilla in Zaragoza Cathedral in 1587 already stipulated that candidates should not only add and sing a third or fifth part to a pre-extant mass section *a* 2 or *a* 4, and compose and sing a motet upon a given plainchant, but also write and sing a villancico upon a given song.[9] Such villancicos were reserved for festive occasions.[10] Singers in the Collegiate Church of San Salvador, Seville, in 1633, for example, were required to sing a Christmas Matins service with nine villancicos and a mass with villancicos on the second day of the Christmas festival.[11] Géry de Gersem, Rimonte's colleague who served as maestro de capilla in Brussels after 1604, received an annual gift of 250 florins in the years 1611-15 "for [composing] the Christmas villancicos."[12]

These new religious villancicos retain the poetic form described by Juan Díaz Rengifo in 1592 in which the opening stanza, the

[9]Dr. Pascual de Mandura, "Libro de me Memorias de las cosas que en la Iglesia se han ofrecido . . . del año 1579 hasta el ño 1601" (Madrid, Biblioteca Nacional, MS 14047), ff. 5-6.

[10]Philip III received high praise for refusing to be entertained by villancicos on the occasion of his state visit to Zaragoza after his accession to the throne. Vincencio Blasco de Lanuza, in his *Historias eclesiasticas y seculares de Aragón* (Zaragoza, 1618), 2:397, col. 2, approves the King's desire to hear only motets and "well-established" music instead of villancicos: " . . . y quiso oyr aquella tarde otra vez en su palacio los Cantores, no permitiendo le cantassen villazicos, sino motetes y cosas fundadas . . . ."

[11]"Libro de Autos Capitulares de el Cabildo desta Colegial de nuestro Señor S. Salvador deesde el año 1633" (Seville, Archivo del Palacio Arzobispal), f. 190: "An de servir el Maestro y Cantores de la Capilla en cada un año las fiestas y asistensias siguientes y los ministrels con ellos . . . Natividad-Calenda-primera y segundas Visperas Maytines connuebe Villancicos=Missa de gallo=y procession primero dia de Pascua=y missa con Villancicos el segundo dia de Pascua . . . ."

[12]Brussels, Archives générales du Royaume de Belgique, Chambre des Comptes, No. 1837, f. 218: ". . . dareis a geri gersen mro de m¹ capilla 2ucientos y cinquanta florines de a veinte placas cada uno . . . de costa de esta vez por los Villancicos de la Navidad del año pass^do. 1613." Similar gifts are recorded on ff. 178v, 353, and in No. 1838, ff. 67v and 92v.

*cabeza* or *estribillo,* sets the main subject and reappears as part of the refrain:

> In the villancicos there is a head and feet; the head is a verse of two, or three or four lines, which the Italians in their *ballatas* call repetition or reprise because one is accustomed to repeat it after the feet. The feet are a stanza of six lines which is like a variation of the idea which is contained in the head.[13]

In Rimonte's *Parnaso,* eight of the opening stanzas (estribillos) are quatrains, six of them using the rhyme scheme *abba.* Only four have shorter estribillos and all of the latter can be allied with pre-extant poetic material. There are invariably two *coplas,* the poetic elaborations of the principal theme, and these are also quatrains, all except number four rhyming *cddc.* Stanzas II and III (*vueltas*) complete the coplas, and involve asymmetrical returns to the estribillo lines and rhyming words by a variety of schemes. Poetically they are a continuation of the sections Rimonte marks copla. In addition to the second copla, Rimonte adds a repeat of the estribillo (marked *Responsion*) and thus his standard poetic villancico form becomes:

|                     |                  |                   |
|---------------------|------------------|-------------------|
| Estribillo          | — Responsion     | = [Estribillo]    |
| Copla I + Vuelta    | — Responsion     | = [Estribillo]    |
| Copla II + Vuelta   | — Responsion     | = [Estribillo]    |

The twelve villancicos follow the new fashion by using spiritual subjects. Many of the texts are conventionally religious and perhaps even mediocre, with the crying or suffering of the Christ Child, the "King of the Sky," the Virgin, or the "new Shepherd" the favored topics. By far the most interesting are those that gloss old estribillos by adding newly written *coplas a lo divino,* a process that links them back into the long popular history of the secular villancico.

One of the finest poems, number three, uses an estribillo that first appears in an anonymous musical setting in a print of 1556:

> ¡Ay, luna que reluces
>    Toda la noche m'alumbres![14]

---

[13] Juan Díaz Rengifo, *Arte poética española* (Salamanca, 1592), cap. XXIX, pp. 30-31: "Villācico es un genera de copla, q̃ solamēte se cōpone para ser cātado. Los demas metros sirvē para representar, para enseñar, para describir, para historia, y para otros propositos; pero este solo para la musica. En los Villancicos ay cabeça y pies; la cabeça es una copla de dos, o tres, o cuatro versos, que en sus ballatas llamā los italianos repetición o represa, por que suele repetir despues de los pies. Los pies sō una copla de seis versos, q̃ es como la glosa de la sentēcia q̃ se cōtiene en la cabeça."

[14] *Villancicos de diversos autores a dos y a tres y a cuatro y a cinco bozes* (Venice, 1556), f. A4; reprinted as *Cancionero de Upsala,* ed. Jesús Bal y Gay, notes and com-

The same estribillo begins a different poem in a Valencian *romancero,* "Los Romancerillos de Pisa," of 1594-98,[15] and is also quoted by the Spanish poet, José de Valdivielso in his "Ensaladilla vuelta al Santísima Sacramento."[16] The poem set by Rimonte uses the same well-traveled estribillo, but this time the moon illuminates a nativity scene:

Ah, shining moon!
All the night you light my way
Resplendent light, clear and brilliant
My sorrow waning
And my good increasing
The Kings of the Orient follow
Your lovely light
And your beautiful star.
The sun discovers them.[17]

"Quiero dormir y no puedo," number four, is another famous estribillo among the *Parnaso*'s poems. Juan Vásquez set it polyphonically in his *Villancicos I Canciones* (1551);[18] it also appears in Miguel Fuenllana's *Orphenica lyra* (1554)[19] and in at least three other manuscript sources.[20]

The one estribillo that would have been recognized instantly by any of Rimonte's contemporaries from erudite scholar to street musician is number nine:

Madre la mi madre
Guardarme queréis

mentaries by R. Mitjana, introductory essay by Isabel Pope (Mexico, 1944), pp. 61-62: "Ay luna que reluces / Toda la noche m'alumbres!/¡ Ay luna tan bella / Alúmbresme à la sierra / Por do vaya y venga!/ Ay luna que reluces / Toda la noche m'alumbres."

The poem is probably of popular origin. The brevity of the two estribillo lines, their metric inequality, the exclamations, the use of present tense, and the assonant rhymes of the copla all point toward an earlier folklike source.

[15]Antonio Sánchez Romeralo, *El villancico* (Madrid, 1969), p. 439.

[16]Quoted in J. M. Aguirre, *José de Valdivielso* (Toledo, 1965), p. 77.

[17]Ff. D3ᵛ-D4: "Luna que reluces / toda la noche me alumbre / Luz resplandeciente / clara y rutilante / A mi mal menguante / y a mi bien cresciente / Los Reyes de Oriente van tras / tu luz bella / y tu hermosa estrella. / El sol les descubries . . . ."

[18]Juan Vásquez, *Villancicos I Canciones* (Osuna, 1551), f. Biiii. The estribillo "I wish to sleep but I can't. Love takes my drowsiness from me," is followed in Rimonte's version by a copla that alludes to the role of the Good Shepherd: "I'm afraid that my flock walks alone." Vásquez offers a different explanation: "The King ordered it announced in Seville and Granada that each one should marry his lover. That would be sorrow indeed for mine is already married."

[19]Miguel Fuenllana, *Orphenica lyra* (Seville, 1554), f. cxxxvii.

[20]Margot Frenk Alatorre, "El Cancionero Sevilliano de la Hispanic Society c. 1568," *Nueva revista filología hispánica* 16 (1962):384, quotes a villancico in the Hispanic Society Library (New York, Hispanic Society, MS B 2486) that begins with the same estribillo. Sánchez Romeralo, *El villancico,* p. 496, cites another poem with this estribillo in Madrid, Biblioteca Nacional, MS 3919. Florence, Biblioteca Nazionale, Pan. 2973, f. 11, contains an "Aria" for the "chitarra spagnola" which begins "Quiero dormir."

Mas si yo no me guardo
Mal me guardaréis

Cervantes, in his *El celoso extremeño* (1613), mentions this estribillo as one known everywhere in Seville:

> . . . the owner took the guitar . . . she put it in the hands of Loaysa, asking that he play and sing some verses which then were very popular in Seville which said

> Madre la mi madre
> Guardas me ponéis.[21]

Cervantes, Lope de Vega, and Calderón all contain other references to the captivating little song[22] (for Cervantes makes it clear that it is to be sung). Gonzalo Correas quotes the estribillo in his *Arte de la lengua española castellana* of 1625 as an example of a *seguidilla*.[23] According to Correas, such seguidillas are an old form newly popular in his own time,[24] they are a poetic quatrain that alternates lines of six or seven syllables with lines of five,[25] and they are sung by common

---

[21]Miguel Cervantes Saavedra, *Novelas ejemplares* (Clásicos Castellanos), ed. Francisco Rodríguez Marín (Madrid, 1917), 2:149: "La dueña tomó la guitarra . . . se puso en las manos de Loaysa, rogándole que la tocase y que cantase unas copillas que entonces andaban muy validas en Sevilla, que decían
    Madre la mi madre
    Guardas me poneis . . . ."
[22]Ibid., p. 149, fn. 18. In Cervantes's *La entretenida* (*Ocho comedias*, f. 189) the text reads:
    "Barbaro: Alto, pues, vayan seguidas
    Cristina: Si, amigo, porque baylemos.
    Musicos: Madre la mi madre . . . ."
The estribillo is also used in Lope de Vega's *El Aldegüela, los melindres de Belisa*, and in the *Entremés de Daca mi mujer*. Calderón includes it in his comedy *Céfalo y Pocris*. J. B. Trend, "Catalogue of the Music in the Biblioteca Medinaceli, Madrid," *Revue hispanique* 71 (1927):551; and Jesús Bal y Gay, *Treinta canciones de Lope de Vega puestas en música* (Madrid, 1935), p. 108; both give still another source, Lope's *El mayor imposible*:
    "Diana: Cantad algo.
    Musicos: Aunque no es nueva, diremos
            . . . .
        Madre la mi madre . . . ."
[23]Gonzalo Correas, *Arte de la lengua española castellana* (1625), ed. and prologue by Emélio Alarcos García (Madrid, 1954), p. 453: "Ai tanbien seghidillas antiguas, i se hazen modernas con el segundo i cuarto verso de à zinco agudas con el azento en la ultima; mas porque aguda vale por dos. Ansimesmo las hallo viexas con primero i terzero de à siete, ocho, i nueve, i segundo i curato de à seis no agudo viene a ser ia verso senario de rredondilla menor . . .
    Madre la mi madre
    guardas me poneis
    que si io no me guardo
    mal me guardereis."
[24]Ibid., p. 441: ". . . las seghidillas, aviendolas antes mui usadas, aunque no tanto como en estos veinte años," and p. 447: " . . . desde el año de mil i seiszientos à esta parte an rrebivido, i an sido tan usadas . . . ."
[25]Ibid., p. 445: "Del verso de zinco silabas i de las seghidillas . . . esto verso de à zinco, como el pie quebrado, no se halla en poesia de por si solo; sino aconpañado con

people[26] who "follow their own pleasure and free life without laws."[27] Seguidillas must have been improvisatory originally, for in Cervantes's *La ilustre fregona* his text speaks of liberties and contradictions, such as *"seguidillas* in print, romances with *estribillos,* poetry without action."[28] Rimonte, however, makes the "Madre" of "Madre la mi madre" analogous to the Virgin, and in this way the roguish seguidilla comes in off the streets and is clothed with clerical respectability.

"Canta, Canta," number eleven, begins with a quatrain that is not of popular origin, but that is intertwined with Spanish tradition:

Gil pues al cantar del gallo
Dios Niño llorando esta
Canta que en mis libros hallo
Que otro gallo nos cantara

Gil is the courtly shepherd figure who appears in many of the secular sixteenth-century villancicos. The cock's crow (*cantar del gallo*) is associated with an important event, an arrival, or an awakening, often to love, in many traditional villancicos.[29] Here the Christ Child cries at the cock's crow, and Gil is to sing that now "another master will awaken us." The midnight mass sung with villancicos at the dawn of Christmas day is the "Missa de gallos," and this villancico was undoubtedly intended for performance at that time.

verso maior, de seis, i siete silabas, de ocho, nueve i diez, en cabezas de cantares i villancicos . . . i en las seghidillas, que son las mas iguales i rregulares, pero todos dulzes i suaves para cantar." Thus the first and third lines are variable while the second and fourth should contain five syllables: "La deven tener segundo i cuarto menores: que estos sienpre an de ser consonantes o asonantes, è iguales adonicos de à zinco silabas" (p. 448).'

Correas also says that seguidillas may be written in two long lines that contain the six or seven syllables (usually of the first and third lines) as well as the five syllables (usually of the second and fourth): "Casi todos escriven las seghidillas en dos versos que viene à ser cada uno onze ú doze silabas . . ." (p. 448). In one of his examples, p. 446, lines one and three contain the five syllables.

[26]Ibid., p. 447: "Son las seghidillas poesia mui antigua . . . que los conopone la xente vulgar i las cantan . . . ."

[27]Ibid., p. 447: "Pues las seghidillas nos dan tan buenas exenplos de los adonicas de à zinco silabas, i las artes poeticas se an olvidado dellas, como de las otras varias coplillas sueltas. . . . de cantares i folias . . . Aunque en este tienpo se han usado mas en lo burlesco i picante, como tan acomodados à la tonada i cantar alegre de bailes i danzas, i del pandero i de la xente de la seghida i enamorada, rrufianes i sus consortes, de quienes en particular nuevamente se les à pegado el nonbre á las seghidillas. I ellos se llamen de la seghida, i de la viga, de la vida seghida, i de la vida airada: porque sighen su gusto i plazer i vida libre sin lei, i su furia, i siguen i corren las casas publicas: . . . ."

[28]Cervantes, *Novelas ejemplares,* 1:239.

[29]A villancico by Vilches in the famous Cancionero de Palacio has this estribillo:

Ya cantan los Gallos            Now the cocks crow
Buen amor y vete               Good love, and see
Cata que amanece               Lo, the dawn begins

(See *La música en la corte de los reyes católicos,* ed. Higinio Anglés, Monumentos de la música española, 5 [Barcelona, 1947], 2:185.) A poem with the same text appears

"Amar y no padecer, no puede ser," is the last of the twelve villancicos. The abrupt statement and metrical inequality of its estribillo
may perhaps be allied to another popular source. The text also bears
a relationship to Luís de Góngora's long poem, "Que pida a un galan
Minguilla . . ." (1581), which uses a refrain, "No puede ser," and the
device of cause-and-effect events. Stanza twenty gives a good idea
of Góngora's mocking irony:

> That a rich miser would amass
> Doubloons by the hundreds
> That well could be
>
> But that his elegant successor
> Would not spend by the thousands
> That can't be.[30]

In the poem set by Rimonte, the estribillo shares the refrain, "No
puede ser," with Góngora's poem, and also the device of contrasting
events; the copla is the usual elaboration. The whole provides an
example of the general quality of the poetry in the *Parnaso*:

> To love and not to suffer
> That can't be
> Cry my Child and my God
> For now man is consoled
> That the cold which freezes him
> You must suffer yourself
> For to love and not to suffer
> That can't be.[31]

These poems lack the wit and skepticism of their sixteenth-century
cousins and instead veer toward the sentimental, but they fulfill the
need for spiritualized texts and the new function of the old, courtly
villancicos.

* * *

The real delight of Rimonte's villancicos lies in the music itself
and in the composer's successful adaptation of a number of new

---

in Elvas, Portugal, MS 11973, no. 54, according to Anglés, Monumentos de la música
española (Barcelona, 1941/1960) 1:127-28. "Gallo" is used in many expressions as a
symbol of the leader, master, or the center of attention.

[30]Luis de Góngora y Argote, *Obras poéticas de D. Luís de Góngora,* ed. R. Foulché-
Delbosc (New York, 1921), 1:10-14: "Que junte un rico avariento / Los doblones
ciento a ciento / Bien puede ser; / Mas que el successor gentil / No los gaste mil
a mil, / No puede ser."

[31]Ff. F3-F3ᵛ: "Amar y no padecer / no puede ser. / Llorad mi Niño y mi Dios /
que ya el hombre se consuela / De que el frio que a el le hiela / haveys de sufrir vos
/ Que amar y no padecer /no puede ser."

musical techniques to enliven his static form. The most obvious source of the villancico's vitality lies in the lilting triple rhythms. Duple meter dominates sixteenth-century villancicos; the dancelike quality of triple meter was explored only slightly by Juan Vásquez (ca. 1510-1560) and then more extensively by Francisco Guerrero (1528-1599). For composers of the generation of 1610-30, however, the C3 sign was the standard choice for villancicos. Rimonte employs it in three-fourths of his; two more, "Quiero dormir," number four, and "Canto, Canto," number eleven, enjoy an interesting alternation between *tempus imperfectum cum prolatio imperfecta* and *proportio sesquialtera.*[32] Only "De la piel de sus ovejas," number seven, moves with the signature of *proportio dupla (tiempo de por medio)* (see table 1). By contrast, Rimonte's madrigals are consistently set in duple meter.

All but two villancicos open off the principal beat. The most frequent opening rhythm ♫ again emphasizes the airy character of these pieces. The notation, with its liberal use of blackened notes, demonstrates another prominent feature: syncopations effected by hemiola, C3 ♩♩♩ = ♩♩♩, agogic accents, C3 ♩♩♩ = ♩♩♩, and ties over main beats by dots of perfection or blackened breves.

Word rhythms play a dominant role in the construction of Rimonte's melodic line. The text settings are generally syllabic with few attempts at word-painting and are clearly differentiated from the technique of the *Parnaso* madrigals, where words are allied with illustrative musical figures at every opportunity. Short scale passages and suspensions are the principal ornaments.

The melodic lines are diatonic, but printed chromatic alterations of the cadential leading tones bend the eight modal settings (see table 1) toward modern major and minor, creating an interesting modal/tonal interplay. Frequent cadences on the first degree give impetus to the sense of a strongly defined tonality. Final cadences are all V-(v)-I with the exception of numbers seven and eight, the compositions in the Phrygian mode, which cadence respectively IV-I and vii⁶-I. All final tonic chords are complete major triads.

These melodic-harmonic aspects are rather conservative and traditional when compared to Rimonte's Italian contemporaries. The

[32]Rimonte uses "3" to indicate a change to the triplet relationship of *sesquialtera* (correctly 3/2) as was customary in Spain as early as 1540. Francisco de Montanos, in his *Arte de música theorica y practica* (Vallodolid, 1592), 2: f. 7ᵛ, says that a ciphered 3 following an imperfect mensuration indicates that three go for two. In *tiempo imperfecto* [C] there are three minims to the *compás*: "Quando delante de algun Tiempo delos ya dichas, ay un tres guarismo. 3. significa y da entender que de aquellas figuras ō con solo el tiempo yuan dos en un compas haviendo el tres vayan tres. En el imperfecto son tres minimas al compas."

TABLE I
Villancicos in the *Parnaso Español* of Pedro Rimonte

| Villancico | Folios | Modality (tonality) | Meter | No. of voices Est/ Copla/ Vuelta | Resp |
|---|---|---|---|---|---|
| 1. Rey del Cielo | Dv-D2 | mix. on g | C3 | a 3 | a 6 |
| 2. De que sirve el disfraz | D2v-D3 | F | C3 | a 3 | a 6 |
| 3. Luna que reluces | D3v-D4 | F | C3 | a 3 | a 6 |
| 4. Quiero dormir y no puedo | D4-E | aeolian on d | C/ C3 | a 3 | a 6 |
| 5. De vuestro divino pecho | E-Ev | mix. on g | C3 | a 2 | a 6 |
| 6. Mal puede estar escondida | E2-E2v | aeolian on a | C3 | a 3 | a 6 |
| 7. De la piel de sus ovejas | E3-E3v | phrygian on e | ₵ "A compas major" | Solo/ a 5 | a 5 |
| 8. Quita enojos son | E3v-E4 | phrygian on e | C3 | Solo | a 5 |
| 9. Madre la mi madre | E4v-F | aeolian on d | C3 | a 2 | a 5 |
| 10. Virgen escogida | F-Fv | dorian on d | C3 | a 2 | a 5 |
| 11. Canta, Canta | F2-F2v | F | C/ C3 | a 3 | a 5 |
| 12. Amar y no padecer | F3-F3v | C | C3 | a 3 | a 5 |

more interesting aspect of his melodic treatment involves motivic manipulation, which serves both as a means of expansion and as a means of relating large sections. "Rey del Cielo," number one, provides the clearest and most obvious model of a fairly consistent procedure. Each of the text phrases of the opening quatrain[33] is provided with a motive of striking rhythmic character. Motive *a* is developed and subjected to imitation, appearing four times in the superius. Motive *b* provides a single answering phrase. The motive for line three, motive *c*, is repeated twice, again imitatively. Motive *d* moves toward the cadence

---

[33]This quatrain, with its even seven-syllabled lines, belongs to the poetic form of *redondillas menor de lira* described by Correas in his *Arte de la lengua española*, p. 441.

by sequential repetition. The responsion is tightly linked to the estribillo, not only by exact repetition of text, but by utilizing the same musical motives, altered and expanded, yet retaining the rhythms and shapes of the first part of the original phrase. The copla is the only section that remains motivically unrelated (see example 1). Text repetitions are rare in Spanish secular music up to 1540. Phrase repetitions become part of the peninsular composer's style after mid-century, as do repetitions of entire sections, but the strong emphasis upon motivic relationships and sequences, such as the chains of sequences painting the

Ex. 1 Pedro Rimonte, "Rey del Cielo" (from *Parnaso Español de madrigales y villancicos*).

2. Assi mi Dios [Assi mi Dios] no lloreis [no lloreis]
   Pues llorando os agraviays, agraviays
   Y de mi alma sacays, sacays
   Y de mi alma sacays, Las lagrimas que verteis.

3. Segun esto [segun esto] no lloreis [no lloreis]
   Pues vos mi vida buscays, buscays
   Que de mi alma sacays, sacays
   Que de mi alma sacays, Las lagrimas que verteis.

A6. Responsion

2. Si venis por mi consuelo, Porque no llorays Rey de Amor?
   Y si vos llorays Señor, Quien ha de alegrar el Cielo?

word "Canta" in number eleven, are arresting new techniques in Rimonte's work.

The *Parnaso* villancicos are unified by motives; they maintain interest by the contrast of opposing sonorities. The responsion is always set for the complete performing force, *a* 5 or *a* 6. The estribillo and copla-vuelta are for a reduced number of voices, three, two, or for solo. The contrast in density is accompanied by a contrast in texture: the responsion is polyphonic; the copla is generally homorhythmic and homophonic, and the estribillo-vueltas distinguish themselves from the copla by widely spaced upper and lower voices. This soprano-bass polarity, in which the lower voice uses motives in imitation but also employs functional leaps, can be seen most clearly in the *a* 2 estribillos.

In the more common *a* 3 settings the two upper voices form an imitative duet above the bass with parts crossing somewhat in the manner of the Italian chamber duets. Thus the overall contrast among sections is typically organized in this way:

| Section | : | Estribillo | Responsion | Copla I |
|---|---|---|---|---|
| No. Voices | : | *a* 3 | *a* 6 | *a* 3 |
| Texture | : | SI, SII | imitative | homophonic |

B

| Section | : | Vuelta | Responsion | Copla II . . |
|---------|---|--------|------------|--------------|
| No. Voices | : | a 3 | a 6 | a 3 . . . |
| Texture | : | SI, SII B | imitative | homophonic . . |

One of the most fascinating aspects of sixteenth-century polyphony in Spain is the manner in which popular tunes as well as poems migrated from composer to composer. This musical travel seems to have slowed in the seventeenth century; thus far, only one of Rimonte's villancicos can be identified as a concordance with a tune found in another collection. "Madre la mi madre," so famous as a poem, was apparently a well-known tune also. An *a* 3 villancico in an early seventeenth-century cancionero in Turin sets the poem to a catchy tune in the alto voice within a simple estribillo-copla form. Rimonte's version, more sophisticated rhythmically and melodically, and expanded formally, quotes the tune in the superius and glosses the poetry of the earlier copla as well.[34]

A probable model for Rimonte's *Parnaso Español de madrigales y villancicos* was Francisco Guerrero's *Canciones y villanescas espirituales* (Venice, 1589).[35] Guerrero's publication, like Rimonte's, divides into two categories of polyphonic music, and all but one of Guerrero's "villanescas" follow the villancico form. Both Guerrero's *canciones* and Rimonte's madrigals are through-composed settings of complex poems with numerous examples of text-painting; both composers invariably set their text in duple meter. The techniques employed by Rimonte show certain striking similarities to those initiated by the older master, particularly in Guerrero's *a* 5 settings.[36] Among Guerrero's twenty *a* 5 villanescas in villancico form, half are in triple meter and three more alternate duple- and triple-meter sections. Guerrero experimented with textures: two-thirds of his villancicos reduce the number of voices in the copla to four, three, or even to solos. Incomplete parts to a villancico by the court composer, Pedro de Pastrana, show that he may have been a pioneer in this new style. As this article has shown, Rimonte also explored the possibilities of triple meters and density contrasts. If he was one of the first of many Spanish composers who were influenced by Pastrana or by Guerrero's enor-

[34]Bal y Gay, *Treinta canciones,* pp. 78-79, 81-85, and 108.

[35]Francisco Guerrero, *Canciones y villanescas espirituales* (Venice, 1589); modern edition in *Francisco Guerrero, opera omnia,* ed. Miguel Querol Galvadá, Monumentos de la música española, 16 (Barcelona, 1955).

[36]For a discussion of Guerrero's forms and style, see Querol, pp. 30-32; and Robert Stevenson, *Spanish Cathedral Music* (Berkeley, 1961), pp. 216-24.

mously successful collection,[37] it is his emphasis upon the newer concerted textures, his motivically-linked "tutti" responsions and the soprano-bass spacing of his fewer-voiced sections that remain Rimonte's own contribution to the new villancico.

A final consideration for these villancicos must be the question of their performance practice. What tempos, if any, were implied by Rimonte's mensuration signs? What role might instruments have played in the original performances? Francisco de Montanos, the theorist who was Rimonte's closest contemporary, supplies some answers to the questions of tempo. He defines the sign C as "the most in use . . . that which we call *Compasillo,*" which is *tiempo imperfecto,*[38] and advises one who would be skillful, singing with enough knowledge for a choir, to learn a variety of rhythms, "taking the beat rather quickly, which is what they call *compasillo.*"[39] Andrés Lorente, writing from the vantage point of a half century later, is unequivocal: compasillo is so named by being sung quickly and lightly.[40] Further, the C with an arabic 3, *tiempo menor de proporción menor*

> is sung three minums in a *compás;* the one on the downbeat, and the other two on the upbeat . . . so that the singing may be the most joyous and light, for ordinarily this *Tiempo de Proporción menor* is that which is most used in the Villancicos and music of happiness and rejoicing . . . .[41]

Clearly, Rimonte's C3 signs should be taken to mean a moderately fast or quick triple time[42] according to the character of the piece. The

---

[37]Tarzona, Archivo musical de la catedral MS 17 contains Altus, Tenor I and II parts for a Pastrana villancico "Senores el ques nascido." The estribillo, *a* 3, is followed by a repeat setting *a* 5; the copla, *bccb,* reduces to three voices and is followed by a vuelta *a* 3 and *a* 5. Pastrana was maestro de capilla to the Duke of Calabria, then was appointed maestro to Prince Philip in 1547. This work is the only identified example of his sacred villancico style and seems to anticipate Rimonte's "Responsion" settings. Stevenson, p. 223, comments upon the widespread imitation of Guerrero's villancicos: "As far away as Peru and Mexico, Juan de Araujo (ca. 1646-1714) and Antonio de Salazar (fl. 1690) were still imitating Guerrero's triple-meter mannerisms at the turn of the century."

[38]Montanos, *Arte de música,* 2: f. 4ᵛ: "Y pues se ha de hazer principio por lo mas facil y por lo mas esta en use, el compas que mas se acostumbra es el que llamamos Compasillo, que su tiempo es el imperfecto . . . . Es el tiempo. C."

[39]Ibid., 3: f. 6ᵛ: "Y advierte que no siempre sean passos largos, mas a vezes semibreves, y a vezes breves sincopados, mezclando lo uno cõ lo otro, que quien en esto estuviere diestro cantando con letra basta para el coro llevando el compas un poco apresurado, que es lo que llaman compasillo."

[40]Andrés Lorente, *El porque de la música en que se contiene los quatro artes de ella* (Alcalá de Henares, 1672), 2:154: "El Tiempo menor imperfecto . . . llamase Compasillo, porque se canta ligeramente, llevado apresurado el cõpas."

[41]Ibid., 2:165: " . . . en este Tiempo de Proporcion menor, se cantan tres Minimas en un compás; la una es al dar, y las dos al alçar . . . porque sea la Cantoria mas alegre, y ligera, por quanto de ordinario este Tiempo de Proporcion menor es el que mas se exercita en los Villancicos Y Músicas de alegría y regozijo. . . ."

[42]A compound measure seems the best solution to modern metric groupings. Two

single composition in duple meter, *tiempo de por medio,* is "De la piel de sus ovejas." It is also one of the loveliest of the villancicos with its elegant melodic curve, haunting Phrygian mode, and subtle introduction of all five voices into the solo estribillo section. Rimonte marks it "A Compás mayor." Montanos is less clear on this meaning but does advise ". . . if passages in *compasillo* are sung with a slow beat it will be the same as if one wrote the figures with doubled value sung in *compás mayor.* . . ."[43] Lorente says that

> in *compás mayor,* which is *Tiempo menor* with a line through it, one sings two Semibreves to the *compás,* and thus the rest of the figures: this *compás* one sings more slowly. . . .[44]

There are no parts for instruments in the *Parnaso* print. However, Rimonte's most famous student, Diego de Pontac, who was maestro de capilla at Granada in 1633, writes in that year that he studied counterpoint and "concierto" with Rimonte as a boy.[45] The latter would seem to have been a special skill, and indeed, Rimonte's villancico style is closely related to the concerted music developed by the late sixteenth-century Venetian masters. It seems logical to assume that instruments would have been used as additions to or substitutes for voice parts in Brussels as they were in Venice, the German courts, and perhaps even in Seville.[46] The estribillos of Rimonte's villancicos, with their wide spacing of voices or solo settings, imply the necessity of filling in harmonic outlines, and continuo parts were undoubtedly supplied as they were to other contemporary Spanish secular villancicos.[47] An Italian treatise of 1607 suggests appropriate accompanying instruments: a group of two or three should have a lute,

---

pieces in a contemporary manuscript, "Tonos Castellanos B" (Madrid, *olim* Biblioteca Medinaceli, MS 13231, ff. 32ᵛ-33 and 58ᵛ-59), begin with all voices entering simultaneously after a written semibreve and minim rest, a clear indication of ₵ [ ₵ ] meter.

[43]Montanos, *Arte de música,* 3: ff. 8-8ᵛ: ". . . si esta liciones de compasillo las cantaren llevando el compas despacio, sera lo mismo que si puntassen las figuras con doblado valor cantados a compas mayor. . . ."

[44]Lorente *El porque de la música,* 2:154: ". . . en compás mayor, que es el Tiempo menor con virgula atravesada, se cantan dos Semibreves al compás, y asi las demás Figuras: este compás se canta mas despacio. . . ."

[45]Diego de Pontac, "Discurso del Maestro Pontac, remitido al Racionero Manuel Correa" (Madrid, Biblioteca Nacional, MS 14069), f. 1: ". . . y con Rimonte en dicha ciudad de Zaragoza empecé a contrapunto sobre tiple, y de concierto . . . ." Lorente, 3:354, specifies that *concierto* is counterpoint *a* 3 in which the [upper] voices sing over the *canto llano* [bass], contending and imitating the subject by different means.

[46]Querol, *Francisco Guerrero, opera omnia,* 1:31-32 and fn. 3.

[47]A similar texture is found in the villancicos of the manuscript "Tonos Castellanos B" (Madrid, *olim* Biblioteca Medinaceli, MS 13231). The bass part on folio 66 is marked "Baxo Tañido," and the one on folio 67ᵛ "Baxo para acompañar."

chitarrone, theorbo, or harp; six or seven will need an organ or harpsichord.[48] Rimonte's villancicos would have utilized the latter; there were few lutenists and no theorbo players at the Brussels court,[49] but two organists, two cornett players, eight minstrels, and two "ynstrumentistas" were available.[50] These forces agree with the clue provided by the frontispiece of the *Parnaso* print itself that shows singers with a complement of viol, cornett, and harp, and a continuo of organ and bass viol. The concerted effect of such contrasting timbres, textures, and densities would have made these villancicos brilliantly successful pieces to adorn the great fiesta of the Nativity.

Eleanor Russell

[48]Thurston Dart, *The Interpretation of Music,* 2d ed. (London, 1962), p. 106. Dart cites the account of A. Agazzari, *Da sonare sopra'l basso* (1607).

[49]Edmond van der Straeten, *La musique aux Pays-Bas* (Brussels, 1872), 2:376-87. A young musician, Phillipe Vermeulen, was sent to Rome by the court of Albert and Isabella in 1612 to learn the theorbo. Monteverdi's *L'Orfeo* was performed at Brussels in 1608 with thirty-five instruments, mostly stringed, but there was no lute (p. 394).

[50]Brussels, Archives générales du Royaume, Chambre des Comptes, No. 1837, f. 22ᵛ. The list of musicians for the year 1612 includes the English organist Peter Phillips. John Bull was also a member of the chapel in 1613-1614 (see Russell, [forthcoming]).

A document from the collection of papers and notes by the Belgian musicologist A. Pinchart indicates that the minstrels were "violons et basses" and that the "ynstrumentistas" were probably "bassoon or trombone" [sackbut?] players (Brussels, Bibliothèque Royale de Belgique, Papiers de Pinchart II, 1200, Carton 10).

# Vocally Inspired Keyboard Music

Secular song has always provided inspiration for stringed keyboard music. No definite tradition for this kind of writing ever developed and not much consistency or pattern shows in its history, yet enough song-inspired keyboard music exists to merit an overall survey of types, composers, and repertoires. Keyboard here refers primarily to the stringed keyboard instruments; song refers to secular song, including solo song, part-song, and even opera arias. The survey covers important, exceptional, or otherwise noteworthy material; it is not intended as an all-inclusive, detailed account of song-inspired keyboard music.

The influence of song on stringed keyboard music has been expressed by many composers in varying degrees and through various musical forms. *Intabulation* (*intavolatura*) is a specific term for describing keyboard arrangements and transcriptions of fourteenth- to sixteenth-century vocal works. The *canzona*—a form popular during the Renaissance and early Baroque—is a contrapuntal keyboard composition based on the rhythmic patterns of Franco-Flemish chansons. The *theme and variation* subjects a song or part of a song to different transformations, dependent on the inherent possibilities of the theme and the imagination of the composer. The term *fantasia* applies to improvisatorial compositions, operatic potpourris, and—in the sixteenth and seventeenth centuries—even strict contrapuntal instrumental forms, like the ricercar. In general, keyboard *arrangements* of vocal compositions are almost note-for-note transliterations; keyboard *transcriptions* are freer interpretations of the original vocal work.

## EARLY KEYBOARD MUSIC

In the early fifteenth century, where this survey begins, composers made very little distinction between harpsichord or clavichord works and organ works. In other words, none of the stringed keyboard instruments had developed enough of a basic style to warrant an independent repertoire. For that reason any discussion of stringed keyboard music prior to the seventeenth century automatically includes all keyboard music.

The fifteenth-century *Codex Faenza*[1] preserves some early examples of song-inspired keyboard composition. It has forty-seven clavier settings, mostly intabulations of vocal music by outstanding French and Italian composers of the fourteenth and early fifteenth centuries: ballades by Guillaume de Machaut (ca. 1300-1377), madrigals by Jacopo da Bologna (mid-fourteenth century), and ballate by Francesco Landini (1325-1397). These keyboard arrangements are usually fashioned in two-part counterpoint, because songs originally written in three voices lose the middle voice in the keyboard arrangement. The tenor remains practically unchanged, and the upper part frequently paraphrases the original.

The *Ileborgh Tablature* (1448)[2]—a manuscript with five short preludes and three *mensurae* (compositions based on a song tenor in measured rhythms)—gives some indication of an emerging keyboard style. A mensura *Frowe al myn hoffen an dyr lyed,* for example, is consonant in its use of thirds and triads; it ends on a major third and has an extensive melodic range that descends gradually by phrases, spanning the range of a twelfth.

Conrad Paumann (ca. 1410-1473), the Nuremberg organist, eventually formulated guidelines for handling instrumental counterpoint. He illustrated his principles in the *Fundamentum organisandi* (1452),[3] a collection of keyboard arrangements including some based on folk songs. Most noteworthy are Paumann's seven arrangements employing German lieder as tenors. These songs all appear in the *Locheimer Liederbuch,* which is in the same manuscript (Berlin [DDR], Deutsche Staatsbibliothek, MS 40613) as the *Fundamentum*: *Wach auff mein hort, der leucht dort her* (*Locheimer Liederbuch* no. 2); *Mit ganczem willen wünch ich dir* (LL no. 31); *Des klaffers neyden* (LL no. 15); *Ellend du hast* (LL no. 5); *Benedicite. Allmechtiger got* (LL no. 34); *Domit ein gut Jare* (identical with *Der Summer,* LL no. 41); and *Mein hercz jn hohen frewden ist* (LL no. 97).

In Paumann's keyboard arrangements the notes of the original lieder are generally broken up into rhythmically free, alternating half, quarter, and eighth notes. Some arrangements—*Des klaffers neyden,* for example—keep the tenor melody, nearly intact, as a foundation and

---

[1] Faenza, Biblioteca Comunale, Cod. 117. Facsimile published as: *An Early Fifteenth-Century Italian Source of Keyboard Music: The Codex Faenza, Biblioteca comunale, 117,* Musicological Studies and Documents, 10 (Rome, 1961). See also Dragan Plamenac, "Keyboard Music of the 14th Century in Codex Faenza 117," *Journal of the American Musicological Society* 4 (1951): 179-201.
[2] Now in the Library of the Curtis Institute of Music, Philadelphia, Pennsylvania.
[3] A modern reprint of the *Fundamentum organisandi* may be found in: Konrad Ameln, *Locheimer Liederbuch und Fundamentum organisandi* (Kassel, 1925).

let the upper voice weave a free counterpoint over it. Other arrangements—the famed *Mit ganczem willen,* for example—show three voices and a paraphrased tenor that is broken up by unrelated notes as it skips back and forth between the low and middle voices.

The *Buxheim Organ Book,*[4] dating from around 1460 and containing 256 compositions, reveals further progress in melodic inventiveness. It is a collection especially pertinent to this survey because the bulk of the manuscript consists of intabulations of vocal works, most of them originally written in three voices. Some songs are anonymous and some are by well-known contemporary composers, such as John Dunstable (d. 1453), Guillaume Dufay (ca. 1400-1474), Wilhelmus Legrant (early fifteenth century), Walter Frye, and Paumgarten. For instance, there are seven arrangements of Gilles Binchois's (ca. 1400-1460) *Je loe amours,* two versions of Dufay's *Se la face ay pale,* also an arrangement of Dufay's *Le Serviteur,* and three arrangements of Dunstable's famous *O rosa bella.*

Many of the secular works in the *Buxheim Organ Book* are truly artistic transcriptions of original German songs. However, the secular works bearing French or Italian titles are often mere arrangements. Numerous compositions call for pedal, but many can be played on any keyboard instrument.

Of the several keyboard styles prominent in the *Buxheim Organ Book,* one resembles that of the *Fundamentum organisandi;* another shows an increase in figurations; a third tends toward simple harmonic texture.

After the *Buxheim Organ Book* German composers seemingly gave little thought to song transcription until almost a hundred years later when Elias Ammerbach (ca. 1530-1597), organist and composer, published three keyboard tablatures (1571, 1575, 1583).[5] The first volume contains transcriptions of vocal pieces by Heinrich Isaac (ca. 1450-1517), Paul Hofhaimer (1457-1537), Ludwig Senfl (ca. 1490-1555), Roland de Lassus (1532-1594), and others. Volume two consists of sacred Latin and German works by Lassus, Thomas Créquillon (d. 1557), Jacobus Clemens non Papa (ca. 1510-1557), and others. Volume three is an amply revised version of the first collection. These volumes and other contemporary tablatures—published by Bernard Schmid, elder (1520-1592) and younger (b. 1548), Jacob

---

[4]*Das Buxheimer Orgelbuch: Handschrift mus. 3729 der Bayerischen Staatsbibliothek, München,* ed. Bertha Antonia Wallner, Documenta musicologica: Reihe II, Bd. 1 (Kassel, 1955); a modern transcription in *Das Erbe Deutscher Musik,* 37-39 (Kassel, 1958-59).
[5]The 1571 edition appears in Monuments of Music and Music Literature in Facsimile, I/34.

Paix (1550-ca 1618), and Augustus Nörmiger—indicate that in the sixteenth century German composers revived the popularity of keyboard
intabulations.

FRANCE

During the years 1530 to 1531 the Parisian music publisher Pierre
Attaingnant printed seven keyboard collections, three of which are
relevant to this survey:

1. *Dix neuf chansons musicales reduictes en la tabulature des
   Orgues Espinettes Manichordions et telz semblables instruments* . . . Jdibus Januarii 1530.
2. *Vingt et cinq chansons musicales reduictes en la tabulature des
   Orgues Espinettes Manichordions et telz semblables instruments
   musicaulx.* Kal'. Februarii 1530.
3. *Vingt et six chansons musicales reduictes en la tablature des
   Orgues Espinettes Manichordions et telz semblables instruments
   musicaulx* . . . 1530.[6]

According to the above titles, these seventy keyboard intabulations may be played on the organ, harpsichord, clavichord, and other
similar instruments. Most of the original chansons are anonymous
secular works from the Franco-Flemish school, and nearly all of them
can be found in other Attaingnant publications. The outstanding
identifiable composer in the collections is Claude de Sermisy (ca.
1490-1562), who wrote thirty-one of the original chansons and possibly
one other.

ITALY

Keyboard composition flourished remarkably in Renaissance Italy,
with a burst of activity unmatched by any other country. Although
this Italian repertoire is on the whole limited to the abstract canzona, ricercar, and fantasia, it also includes some fine examples of song-
inspired keyboard compositions.

In 1517 Andrea Antico published the first book of tablatures to be
printed in Italy: the *Frottole intabulate da sonare organi libro primo,*
a collection of twenty-six intabulations.[7]

Another early collection, the *Recerchari Motetti Canzoni* (1523)[8]
by Marco Antonio Cavazzoni (1480-1559), also known as Marc' An-

---

[6]Pierre Attaingnant, pub., *Transcriptions of Chansons for Keyboard,* ed. Albert
Seay, Corpus mensurabilis musicae, 20 (Rome, 1961).
[7]Six transcriptions printed in Knud Jeppesen, *Die italienische Orgelmusik am An-
fang des Cinquecento* (Copenhagen, 1943).
[8]Ibid.

tonio da Bologna, has only eight compositions: two ricercars, two transcriptions of motets, and four transcriptions of French songs. The four keyboard canzonas have French titles—*Perdone moi sie folie, Madame vous aves mon cuor, Plus ne regres, Lautre yor per un matin* —and are imitations of vocal works from the Josquin period, but no specific originals are identified.

In 1543 Girolamo Cavazzoni (ca. 1500—ca. 1560), son of Marco Antonio and one of the first composers to develop scope and style in keyboard technique, published a collection of *Recercare, Canzoni, Himni, Magnificat.*[9] The two canzonas derive from well-known contemporary French chansons: *sopra Ille bel e bon* from Passereau's (early sixteenth century) *Il est bel et bon,* and *sopra Falte dargent* from Josquin's *Faulte d'argent.* In his keyboard paraphrases, Girolamo skillfully draws on motifs from the original French chansons to create a new imitative contrapuntal texture.

Girolamo established a canzona format for future composers: a vivacious movement in four-part counterpoint, treated imitatively, and with distinctive, concise subjects. In almost every instance, the initial subject employs the traditional threefold tone repetition.

Renaissance Italy produced three great masters of instrumental music: Andrea Gabrieli (ca. 1510-1586), his nephew Giovanni Gabrieli (1557-1612), and Claudio Merulo (1533-1604). Both the elder Gabrieli and Claudio Merulo composed song-inspired keyboard works.

Andrea Gabrieli's two 1605 posthumous collections of canzonas contain mostly simple intabulations—*Suzanne un jour d'Orlando, Un gai berger di Créquillon, Petit Jacquet, Le bergier, Con lei foss'io*— differing from the original songs only by the addition of some colorful ornamentation. A few—*Martin menoit di Janequin, Orsus au coup di Créquillon, Pour ung plaisir di Créquillon*—that he calls *ricercari ariosi* are imaginative transcriptions of the original chansons.[10]

Claudio Merulo, one of the finest organists of his day, published three keyboard collections (1592, 1606, 1611)[11] totaling twenty-three keyboard canzonas, five of which are somewhat naïve arrangements of French chansons: *Petit Jacquet, Petite Camusette, Languissans di Créquillon, Content di Créquillon, Suzanne un giour di Orlando Lasso.*

---

[9]Included in volume 1 of *Antologia di musica antica e moderna per pianoforte,* ed. Gino Tagliapietra (Milan, 1931-32).

[10]Examples included in *Andrea e Giovanni Gabrieli e la musica strumentale in San Marco,* vol. 1, ed. Giacomo Benvenuti (Milan, 1931-32).

[11]Works included in *L'arte musicale in Italia,* 1 and 3, ed. Luigi Torchi (Milan, 1897, 1902; reprint, Milan, 1959, 1968). See also *Antologia* vol. 2.

SPAIN

Antonio de Cabezón (1510-1566), Spain's greatest keyboard-music composer during the later Renaissance, greatly enriched keyboard literature by his playing and his composing. He designed his music for keyboard (*tecla*), harp (*arpa*), and guitar (*vihuela*) without indicating which instrument was most appropriate.[12]

Cabezón's nine sets of variations (*diferencias*) include three sets based on the widespread popular theme *Guárdame las vacas,* one based on the *Canto llano del caballero,* one on the *Canto de la Dama le demanda,* and one on a villancico entitled *¿De quién teme enojo, Isabel?*

Cabezón handled variation form as one continuous unit by using transition passages to connect the variations. Ordinarily the theme first appears in a simple four-part contrapuntal setting. Then it undergoes various changes: it may appear in the soprano voice or in other voices, surrounded by instrumental counterpoint; it may appear ornamented in the top voice; or it may be so transformed as to be barely recognizable.

Occasionally Cabezón treated song themes to more lavish contrapuntal elaboration: Créquillon's chanson *Qui la dira,* for example, provides material for a *tiento* (ricercar).

Showing much more imagination, Spanish composers of the late sixteenth and early seventeenth centuries enlivened the original vocal scores with clever, highly stylized figurations. Early examples—*Susana un jur* and *Dulce memoriae*—were written by Hernando de Cabezón (d. 1602), son of Antonio, and included by him in his edition of his father's *Obras de música.*

Although Francisco Corrêa de Araujo's (ca. 1576-1663) career straddles both the Renaissance and Baroque eras, his artistic, well-developed instrumental ornamentation marks him as a typical composer of the early Baroque. Corrêa de Araujo's *Facultad orgánica* (1626)[13] contains sixty-nine compositions, including three sets of *diferencias* on popular themes: *Dexaldos mi madre; Todo el mundo;* and the celebrated *Guárdame las vacas,* in which he first sustains the theme with simple harmonies and then submits it to sixteen variations. Among the keyboard settings of songs included in this manual, that of Créquillon's *Gay bergier* is especially interesting because of the lively figuration.

[12]Cabezón's *Obras de música,* originally edited by his son Hernando, appears in *Hispaniae schola musica sacra,* 3, 4, 7, 8, ed. Felipe Pedrell (Barcelona, 1894-98).

[13]Francisco Corrêa de Araujo, *Libro de tientos y discursos de musica practica, y theorica de organo intitulado Facultad orgánica* (Alcalá, 1626), 2 vols., ed. Santiago Kastner, Monumentos de la música española, 6, 12 (Barcelona, 1948-52).

ENGLAND

From the latter part of Henry VIII's reign (1509-1547) to about 1575, English composers turned to keyboard composition with an increasing intensity that finally culminated in the great body of keyboard works produced in the late sixteenth century. Samples from the beginning of this period exist in several manuscripts, notably the *Mulliner Book*,[14] a manuscript partly compiled around 1550 with works by John Taverner (ca. 1495-1545), Richard Farrant (d. 1581), and John Redford (ca. 1485-1547). Another more recent addition lists compositions dated as late as 1575, including works by John Munday (d. 1630), Christopher Tye (ca. 1500-1578), Thomas Tallis (ca. 1505-1585), and William Blitheman (d. 1591). The *Mulliner Book* has forty-six keyboard arrangements of songs and nine transcriptions of madrigals. The song arrangements have such titles as *Bittersweet, La Brunette, When Cressid went from Troy, In going to my, naked bedde, O ye happy dames.*

English composers were the first to liberate stringed keyboard music from organ music and to form a distinct harpsichord (virginal) style independent of organ technique. The *Fitzwilliam Virginal Book* (compiled ca. 1621)[15] and other similar manuscripts and editions[16] from that great era of English keyboard writing belong to a time when English musicians employed at various European courts introduced abroad the treasures of English folk song, such as *Fortune my Foe, Greensleeves, Packington's Pound,* and *Walsingham.* With nearly three hundred compositions written by representative composers of the English keyboard school, the *Fitzwilliam Virginal Book* provides an excellent means for studying the devices, techniques, and musical forms of that time.

In the *Fitzwilliam Virginal Book* and other contemporary collections, the variations based on secular song are significant from a qualitative point of view. Although not as prolific in variations on songs as in variations on dance themes, the virginalists nevertheless instilled their special originality and powerful expression into their song-inspired compositions. Some of these have quasi-polyphonic texture, others vary a melodic line supported by chordal accompaniment.

[14]*The Mulliner Book*, 2d rev. ed. Denis Stevens, Musica Britannica, 1 (London, 1962).

[15]A complete and convenient edition is available from Dover Publications: *The Fitzwilliam Virginal Book*, 2 vols., ed. J. A. Fuller Maitland and W. Barclay Squire (Leipzig, 1899; reprint, New York, 1963).

[16]*My Lady Nevells Booke* (1591), ed. Hilda Andrews (London, 1926); *Parthenia; or, The maydenhead of the first musicke that ever was printed for the virginalls* (1611), ed. Kurt Stone (New York, ca. 1951); and *Twenty-five Pieces for Keyed Instruments from Benjamin Cosyn's Virginal Book,* ed. J. A. Fuller-Maitland and W. Barclay Squire (London, 1923).

For examples of variations with quasi-polyphonic texture see William Byrd's (1542-1623) fourteen variations on *The Woods so wilde* (*Fitzwilliam Virginal Book* 1:263), Orlando Gibbons's (1583-1625) virtuoso variations on the same theme (*FVB* 1:144), Byrd's variations on *Walsingham* (FVB 1:267), and Byrd's setting of *The Maydens Song* (*FVB* 2:67).

The virginalists, at least those represented in the *Fitzwilliam Virginal Book,* composed only a few sets of melodic variations. One of these, however, is perhaps the best known of all virginal compositions: Byrd's *The Carmans Whistle* (*FVB* 1:214). Taken from a popular song, the theme undergoes eight transformations, each one preserving the bouncy rhythm of the original melody, and although this theme is still present in the final variation, it lies buried beneath a series of ponderous chords.

William Byrd wrote at least fifteen sets of variations (seven appear in *My Lady Nevells Book,* eight in the *Fitzwilliam Virginal Book*) on themes taken from popular song: for example, *Walsingham* (*FVB* 1:267); *Jhon come kisse me now* (*FVB* 1:47); *The Carmans Whistle* (*FVB* 1:214); *Callino Casturame* (*FVB* 2:186), the title being a distortion of the Irish song *Cailinog a stuir me* ("Young Maiden, My Love"); and *Fortune* (*FVB* 1:254), deriving from the popular tune *Fortune, my foe,* which in turn may have been inspired by Antoine Busnois's (d. 1492) chanson *Fortuna desperata.*

Byrd's keyboard variations are seldom pedantic. He preserved the essential character of the original melodies, even those he chose to adorn with ornate contrapuntal designs. His musical texture, usually constructed from solid harmonies blended with polyphonic elements, indicates technical proficiency and expressive vitality.

Peter Philips (ca. 1560-ca. 1635), an English religious refugee employed as organist and composer at the court of Archduke Albert in Brussels, built up a considerable repertoire of song-inspired transcriptions. The *Fitzwilliam Virginal Book* contains at least eight splendid Philips compositions based on chansons and madrigals by well-known composers of his time: *Chi fara fede al cielo* (*FVB* 1:312) by Alessandro Striggio (ca. 1535-1587); *Amarilli* (*FVB* 1:329) from Giulio Caccini's (ca. 1550-1618) famous *Le nuove musiche;* *Bon jour, mon cueur* (*FVB* 1:317) by Lasso; *Così morirò* (*FVB* 1:286), *Freno* (*FVB* 1:283), and *Tirsi* (*FVB* 1:280), all three from Luca Marenzio (1553-1599) madrigals; and *Margott laborez* (*FVB* 1:332) and *Le Rossignol* (*FVB* 1:346), both based on Lasso originals.

John Bull (1562-1628), another English religious refugee who found shelter in Belgium, possessed both technical ability and innate musical sensitivity. His high reputation for composing variations is well supported by the thirty variations on the theme of *Walsingham* (*FVB* 1:1), in which he subjects the melody and its framework to most of the keyboard devices known at that time. Bull's variations on *Go from my window* (Musica Britannica, 19) further prove his talent for this type of writing.

In an entirely different vein, Bull arranged three Dutch folk tunes—*Den lustelijcken Meij, Een Kindeken is ons geboren* (three versions), and *Laet ons met herten reijne* (all found in Musica Britannica, 14)—using simple contrapuntal textures and ornamental repetitions for variations. *Laet ons,* with its unexpected opening prelude, is the most beautiful of these settings.

Giles Farnaby (ca. 1560-1640) was a more spontaneous composer than either Philips or Bull. He preferred brief, lively tunes for variation themes and he found a generous supply in the English popular-song repertoire—like *Bony sweet Robin* (*FVB* 2:77), *Loth to depart* (*FVB* 2:317), and *Tell mee, Daphne* (*FVB* 2:446). Using trills, tone repetition, arpeggios, and new figurations, Farnaby fashioned graceful, vivacious music that now seems to sound more "modern" than the music of his contemporaries.

Other virginalists also worked with song themes. Thomas Morley's (1557-ca. 1602) variations on the folklike *Nancie* (*FVB* 1:57) rely primarily on runs and trills. John Munday (d. 1630) treated the structure as well as the melody of his themes. In his *Robin* (*FVB* 1:66) two figured variations treat the theme with unusual freedom, as do the eight variations in *Goe from my Window* (*FVB* 1:153). The latter also appears in the *Fitzwilliam Virginal Book* (*FVB* 1:42) as a work by Thomas Morley.

## THE BAROQUE ERA

### THE NETHERLANDS

For more than forty years Jan Pieterszoon Sweelinck (1562-1621) presided daily at the organ of the Oude Kerk in Amsterdam, establishing an important reputation through his playing, composing, and teaching. In keeping with the times, Sweelinck does not indicate whether his keyboard pieces are intended for organ or harpsichord or clavichord. His keyboard repertoire includes six variations on popular tunes.[17]

---

[17]Jan Pieterszoon Sweelinck, *Werken voor Orgel en Clavicimbel,* ed. Alfons Annegarn, et al. Werken, 1 and supplements (Amsterdam, 1894, 1943, 1958).

These six variations on well-known tunes are all extremely di-
verting: *Est-ce Mars?* (an *air de cour* by Guédron); *Ick voer al over
Rhijn; Mein junges Leben hat ein End'*; the student song *More Palatino; Onder een linde grone*, derived from the English ballad *All in
a garden green; Engelsche Fortuyn* (the same theme that Byrd and
others used).

Sweelinck adapted the English variation technique to his own
use, personalizing it with his concept of counterpoint and harmonic
cadential treatment. He chose binary tunes with both sections repeated.
Usually he omits the theme itself, beginning his keyboard work with
the first variation, and limits his treatment to either different settings
of an unaltered soprano melody or an ornamented soprano melody.
His music is not monotonous, however, because he had inexhaustible
resources for creating motivic variety in the lower parts.

Apart from Sweelinck's works, there is little evidence of significant keyboard composing in the Low Countries—Belgium and Holland—during the early seventeenth century.

The *Gresse Manuscript*[18] contains two allemandes, a pair of three-
movement suites, and some keyboard arrangements of excerpts from
Lully's operas.

Another collection, thirty-three pieces originally written out
for a certain Anna Maria van Eyl, was compiled in 1671 by Gisbert
Steenwick (d. 1679), organist and carilloneur at the Groote Kerk
in Arnhem from 1665 to 1674.[19] Almost all of the transcribed tunes
derive from folk music. One composition signed by Steenwick is yet
another arrangement of the popular student song *More Palatino*. The
anonymous composition *Bel Isis* is an arrangement of an air from
Lully's *Ballet de l'impatience* (1661).

GERMANY

Throughout the sixteenth and early seventeenth centuries, German
and Austrian composers had little inspiration or inclination to write
for any keyboard instrument except the organ. Religious conflicts and
the rise of two distinct theologies and philosophies created an atmosphere wholly unsympathetic to the mood of the sonatas and dances
that enrich any stringed keyboard repertoire. As a result, most composers devoted their talents to music suitable for the divine services.

Of course there were exceptions. The illustrious Samuel Scheidt
(1587-1654) from Halle, in northern Germany, occasionally wrote

---

[18]A modern edition may be found in volume 3 of *Monumenta musica neerlandica*, ed.
Alan Curtis (Amsterdam, 1961).

[19]A modern edition may be found in volume 2 of *Monumenta musica neerlandica*,
ed. Frits Noske (Amsterdam, 1959).

secular music. Because of his studies with Jan Sweelinck in Amsterdam, Scheidt was able to introduce into his own country the essence of Sweelinck's basic style: a fusion of the warm-textured, suavely melodic language from Italy with the delightful patterned variation technique taken from the English virginal composers.

Like his teacher, Scheidt composed some variations on songs and dances: on the Netherlands song *Ach du feiner Reiter;* seven effective variations on *Est-ce Mars?;* on *Fortuna;* and on *Weh, Windchen weh,* a Netherlands folk song that Scheidt subjects to twelve masterful variations displaying imagination and skill.[20]

In Fantasia *super Io son ferito lasso,* Scheidt artistically transforms the opening theme of Palestrina's (ca. 1525-1594) madrigal into a powerful quadruple, four-voice fugue: the first subject comes from the madrigal; the countersubject is the madrigal subject in retrograde.

German harpsichord music made great progress under the guidance of Johann Jacob Froberger (1616-1667). His harpsichord style blends organ technique with variation patterns, in the manner of Sweelinck and the early English virginalists. One of his best-known keyboard works, a suite based on the song *Auff die Mayerin,*[21] has a simple theme followed by seven variations woven around different dance forms. The second variation is a gigue; the fifth, called Partita cromatica, is based on alternating ascending and descending chromatic progressions; the sixth variation is a courante; and the last is a sarabande. Characteristic of Froberger, this suite lacks ornaments; obviously the performer must supply them.

It is worth noting here that another German clavierist and composer, Johann Reinken (1623-1722), also composed a set of attractive variations (*Partite*) on *Auff die Mayerin.*[22]

Dietrich Buxtehude (1637-1707), the Danish-born composer who worked most of his life in Germany, created a harpsichord repertoire—nineteen suites and six sets of variations[23]—that is characteristic of his general musical style: imaginative, vigorous, and expressive.

Some of Buxtehude's variation themes come from his own writings: Aria in C Major, for example. Some derive from other composers' works: *Rofilis* is a melody from Lully's *Ballet de l'impatience.* Other themes are taken from well-known folk songs: *More Palatino,* the Latin students' song set by so many composers; *La Capriccioso,*

---

[20]Published in *Tabulatura nova,* Hamburg, 1624, 2 vols., ed. C. Mahrenholz, Samuel Scheidt Werke, 6-7 (Hamburg, 1953).
[21]The complete harpsichord works of Froberger edited by Guido Adler are in *Denkmäler der Tonkunst in Österreich,* 8, 13, and 21 (Vienna, 1897, 1899, 1903).
[22]Reinken's *Diciotto Partite diverse sulla "Mayerin"* is included in *Antologia,* vol. 7.
[23]In Dietrich Buxtehude's *Klavervaerker,* 2d ed. Emilius Bangert (Copenhagen, 1944).

a bergamasca tune also used by Sweelinck, Scheidt, and others. (It appears again in the last variation of J. S. Bach's *Goldberg Variations* as the folk song *Kraut und Rüben*.)

## THE CLASSIC ERA

For nearly seventy-five years—from about 1700 to 1775—most German composers semed to ignore vocally inspired keyboard music. Late Baroque composers apparently were not interested in this type of composition. A true piano literature began with the Clementi (1752-1832) sonatas published in 1770, and Classic composers were too intrigued by the latent possibilities of the abstract sonata to give much thought to anything else in the instrumental field.

This barren period, however, was relieved by Wolfgang Amadeus Mozart's (1756-1791) seventeen independent sets of variations for solo clavier (distributed throughout K. 24 to K. 613), many based on folk songs, ariettes, and popular tunes. For example, K. 180 is based on an arietta by Salieri; K. 264 derives from *Lison dormait;* K. 265 is an entrancing version of *Ah, vous dirai-je maman;* K. 353 is based on *La belle Françoise;* K. 354 on *Je suis Lindor;* K. 359 on *La Bergère Célimène;* K. 455 on *Unser dummer Pöbel meint* from Gluck's *Pilger von Mekka;* and K. 613 on *Ein Weib ist das herrlichste Ding* from a farce created by Mozart's librettist Johann Emanuel Schikaneder (1751-1812).[24]

The theme-and-variations form that reached Mozart's hands had developed primarily in Paris. In this form, when the theme had duple time, usually one variation would be in triple meter; when the theme was in a major key, one variation would be in minor mode and one variation would be an adagio. Like those of his contemporaries and immediate predecessors, many Mozart variations are charming, ear titillating, and graceful.

Johann Christoph Friedrich Bach (1732-1795), eldest surviving son of Anna Magdalena and Johann Sebastian Bach, produced numerous instrumental and keyboard works. His Allegretto con variazioni[25] on the folk song *Ah, vous dirai-je maman* is especially gracious and artful.

## THE NINETEENTH CENTURY

In a complete reversal, nineteenth-century composers (in Germany and elsewhere) began an almost feverish activity in song transcrip-

---

[24]Mozart's variations are found in Serie 21 of his *Sämtliche Werke.*
[25]Modern edition by Henriette Barbé, published by Hug (available through C. F. Peters).

tion, with new versions ranging from rather straightforward transliterations to ornate paraphrases. That indefatigable transcriber Franz
Liszt (1811-1886) produced an enormous body of these works, notably six *Lieder von Goethe* and *Adelaide* by Beethoven; six *Chants
polonais* by Chopin; eleven songs by Schumann; nine songs by Mendelssohn; fifty-six songs by Schubert; the *Soirées musicales* by Rossini; and many of his own songs.[26]

While transcriptions were the fashion, other composers and pianists,
well known and otherwise, added to the repertoire. Sigismond Thalberg (1812-1871) transcribed Beethoven's *Adelaide* (different composers have done at least five other versions) and wrote a delightful
keyboard piece based on Giovanni Battista Pergolesi's (1710-1736)
*Tre Giorni son che Nina.*[27] Max Reger (1873-1916), Hermann Kel-
ler (d. 1885), Cornelius Gurlitt (1820-1901), and others chose
many of Brahms's lieder for keyboard transcription. Carl Czerny
(1791-1857) transcribed Mendelssohn songs. Niels Gade (1817-1890)
brought out an album of *Folkedanse* and one of Scandinavian Folksongs for piano.[28] And Edvard Grieg (1843-1907) composed two interesting collections of folk melodies for piano—Norwegian Dances
and Songs, op. 17 and Norwegian Folk Melodies, op. 66.[29]

Some composers of the time went beyond mere song arrangements.
Joachim Raff (1822-1882) composed a Concert Paraphrase on Schu-
mann's *Abendlied* and Two Paraphrases on Songs of Liszt, op. 18.[30]
Grieg wrote a Ballad in the Form of Variations on a Norwegian
Folksong, op. 24 and Improvisations on Norwegian Folksongs, op. 29.

Operatic transcriptions and opera fantasias also came into vogue,
and thus we now find keyboard transcriptions of arias from most
of the well-known nineteenth-century operas. Georges Bizet (1838-
1875) made a surprising number of operatic transcriptions: on Mozart's *Don Giovanni,* on Gounod's operas, and one on *Mignon* by
Ambroise Thomas (1811-1896).[31] Adolfo Fumagalli's (1828-1856)
transcription—for left hand only—of the *Casta Diva* from Bellini's

---

[26]The largest available selection of Liszt's piano compositions is published by C. F.
Peters. The variations are not included in Liszt's *Musikalische Werke.*

[27]Both *Adelaide* and *Tre Giorni* were originally included in a collection entitled
*L'Art du chant appliqué au piano* (Boston, 1850). A modern reprint of *Tre Giorni*
is published by Musical Scope Publishers.

[28]Most of Gade's music is published by Wilhelm Hansen of Copenhagen, available
through G. Schirmer, Inc.

[29]C.F. Peters publishes a complete edition of Grieg's piano music.

[30]Raff's Schumann paraphrase was published by Schuberth.

[31]Heugel of Paris published Bizet's transcriptions of Mozart and Thomas; Choudens
published the Gounod transcriptions.

*Norma* stands as one of the more bizarre items in the vocally inspired keyboard repertoire.[32]

There are far too many keyboard adaptations of operatic excerpts to make anything but a general listing: transcriptions of arias from Gluck's *Alceste* and *Orfeo;* countless arrangements and fantasias based on Mozart's operas—*Così fan tutte, Don Giovanni, Die Zauberflöte, Le nozze di Figaro*—by Liszt, Thalberg, Louis Diémer (1843-1919), Félix Le Couppey (1811-1887), and others; and diverse transcriptions of Donizetti's *Lucia di Lammermoor,* including some by Liszt and Thalberg.

Far more satisfying than most operatic transcriptions are the keyboard variations based on themes from folk songs, arias, and lieder. Ludwig van Beethoven (1770-1827) composed numerous variation sets, but they are rarely heard now. Written between 1782 and 1823, they vary from the infantile Variations on a March by Dressler to the powerful Variations on a Waltz by Diabelli, op. 120. Within this period he produced no less than twelve keyboard variations on vocal themes, usually themes written by composers forgotten today: two themes and variations from Giovanni Paisiello's (1740-1816) *Die schöne Müllerin;* variations on themes from operas by André Grétry (1741-1813), Peter von Winter (1754-1825), and Franz Süssmayr (1766-1803); and variations on *Ich hab' ein kleines Hüttchen nur, Rule, Britannia,* and *God save the King.*[33]

Frédéric Chopin's (1810-1849) variations, all composed early in his career, are not equal to his best writing: for example, the Variations on *Là ci darem la mano,* op. 2; the superficial *Variations brillantes,* op. 12 on the air *Je vends des scapulaires* from the opera *Ludovic* by Louis Hérold (1791-1833) and Jacques Halévy (1799-1862); and the boring Grand Fantasy on Polish Airs, op. 13. The one notable exception is the brilliant, colorful Krakoviak, op. 14.[34]

Johannes Brahms (1833-1897) composed his Variations on a Hungarian Song, op. 21, no. 2 in 1853 while on tour with the Hungarian violinist Eduard Reményi (1830-1898). The vivacious song theme—in alternating $\frac{3}{4}$ and $\frac{4}{4}$ time — supports a series of expertly tailored variations, each one proceeding logically to the next in Brahms's predictable manner.[35]

Quaint is the only word to describe such keyboard transcriptions

---

[32]Fromont originally published Fumagalli's *Norma* transcription.

[33]These variations are included in *Ludwig van Beethoven's Werke,* Serie 17.

[34]The Chopin variations are included in the *Complete Works,* vol. 13 (Warsaw, 1959).

[35]The variation is included in *Johannes Brahms Sämtliche Werke,* Band 13 (Leipzig, 1927).

as Anton Rubinstein's (1829-1894) *Variations sur l'air américain Yankee Doodle* [36] or Thalberg's variations on *The Last Rose of Summer* and *Home, Sweet Home*.[37]

## THE TWENTIETH CENTURY

The musical ambience of the twentieth century has not been sympathetic to vocally inspired keyboard music. Techniques like dodecaphony, microtonality, and musique concrète are essentially incompatible with the inherent simplicity of folk song, popular song, or even the melodic line of lieder and operas. On the whole, only those composers who have been nationally oriented or those who have found natural inspiration in song have composed much song-derived keyboard music.

Thus the Hungarian Béla Bartók (1881-1945), with his passionate interest in native folk music, converted many simple Hungarian folk tunes into interesting keyboard paraphrases. *For Children,* a collection of eighty-five settings of Hungarian and Slovakian melodies, keeps the original melodies intact, merely repeating them once or twice with varied accompaniments taken from the melodies themselves. In Romanian Christmas Songs of Hungary—two series having ten pieces each, all to be played without pause—Bartók uses many different means to create appealing music. Fifteen Hungarian Peasant Songs contains settings of songs from Bartók's ethnological collections.[38]

Other talented Hungarian composers turned to their native music for inspiration. Zoltán Kodály (1882-1967), who became an expert in Hungarian folk music, was so deeply affected by Magyar music that it dominated most of his writings. *Gyermektáncok,* a keyboard collection of twelve children's dances based on Hungarian folk tunes, is played entirely on the black keys. Kodály's Dances of Marosszek also derives from peasant tunes.[39]

Although Ernö Dohnányi's (1877-1960) keyboard style springs from the fount of German Romanticism, his interpretation of his native Hungarian folk idiom can be charming, as he so well proves in Variations on a Hungarian Folk Song, op. 29 and *Ruralia Hungarica,* op. 33a. An entrancing exception to the Hungarian nationalist approach occurs in Dohnányi's Variations on a Nursery Tune for piano

---

[36]Rubenstein's variations were published by Hamelle.

[37]Hamelle published both sets of Thalberg's variations.

[38]Boosey & Hawkes publishes the complete piano music of Bartók.

[39]Boosey & Hawkes publishes *Gyermektáncok,* Universal Edition the Dances of Marosszek.

and orchestra in which he cloaks the folk tune *Ah, vous dirai-je maman* with clever transformations.[40]

Only Spain has matched Hungary's nationalist fervor. In the late
nineteenth and early twentieth century the Spanish composers Isaac
Albéniz (1860-1909), Enrique Granados (1867-1916), and Manuel
de Falla (1876-1946) discovered the tremendous creative resources
available in their national idiom. None of the Spanish composers
seemed to care much about using specific native songs, preferring instead to evoke the Spanish mood and spirit. Granados's Six Pieces
on Spanish Folk Songs and Ernesto Halffter's (b. 1905) effective
piano transcription of Falla's *Siete canciones populares españolas* are
rare exceptions.[41]

There are a few isolated instances of song-inspired keyboard works
in other countries: in Finland, Selim Palmgren's (1878-1951) Fin-
nish Folksongs[42] in piano transcription; in Brazil, the extravagant
Heitor Villa-Lobos's (1887-1959) *Cirandinhas* (a suite based on
children's songs), Ten Pieces on Popular Children's Folk Tunes of
Brazil, and his useful eleven-volume *Guia prático,* with its many folk
song settings;[43] in Argentina, Alberto Ginastera's (b. 1916) fanciful
Rondo on Argentine Children's Folk Tunes;[44] and in Australia, Percy
Grainger's (1882-1961) numerous settings of Australian, English, and
Irish folk songs.[45]

Austrian-born Ernest Krenek (b. 1900) has a collection quite out
of style with his later twelve-tone works and experimental works:
the 1958 *Echoes from Austria,* seven keyboard compositions based
on folk songs.[46]

The American Arthur Farwell (1872-1952), a strong champion of
nationalism, made numerous keyboard settings of Indian melodies,
which were published by the now historic Wa-Wan Press; for example, *The Domain of Hurakon, Navajo War Dance No. 2,* and

---

[40]Dohnányi's two solo works are published by E. B. Marks; the Variations are
available through Associated Music Publishers.

[41]Unión musical española publishes the Granados pieces (distributed through Associated Music Publishers); Max Eschig publishes the Halffter transcriptions of Falla's
songs (available through Associated).

[42]Finnish Folksongs are published by Wilhelm Hansen (available from G. Schirmer, Inc.).

[43]Max Eschig publishes *Cirandinhas;* Mercury Music Corp. publishes the Ten Pieces.
The volumes comprising *Guia prático* are published by various companies: Max Eschig,
Mercury Music Corp., Consolidated Music Publishing, and Southern Music Co.

[44]Boosey & Hawkes publishes the Ginastera Rondo.

[45]The best available collection is *The Young Pianist's Grainger* published by Schott
(available through Belwin-Mills).

[46]*Echoes from Austria* is published by Rongwen Music, Inc. (available through
Broude Bros.).

*Pawnee Horses.*[47] The esteemed American composer Roy Harris (b. 1898) overtly expressed his patriotic feelings in *American Ballads,*[48] five expertly designed settings of American folk tunes. In a more modern vein, Ellis Kohs (b. 1916) has created a set of Variations on *l'Homme armé,*[49] wherein the famous Renaissance song undergoes eighteen well-knit transformations.

This survey of vocally inspired keyboard music most appropriately concludes with the significant contributions of Halsey Stevens (b. 1908), who has composed more folk-music settings than any other American composer. His settings of Magyar, Romanian, French, Russian, Portuguese, Ukranian, Hungarian, Czech, and Swedish folksongs are achieved with utmost care and obvious concern for preserving the spirit and beauty of the original vocal models.

Halsey Stevens, an articulate and sensitive composer, demonstrates that in our time the art of writing vocally inspired keyboard music can be accomplished with the same artistry as that shown by the Renaissance pioneers in this field.[50]

John Gillespie

[47]*The Domain of Hurakon* has been reprinted by Arno Press. Mercury Music Corp. publishes the *Navajo War Dance, No. 2;* G. Schirmer, Inc. publishes *Pawnee Horses.*
[48]*American Ballads* is published by Carl Fischer.
[49]Mercury Music Corp. publishes Kohs's Variations.
[50]The American Composers Alliance publishes most of the keyboard music of Halsey Stevens. For further publication information on the music of Stevens and the foregoing composers, see Maurice Hinson, *Guide to the Pianist's Repertoire* (Bloomington, Ind., 1973).

# Manuel de Zumaya (ca. 1678-1756): Mexican Composer for Church and Theater

The earliest known opera performed in North America was composed by Manuel de Zumaya (Sumaya), born and trained in Mexico near the end of one of the most creative periods in its musical history. In Mexico during the Baroque era, as in Spain, there were three major fields for composers: church service music, the musical theater (both secular and sacred), and an important, peculiarly Spanish area between those two, that of the devotional/popular villancicos and chanzonetas. Zumaya's contributions to all these areas were major ones, and his career also included contact with many of the other outstanding figures in Mexican Baroque music and literature. A discussion of the life and work of this colorful figure, the earliest important native-born composer on the North American continent, can therefore illuminate the musical life of Nueva España in one of its most brilliant capitals.

Zumaya was born ca. 1678 and, in the normal fashion for that time and place, received his early music training as a *seise* (choirboy). He was taught to sing plainsong and polyphony and also received a thorough grounding in counterpoint. The boy served in the great new Cathedral of Mexico City, a magnificent building still in active use, which replaced an earlier structure erected in 1525. The Cathedral had been solemnly dedicated in 1656 and again, upon completion of the interior, in 1667; both events occurred during the tenure of the important chapelmaster-organist, Francisco López y Capillas.[1]

Zumaya began his career as a seise under the chapelmaster Joseph de Agurto y Loaysas, who is best known as one of the principal composers of villancico sets (*juegos*) by the famed Mexican poetess and

---

[1]Robert Stevenson, "Mexico City Cathedral Music: 1600-1750," *The Americas* 21 (1964): 121-25.

nun, Sor Juana Inés de la Cruz (1651-1695).[2] One of the finest poets in the Spanish language, internationally famed even during her lifetime as "the tenth Muse," Sor Juana possessed a brilliant mind and vast learning in the arts and sciences. It is possible that the young Zumaya participated in the brilliant performances of the villancicos for Assumption of 1685 and 1686 at matins in the cathedral; he certainly performed in the later sets composed by the new *maestro de capilla*, Antonio de Salazar.

The Spaniard Salazar, a skilled and important composer, had won the coveted post of chapelmaster of the great Cathedral of Puebla (Mexico) in July 1679.[3] In September 1688 he was appointed chapelmaster of the Mexico City Cathedral, having easily bested his rivals in the customary demanding and public contest for the position. From this time on, Salazar's career was intimately associated with that of his talented young protégé, Zumaya, who served his mentor successively as counterpoint pupil, organist, teaching assistant, collaborator in compositions, and eventually as substitute and acting chapelmaster.

In May 1694, having reached the graduating age for seises, Zumaya petitioned for dismissal from cathedral employ with the customary terminal pay. The cathedral authorities also granted his additional request for help in learning to play the organ. Noting his exceptional musical talent and hoping to forestall any decision on his part to become a friar through economic necessity, the cathedral chapter recommended that the young musician be given a clothing allowance and a yearly salary while taking daily organ lessons and assisting in cathedral services when required. Zumaya's teacher, principal organist for the Cathedral, was Lic. Joseph Ydíaquez, distinguished teacher of a long line of church organists in Mexico and an exceptionally fine performer, who was cited in the archives as a great player of *tientos*.[4] Zumaya's interest in the organ must also have been stimulated by the excitement surrounding the arrival (1692), tuning, testing, and final installation (1695) of the great new organ, ordered at

---

[2] Sor Juana Inés de la Cruz, *Obras completas*, ed. Alfonso Méndez Plancarte (México, 1952), 2: 355, 365, 368, 378, 388, 397, 401, 469, 499. By Sor Juana, with music by Agurto y Loaysa are sets for *Asunción* (Assumption) 1676, 1679, and 1685; *Concepción* (Conception) 1676; and *San Pedro Apóstol* (St. Peter the Apostle) 1683. Attributed to Sor Juana are *Asunción* 1677 and 1686. Agurto y Loaysa was probably also the composer for Sor Juana's villancico sets for *San Pedro Nolasco* 1677 and *San Pedro Apóstol* 1677.

[3] Biographical information is included in my articles on Salazar, Zumaya, and Puebla for the forthcoming sixth edition of *Grove's Dictionary of Music and Musicians*, and is used by permission of Macmillan, the publishers. For further details and specific references, see also Stevenson, pp. 125-35.

[4] *Actas capitulares* 24 (1695-1697), f. 29.

Salazar's instigation and built in Madrid by the famous Jorge de Sesma.[5]

In 1708 Zumaya, by then a priest, was one of the three cathedral organists also obligated to teach polyphony to talented choirboys. The cathedral authorities had long practiced a systematic plan of training and supporting outstanding young musicians, believing that a continuing stream of new candidates should be prepared to take over important church positions. Zumaya himself had benefited from this plan. Early in 1710 he was also asked to teach counterpoint twice a week at the *escoleta* in order to free the aging Salazar of his duties there. Salazar agreed to continue teaching the particularly talented pupils at his home. In addition, Zumaya was selected to serve as substitute chapelmaster, much to the chagrin of the older composer Francisco Atienza y Pineda, who had previously substituted for Salazar and who soon left to become chapelmaster in Puebla.

In the meantime, in spite of his busy schedule in the cathedral, Zumaya was attracted to the musical theater, which in the colonies—as in Spain—was a vital and richly varied adjunct of life in the streets, at court, and in the church. His contributions to the field came at a period of great stylistic change. His earliest known musical play and a large number of his Spanish villancicos were rooted in Hispanic traditions that had peaked during the late seventeenth century but continued to flourish during much of the eighteenth. The young Mexican, however, was also one of the earliest composers in the colonies to embrace the newly fashionable Neapolitan opera and the Italian cantata style.

Although the Baroque musical theater in the Spanish language was an exciting one, with unique native features, it has been so neglected in general studies of music history that a brief background discussion seems necessary. Spanish drama, poetry, music, and dance enjoyed a continuous line of development and interaction from the Middle Ages through the Renaissance and well into the Baroque era. During all this long span, courtly, sacred, and popular elements were intermingled to a degree far greater than was typical of other West European cultures.

The Spanish and the Mexican public of Zumaya's time, especially in the larger cities, enjoyed a colorful spectrum of religious theater and near-theater that featured popular song and dance types as well

[5]Stevenson, pp. 128-30. See also Colin C. Kerr, "The Organ at the Cathedral of Mexico City," *The Organ* 36 (1956-57): 52-62; this article describes the two great organs (1695 and 1735) in detail, although the dates given are incorrect. See also corrections in *The Organ* 37 (1957-58): 46; and the articles by M. A. Vente and W. Kok, "Organs in Spain and Portugal," *The Organ* 35 (1955-56): 58; and 36 (1956-57): 203.

as some liturgical music. Church and civic festivals were celebrated with lavish processionals—such as that of Corpus Christi—and with sumptuously staged and costumed *máscaras* (pageants) performed in the streets and the great plazas. As an extra feature, elaborately costumed portrayals of the battles of the Moors and the Christians were special favorites.[6] In the colonies, local color was sometimes added by throngs of Indians, brilliantly costumed and wearing plumed headdresses, who contributed their own ancient and highly developed traditions of ceremonial music and dance. The cathedral choir and choirboys normally participated in the pageants and processionals, with singers and instrumentalists often performing on decorated carts. In addition, they frequently took part in allegorical plays that included singing and dancing and were staged in churches and convents. Popular and theatrical elements also entered the church in the brilliant and festive performances of chanzonetas and villancicos, a regular feature of important liturgical days in the Spanish church.

During the Baroque era, the major type of religious, musical drama was the *auto,* an important one-act play in verse on a sacred or allegorical theme. Autos were written and printed by the hundreds on both sides of the Atlantic; major examples from Mexico included those by Sor Juana and by González de Eslava.[7] They were elaborately staged, normally on large decorated carts in the public plazas, and usually featured a considerable amount of incidental music that included solo airs and arias, choral and ensemble numbers, and instrumental music. Most of this music has been lost, but some is extant, especially for the autos by the great Spanish dramatist Calderón de la Barca (1600-1681) and written by leading Spanish composers.[8] The strong popular elements that had typified Spanish religious drama since the Middle Ages were also retained by the autos; these were evidenced in scenes of roguish street humor and exuberant vitality; in the rich diversity of characters that included shepherds, gypsies, soldiers, merchants, courtiers, students, peasants, and friars; in the use of dialects (special favorites being Negro, Basque, and regional Spanish); and above all, in the emphasis given such popular song and dance types as the *seguidilla,* the *ciacona,* the *jácara* and, most importantly, the villancico and romance.

[6]For more detailed descriptions of such pageants in Baroque Mexico, see Alice Ray [Catalyne], "The Double-choir Music of Juan de Padilla" (Ph.D. diss., University of Southern California, 1953), chapter 6; and Carlos de Sigüenza y Góngora, *Glorias de Querétaro* (Mexico, 1680), p. 48, translated in Irving Leonard, *Baroque Times in Old Mexico* (Michigan, 1959), pp. 125-29.
[7]Arturo Torres-Rioseco, *New World Literature: Tradition and Revolt in Latin America* (Berkeley, 1949), p. 41.
[8]Patricia J. Connor, "The Music in the Spanish Baroque Theater of Don Pedro Calderón de la Barca" (Ph.D. diss., Boston University, 1964), pp. 85-102, 175-81.

The villancico and romance were Spanish song types that dated back to the Middle Ages and displayed both courtly and popular elements. Until the end of the Baroque era they continued to flourish as typical forms for songs with Spanish texts, whether composed for the theater, the court, or the church. Spanish poetry for song and theater employed specific and extremely varied metrical and stanzaic designs, too complex to be considered here. In general terms, however, the villancico was characterized by a series of *coplas* (stanzas) set strophically and repeated *estribillo* (refrain) that was sung before and after the coplas, sometimes after each one. The romance was a ballad with several four-line *estrófas* (strophes), all sung to the same music. The romance had no refrain, but during the seventeenth century, while retaining its other poetic features, it often absorbed the estribillo of the villancico.[9] The jácara was like a mischievous, picaresque romance but was also a popular dance type, frequently performed by a woman in the stage forms.

The lively secular theater, with its strong reliance on music and dance, also enjoyed enthusiastic public support during the Baroque era.[10] Its major dramatic type was the three-act *comedia,* performed in public theaters called *corrales* or *coliseos.* The comedia was a continuous, fast-paced show that lasted more than two hours and included lively musical interludes before and between the acts. The most elaborate of these interludes was the *entremés* or *jácara entremesada,* usually given after the first act; it was a little farce in verse, presented in spoken dialogue, singing, and dancing, like a miniature comic opera. Other interludes and finales became veritable recitals of popular song and dance, presenting a fiesta of seguidillas, zarabandas, jácaras, ciaconas, and villancicos. Brief dramatic types in verse, as was the comedia, included the *loa* (prologue) and the *sainete* (a one-act farce, often played between acts). As a rule, the three acts

---

[9]For the developing forms of the villancico and romance, see ibid., pp. 127-48; Miguel Querol Gavaldá, *Música barroca española,* t. 1, Monumentos de la música española, 32 (Barcelona, 1970); Méndez Plancarte, ed., 2:vii-lxxviii; and Isabel Pope, "The Musical Development and Form of the Spanish Villancico," *Papers of the American Musicological Society, 1940* (1946): 11, which is a translation and condensation of the introduction in *Cancionero de Upsala,* eds. R. Mitjana, J. Bal y Gay, and I. Pope (Mexico, 1944).

[10]For further discussion of music in the Renaissance and Baroque Spanish theater see Gilbert Chase, *The Music of Spain,* 2d ed. (New York, 1959), pp. 90-105, 121-24; Connor includes music examples and a brief history of music in the theater before Calderón; Emilio Cotarelo y Morí, "Colección de entremeses (Loas, Bailes, etc.)," *Nueva biblioteca de autores españoles* (Madrid, 1911), vols. 17-18, and idem, *Historia de la zarzuela* (Madrid, 1934); Francis C. Hayes, *Lope de Vega* (New York, 1967), pp. 43-51, 55-57, 72-75, 84-89; Felipe Pedrell, *Teatro lírico español anterior al siglo XIX* (La Coruna, 1897), 5 vols.; Miguel Querol y Galvadá, *La música en las obras de Cervantes* (Barcelona, 1940); Robert Stevenson, *Music in Mexico* (New York, 1952); José Subirá, *Historia de la música española o, hispanoamericana* (Barcelona, 1953), and idem, *Historia de la música teatral en España* (Barcelona, 1945).

of the comedia itself also employed a considerable amount of incidental music, some of it quite elaborate. Villancicos and romances were almost always included, but other solo and choral songs of all types were also an important part of the drama.

The basic characteristics of this national musical theater were established by the imaginative and incredibly prolific Lope de Vega (1562-1635), but additional important contributions were made by the Mexican dramatist Juan Ruíz de Alarcón y Mendoza (1581?-1629), one of the foremost figures of the Golden Age of Spanish literature and much admired by Corneille. From the middle of the seventeenth century, however, the dominant figure in all Spanish theatrical-musical forms was Calderón de la Barca. His works, many of them written for the court, made an increasingly important use of music, composed by the major Spanish musicians of his time. Many of his dramas, which combined mythological, pastoral, and popular elements, were near-operas or full operas, set with recitatives, arias, ensembles, and important choral numbers. One of Calderón's librettos, *La Púrpura de la Rosa* (1660), was also set to music in Peru by Tomás de Torrejón y Velasco. Performed at the viceregal court of Lima in 1701, it became the earliest known opera composed and performed in the New World; its attractive music is extant.[11] At the end of the seventeenth century, the finest works were those by the Mexican poetess Sor Juana Inéz, whose autos, loas, sainetes, and comedias stand out as the flowering of the highly refined culture that flourished in colonial soil.

In spite of the importance of the comedias and autos in Mexican life, virtually none of its Baroque theater music has survived. Two brief songs from this sophisticated musical stage, however, are preserved in manuscripts now in the National Archives of Mexico. Although they were performed in Mexican theaters, both are by Spanish composers and both are villancicos for solo voice and a basso continuo, which in Hispanic tradition was usually played by harp and guitar. The earlier of the two, from the late seventeenth century, is a *solo humano* (secular song) by Manuel de Villaflor, one of the composers for the musical stage at the Madrid court. *Huyendo del verde margen* (example 1) shares with other seventeenth-century songs the use of a flowing triple meter with occasional flexible changes to duple, as in the estribillo; but its lilting melodic style and its characteristic use of syncopations, hemiola, dotted rhythms, and shifting accents to impart rhythmic interest are typically Spanish. The complete

---

[11]Robert Stevenson, "Opera Beginnings in the New World," *Musical Quarterly* 45 (1959): 8-25; idem, *The Music of Peru* (Washington, 1960), chapter 4; idem, *Renaissance and Baroque Musical Sources in the Americas* (Washington, 1970), pp. 112-13.

Ex. 1 Manuel de Villaflor, *Huyendo del verde margen.*

da Ca - de - na con que o - prime infiel des - ti - no en ma - te - riales la - zos

La dul___ -ce unión del al - ma al cie___ - lo mi - ra

la dul___ -ce unión del al - ma al cie___ - lo mi - ra.

COPLAS
1. Fleeing from the green pasture and from the pleasing hubbub,
   Bireno moved his habitation to the horror of the crags.
2. The echo in the air's arms sometimes brought to his ear the confused
   murmur of voices from the merriment in the valley.
3. It was a torment to his anxieties, that hint that others lived
   happily, living without his martyrdom.
4. Weary of the remote, faintly heard merriment, he (Bireno) desires a
   solitude where his feelings can gush forth.

ESTRIBILLO
   And this unhappy being, restored, -although hanging in the prisons of the
living,- by the momentary pleasure of deep contemplation, says: Ah! sad life!
the chain with which treacherous destiny represses, with material bonds, the
sweet union of the soul looking to heaven.

song is included in example 1 to illustrate a representative villancico
format;[12] in this case, the estribillo would be repeated after each copla.
    The second villancico, *Deidad que postrada* (example 2), was
composed by Antonio Literes, one of the most famous early eighteenth-
century Spanish composers for the theater and church, probably best
known for his heroic zarzuela, *Acis y Galatea.* This lighthearted song
has a somewhat different but equally common formal design: it opens
with an estribillo of twelve lines addressed to the goddess whose un-
conscious state is imperiling the very light of the sun. Four coplas
plead with the beautiful nymph to "wake the two suns, the lights
beneath your lashes, or the dawn itself will be lazy" and "come back

[12]The transcriptions in examples 1 and 2, previously unpublished, were made from
manuscript facsimiles printed as a supplement to *Boletín del archivo general de la nación*
16, no. 4 (Mexico, 1945).

from breakfast, breathe again, so that the one who loves you can live." Each copla concludes with a refrain that is the very slightly modified ending of the estribillo; the entire estribillo may have been repeated after the fourth copla to conclude the villancico.

It is not presently known whether Zumaya composed for the numerous autos, comedias, loas, or sainetes of the time, although it would have been natural for a cleric to do so. He was, however, sufficiently involved in the theater and the life at court to compose and produce the musical drama *El Rodrigo,* performed in 1708 at the viceregal palace in Mexico City to celebrate the birth of Prince Luis Fernando.[13] The play was printed in Mexico in 1708 by Ribera, but the music has not survived. Its loss is particularly unfortunate because it is an early musical setting of one of Spain's oldest and richest epics, that of Rodrigo, last king of the Visigoths, whose defeat brought about the Moorish invasion of Spain in the eighth century. The Rodrigo legend's popularity can only be compared with that of the Cid in terms of instigating literary works.[14] Presumably, the musical style for *El Rodrigo* approximated that used for the comedias (discussed and illustrated above) and for the Calderón musical dramas; many of Zumaya's extant villancicos resemble this theater music in both solo and choral styles (see example 3).

Zumaya's next works for the musical stage, however, came under the influence of the Neapolitan opera style. On 15 January 1711 Mexico City welcomed as its new viceroy the Duke of Linares, Don Fernando de Alencastre Noroña y Silva, who was a cultivated devotee of the Italian opera, newly fashionable at the Madrid court. The new ruler apparently recognized Zumaya's gifts in dramatic music immediately. It is not clear how Zumaya learned Italian, but, according to the colonial chronicler Beristaín y Souza, he "translated several Italian operas into Castilian and put them to music for the diversion of the Duke."[15] Only one of these, *La Partenope,* was specifically named; a full three-act opera with music by Zumaya, it was performed at the viceregal palace on 1 May 1711 and thus became the earliest known complete opera composed and performed on the North American continent. Its Spanish libretto was a translation of Silvio Stampiglia's *Partenope,* which had been set to music in Naples in 1699 and in a slightly modified version was also set by Handel in 1730. Both the Spanish and Italian versions were printed in Mexico by Ribera in 1711.

---

[13]José Mariano Beristaín y Souza, *Biblioteca hispanoamericana setentrional,* 2d ed. (Amecameca, 1883), 3: 325.
[14]See Ramón Menéndez Pidal, *El Rey Rodrigo en la literatura* (Madrid, 1925); and vols. 62 and 71 of *Clásicos castellanos,* ed. Menéndez Pidal.
[15]Ibid.

Ex. 2 Àntonio Literes, *Deidad que postrada.*

(Alienta, alienta! Take courage, rouse yourself! for if you are not here,
the light dies, the day fails, and the sun fades away.)

The music unfortunately has been lost, but it was presumably as Italianate in style as the recitatives and arias Zumaya composed for many of his villancico-cantatas (see examples 4 and 5). It is not known whether Zumaya continued to compose for the musical theater. Although opera on the scale of *La Partenope* would have undoubtedly required the support of the viceregal court, public coliseos for comedias were operating in Mexico City. The newest of these theaters, built in 1725, contracted in Cádiz for several singers, dancing instructors, and orchestral musicians (including players of violins, transverse flutes, French horns, and violons) in 1742.[16] Among those who were

---

[16]Luis Gonzáles Obregón *México viejo: 1521-1821* (Mexico, 1945), pp. 343-46.

brought back to the Mexico City Coliseo was the well-known Italian violinist and composer, Ignacio Jerusalem, Zumaya's eventual successor as chapelmaster of the Cathedral.

In 1711, the same year that he was honored by the performance of his opera at the viceregal court, Zumaya was appointed acting chapelmaster at the Cathedral, for the aging Salazar was ill and had resigned from his duties. In 1715, between May 27 and June 7, the usual public examinations were conducted for the post of maestro de capilla, apparently vacated by Salazar's death. In addition to tests in plainsong and counterpoint, the authorities customarily gave the candidates the text of a Latin motet and a Spanish villancico to be set to music and performed for the judges in a brief and specified time. Zumaya was the victor, and his *opocisión* (examination) villancico, *Solfa de Pedro es el llanto,* is still preserved in the Guatemala Cathedral archives.[17]

The twenty-four years of Zumaya's service in the Mexico City Cathedral as its chapelmaster were brilliant and productive. The climaxing event was the installation of still another grand organ, built by Joseph Nazarre to match the great Sesma organ of 1695 and to face it across the *coro*.[18] Nazarre had recently completed an organ of 2,226 pipes for Guadalajara, but the new organ, with its 86 *mixturas,* was even more impressive. The spectacular inauguration ceremony on 15 August 1735 was attended by thousands, and the great organs were considered among the wonders of the New World. During the following months, leading organists from other important churches in the capital and throughout the country were invited to perform on the *nuevo famoso órgano.*

Zumaya's duties as chapelmaster included the composition of Latin liturgical music. Numbered among his extant examples are: (in Mexico City) a Lamentation, three Magnificats, Tones I, II, III, and numerous motets, psalms, and hymns, several of the latter in collaboration with Salazar; (in Oaxaca) a beautifully copied Missa Te Joseph celebrent[19]; and (in the Newberry Library in Chicago) a very simple Mass *a* 4. A considerable number of the works by earlier composers also owe their preservation to Zumaya, who ordered their collecting and professional copying for choirbooks still held in the Cathedral archives. All of these liturgical compositions employed the traditional, equal-voiced counterpoint of the *prima prattica,* featuring

---

[17]Stevenson, *Renaissance,* p. 105.

[18]See note 5; see also Stevenson, "Mexico City Cathedral Music," pp. 132-33, and idem, *Music in Mexico,* pp. 153-54.

[19]Stevenson, *Renaissance,* p. 207.

imitative polyphony and frequent polychoral techniques and displaying the reserve and decorum that characterized Spanish cathedral
music until almost the middle of the eighteenth century.

In sharp contrast to these works were the Spanish villancicos and
chanzonetas, which for more than a century Hispanic chapelmasters
had also been expected to compose as a regular part of their duties.
These colorful works employed many of the same popular elements
that characterized the Hispanic musical theater, but there seems to
be no reason to assume that the villancicos were acted or costumed.
They were usually given festive and elaborate performances at matins
on such important liturgical festivals as Christmas, the Birth of Mary,
Assumption, Corpus Christi, and the various saints' days, particularly
that of San Pedro. From the early seventeenth century until near the
middle of the eighteenth, all the best (as well as the poorest) Spanish
poets on both sides of the Atlantic were feverishly engaged in the production of villancicos and villancico sets to be sung in these special
church services. During the second half of the seventeenth century
and lasting through the first decade or so of the eighteenth, villancico sets or cycles (*juegos*) such as those by Sor Juana Inéz de la Cruz
were the most popular type. These usually consisted of nine villancicos,
three for each nocturn of matins; most of the individual poems retained the traditional format of a repeated estribillo and from four
to twenty or more coplas. The sets included such familiar popular
types as the romance, jácara, *negrilla* (using Negro dialect), *gitanella*
(gypsy), *tocotín* (a dance song in the Aztec language), *pastoriles*
(shepherds), and *ensalada* (medley). Playful dialogues, picaresque
characters, and colloquial speech were mixed with sophisticated allu-
sions, flowery figures of speech, metaphors (many of them musical),
and elaborate Baroque *góngorisms*. As choirboy, organist, and singer,
Zumaya certainly participated in the at least twenty elaborate villancico sets known to have been composed by Salazar and performed in
the Mexico City Cathedral between 1689 and 1704.[20] Three of these
were by Sor Juana or are authoritatively attributed to her.[21] Generous contributions from wealthy patrons assured performances that
were appropriately sumptuous and festive. Solo, ensemble, and choral
singing was featured in a variety of combinations, with instrumental
accompaniments and interludes of many kinds. The musical style
ranged from sweet lyricism to playful vivacity or brilliant virtuosity,
but it was generally bright and tuneful, with frequent dancelike

---

[20]J. T. Medina, *Imprenta en México,* vol. 14, no. 3 (Chile, 1908; reprint ed., Amsterdam, 1962), pp. 53, 68, 81, 82, 98, 142-44, 156, 158-59, 180, 182, 218, 237, 325,
358, 364.
    [21]*Asunción* 1690; *San Pedro* 1691 and 1692. Méndez Plancarte, ed., pp. 427, 512, 517.

rhythms and strong syncopations. In the period of Zumaya's maturity, the florid Italian style was increasingly fashionable, and the composite cantata structure with its recitatives and da capo arias for solo voice and instruments began to supersede the villancico cycles with vocal ensembles (see examples 4 and 5). The basic villancico format of coplas-estribillo was normally retained, however, for at least one aria.

More than forty villancicos by Zumaya survive; his fame gave his works wide dispersal, and the villancicos are now found in archives in Mexico City, Oaxaca, Morelia, Guatemala City,[22] and in private collections. As might be expected in such a transitional period, these works employed a great variety of styles and resources. Some re-

Ex. 3 Manuel de Zumaya, *Como es Príncipe Jurado.*

As a prince, attested to be in the highest hierarchy, the divine intelligences
come to acclaim Peter -
Viva! Viva! offering for his applause, as sacred insignias, the lofty palms,
the pure white lilies, the brilliant crowns, the hidden lights . . . . .

---

[22]Stevenson, *Renaissance,* pp. 105-6, 166, 192, 206-7.

semble the earlier villancicos in format, featuring four- and eight-part ensemble/choral writing, alternating frequently with duos and solo songs; all sections are instrumentally accompanied. Example 3, from a villancico for San Pedro (1715), illustrates one of these.[23] The stylistic variety may be suggested by brief descriptions of two additional examples: *Resuenen los clarines* (The trumpets resound *a* 8, with continuo; for Santa Cecilia) is brilliant antiphonal procession music with brisk march rhythms and simple harmonies.[24] *Albricias mortales* (Good tidings for men; for Easter) has an estribillo for two groups, SATB and SAT, and coplas for alternating soloists, with instrumental parts for two violins, clarin, and continuo.[25]

Although Salazar composed four sets of villancicos (1690, 1695,

[23]From a facsimile reproduction in Gabriel Saldívar, *Historia de la música en México* (México, 1934), pp. 112-13.

[24]Stevenson, *Renaissance,* p. 105.

[25]Ibid., p. 206.

1696, 1697) dedicated to the "Glorious Apparition of Our Lady of Guadalupe of Mexico,"[26] the music is lost. Zumaya's two villancicos for the Virgin of Guadalupe are therefore the earliest known extant pieces composed in her honor. One of these, *Al Alva que brilla*,[27] is a stylistically transitional work. A large-scale piece, it alternates four-part writing and brilliant baritone solos. The rhythms are jaunty and brisk, and the soloist's references to the fragrant gardens and brightly colored birds that surrounded Our Lady of Guadalupe seem to demand the use of the *pajaritos* (warbling birds) stops on the Cathedral organs.[28] Modern features in this villancico include the brilliant coloratura sequences for the soloist and the use of violins as the accompanying instruments.

Instrumentalists in considerable numbers were hired for the Cathedral choir. During the sixteenth and seventeenth centuries, Spanish traditions, which were followed even more enthusiastically in the colonies, favored such instruments as recorders, *chirimías* (shawms), *cornetas*, viols, bassoons, and trombones to double or replace melodic lines in the polyphonic liturgical music and to perform versos for such types as the Magnificats and Psalms. The accompaniment, or continuo part, was usually played by the harp and organ—sometimes with the guitar. The great organs, such as those in the Mexico City Cathedral, also added color with a wide variety of flute, reed, string, and brass stops, plus such extra stops as drums and kettledrums (*tambores, timbales*), large and small bells (*campana, cascabeles*), and the *pajaritos* described above. Instrumental accompaniments and interludes were even more important in the villancicos and chanzonetas. Some indication of their color on festive occasions may be gathered from the following playful poem, villancico number 7, from the 1691 set for Saint Peter, attributed to Sor Juana, set to music by Antonio Salazar, and performed in the Mexico City Cathedral.[29]

## VILLANCICO VII (Tercero Nocturno), SAN PEDRO, 1691

### ESTRIBILLO

| - ¡ Qué bien la Iglesia Mayor | How well the Cathedral |
|---|---|
| le hace fiesta a su Pastor! | puts on a fiesta for its Pastor |

[26]Medina, pp. 69, 144, 158-59, 182.

[27]Stevenson, *Renaissance*, p. 206.

[28]*Pajaritos*: "This stop consists of a number of small tanks of water into each of which are dipped the ends of several inverted metal pipes. The stop-tablet supplies wind to all of these at once, and the resulting sound is a warbling chord containing the unison and fifth. This stop is similar to the nineteenth-century nightingale stop." C. C. Kerr, p. 60.

[29]Méndez Plancarte, ed., pp. 339-41, 516.

Oíd los repiques; veréis cómo
  dan: ¡ Tan tan, talán, tan,
  tan!

Oíd el clarín:
  ¡ Tin tin, tilín, tin, tin!

- Mejor suena la trompeta,
  el sacabuche y corneta,
  el órgano y el bajón.
- ¡ Jesús, y qué confusión!

Con los repiques que dan,
  templar no puedo el violín.
    ¡ Tan tan, talán, tan, tan!
      ¡ Tin tin, tilín, tin, tin!

Hear the bells clanging, see
  how they go: Tan tan
  talán, . . .

Hear the bugle:
  Tin tin, tilín, . . .

Even greater sounds the trumpet,
  the trombone and cornet,
  the organ and the bassoon.
- Jesus! what confusion!

With the bells clanging like that,
  I can't tune the violin.
    Tan tan, talán . . . .
      Tin tin, tilín. . . .

## COPLAS

1) De Pedro el sacro día,
   para más lucimiento,
   uno y otro instrumento
   forme dulce armonía;
   suene la chirimía
   y acompañe el violín:
   ¡ Tin, tilín, tin, tin!

2) Porque el rumor se escuche,
   retumbe la trompeta,
   gorjee la corneta
   y ayude el sacabuche;
   una con otra luche,
   voces que entrando van:
   ¡ Tan talán, tan, tan!

3) Rechine la marina
   trompa, con el violón;
   déles tono el bajón
   y el eco que refina
   la cítara, que trina
   apostando al violín:
   ¡ Tin, tilín, tin, tin!

4) El tenor gorgoree
   la vihuela discante,
   el rabelillo encante,
   la bandurria vocee,

1) For Peter the sacred day,
   for more brilliance,
   one with another instrument
   forms sweet harmony;
   let the shawm sound
   and the violin accompany:
   ¡ Tin, tilín, tin, tin!

2) So that we can listen to the
   murmur, sound out the trumpet,
   trill (warble) the cornet
   and add the trombone;
   one battles with the other,
   voices that entering go thus:
   Tan, talán, tan, tan!

3) The marine trumpet squeaks,
   with the bass viol;
   the bassoon sounds the tone
   and the echo is refined by
   the cittern, that reinforces
   the trills of the violin:
   Tin, tilín, tin, tin!

4) The tenor vocalizes roulades,
   the guitar sings,
   the little rebec adds charm,
   the bandore gives voice,

| el arpa gargantee, | the harp quavers (warbles) |
| que así rumor harán! | that thus all will create the |
| ¡ Tan talán, tan, tan! | murmur: Tan, talán, tan, tan! |

The cathedral archives of the early eighteenth century reflect the radical changes in taste. String players were increasingly more desired than the formerly popular performers on the chirimía, corneta, and bajón. A 1736 list, for example, recorded the hiring of players on the violin, viola, cello, bass viol, trumpet, clarín, and other instruments.

This new emphasis on strings, mainly on the violins, is also demonstrated in the Zumaya villancicos, particularly those in solo cantata form. Typical examples, showing the influence of the Italian vocal style and the Italian violin, are illustrated in examples 4 and 5, excerpts from two villancico-cantatas by Zumaya, apparently part of a set for Assumption, 1715.[30] The first of these works, *Y a la gloria âccidental,* was written for tenor solo, two violins, and a basso continuo; its formal plan is as follows: aria #1 (fast, F major, measures 1-21); recitativo secco (measures 22-36); and a da capo arieta-fuga (fast, section A: measures 37-51, ending in F major; section B: measures 52-62, ending in A major; section A, da capo). Example 4a is the opening of aria #1; example 4b shows the end of the recitative and the beginning of the arieta-fuga; and example 4c illustrates the sweeping coloratura passages, an admired feature of the florid style, that conclude section B of the arieta-fuga.

The second villancico, *Oy sube arrebatáda,* was composed for a tenor soloist, basso continuo, and two alternating instrumental groups; the first of these, which generally parallels the voice rhythmically, consists of a soprano and a bass instrument—probably winds such as a chirimía and bassoon. The second group, employed between vocal phrases, consists of two violins and a bass—probably also a string instrument. In form, this villancico-cantata follows the old format: a brilliant estribillo (F major, measures 1-31); four coplas, set strophically in a much simpler style; and a repeat of the estribillo. Example 5 shows the fanfarelike opening of the estribillo.

Zumaya's villancico style is notable for its utilization of contrasts in texture, rhythms, registers, and harmony. His harmonic usage

---

[30]My transcriptions of these two cantatas were made from manuscripts originally in the Mexico City Cathedral and now in a private collection; they are previously unpublished. *Y la gloria âccidental* was first performed in modern times on 30 April 1961 by Richard Robinson, tenor; John Korman and Joan Cruckenmiller, violins; and Roger Wagner, conductor, for a festival on the campus of the University of California at Los Angeles; it was also included in the 1966 recording *Salve Regina* (Angel S36008), Roger Wagner, musical director.

Ex. 4 Manuel de Zumaya, *Y a la gloria âccidental.*

a)   from Aria #1

b)    from the Recitado, Arieta-Fuga

c)   from the Arieta-Fuga (conclusion of section B)

Ex. 5 Manuel de Zumaya, *Oy sube arrebatáda*.

En a - las de che-
(on the wings of the cherubim)

ranges from an emphasis on simple fundamental chords in the march-like pieces to a sophisticated vocabulary that employs the diminished-seventh chords, the Neapolitan sixths, and the pleasantly sweet sonor-ities of the Neapolitan opera style. A brief reference to a few addi-tional solo cantatas will also illustrate the variety of the composer's formal designs. A Christmas cantata, for alto solo with violins and continuo, consists of an introduction, da capo aria #1 (in D minor, Grave ending), aria #2 (G minor, fast), recitative, and four coplas that are seguidillas (E-flat major).[31] A San Pedro cantata, for alto, violins, and continuo, presents two arias in a balanced design of seven sections, beginning and ending with Largos in G minor and 6/8 meter.[32] An expressive and harmonically rich Christmas cantata (1738), one of Zumaya's latest and most modern works, was written for tenor solo, two violins, a viola, and continuo; it consists of an in-troduction, da capo aria #1 (E minor), recitative, and da capo aria #2 (A minor).[33]

In 1739 Zumaya made a decision that radically changed his life; his reasons are unknown, but—then past sixty—he may have desired a more tranquil and reflective existence. A close friend, who had left

---

[31]*Y la naturaleza redimida*. Stevenson, *Renaissance*, p. 207.
[32]*Si yâ â aquella Nave que calman los vientos*. Ibid.
[33]*Dela celeste esfera que portento*. Ibid., p. 105.

the capital the previous year to become bishop in the southern city of Oaxaca, invited Zumaya to join him. The chapelmaster did so without asking permission from the Cathedral authorities, whose frequent pleas to return he consistently ignored even as late as 1743. Beristaín y Souza stated that in Oaxaca Zumaya devoted himself to religious duties and translated from Italian into Spanish a biography of the Jesuit Sartorio Caputo.[34] The composer obviously also continued his musical activities. While his friend Bishop Montaño was alive, Zumaya held the post of *cura interino del Sagrario,* but near the end of 1744 this was given to another.[35] In order to keep the famous musician in Oaxaca, where he had been acting as a musical consultant, the Cathedral authorities on 11 January 1745 offered the *"buen eclesiastico"* Zumaya the post of chapelmaster, with the duties of composing and of teaching the choirboys. Although there are more than twenty-five compositions now in the Oaxaca archives, it is not known whether any were written there; the dated ones (1719-1738) were composed for the Mexico City Cathedral. The Oaxaca archives record the usual cycle of activities and the esteem and honor accorded the chapelmaster for his abilities, his character, and his conscientious attention to fulfilling his duties. Zumaya died in 1756, probably between May 1 and 6.

Manuel de Zumaya's contributions to Mexican Baroque music for church and theater should ensure him recognition as the earliest important composer of Western music born on the North American continent, one who reached the highest pinnacles of achievement and who was accorded the greatest musical honors possible to his time and location.

Alice Ray Catalyne

---

[34]Beristaín y Souza, p. 325.
[35]Robert Stevenson, "Mexican Colonial Music Manuscripts Abroad," *MLA Notes* 29 (1972-73): 212.

# PART III

# Barthold Feind's
# "Gedancken von der Oper":
# An Early Eighteenth-Century
# View of Drama and Music

In 1708 Barthold Feind, a prolific Hamburg writer and frequent collaborator of Reinhard Keiser, published a large volume of writings entitled *Deutsche Gedichte*.[1] The title page, ample in its description of the contents, gives some indication of the scope of the author's interests.

> Musical Dramas/Eulogistic, Congratulatory, Love and Moralistic Poems/Serious and Facetious Epigrams and Epitaphs/Satires/Cantatas and a variety of other Types. Together with a Preface on the Temperamental and Emotional Idiosyncrasies of a Poet/and Thoughts on Opera.[2]

It is the final item, a tightly written essay of some forty pages, that commands our attention, for in the course of his examination of the musical theater of his day, Feind probed local practices, national characteristics, and musical as well as dramaturgical problems with a practiced eye and a keen wit.

By the early years of the eighteenth century the German opera company of the flourishing Hanseatic capital had already enjoyed several decades of preeminence, but despite the popularity of the venture, the signs of its decline were clearly visible and the ultimate success of the ubiquitous Italians was only a matter of time. This was to prove true, of course, not only in Hamburg, but also in other German

---

[1]Barthold Feind, *Deutsche Gedichte* (Hamburg, 1708). The essay, *Gedancken von der Oper*, has been reprinted in *Encyclopädie der deutschen Nationalliteratur oder biographisch-kritisches Lexicon der deutschen Dichter und Prosaisten*, ed. O. L. B. Wolff (Leipzig, 1837), 2:317-24.

[2]Musicalischen Schau-Spielen/Lob-Glückwünschungs/Verliebten und Moralischen Gedichten/Ernst- und schertzhafften Sinn- und Grabschrifften/Satyren/Cantaten und allerhand Gattungen. Sammt einer Vorrede Von dem Temperament und Gemühts-Beschaffenheit eines Poeten/und Gedancken von der Opera.

127

cities and courts such as Leipzig, Hannover, Braunschweig, Weissen-
fels, Wolfenbüttel, and Stuttgart, all of which supported, however
sporadically, the performance of German opera. By the late 1730s,
the Hamburg opera and most of the other German houses had closed
their doors, yielding at last to the pressure of changing tastes and the
persistent lure of imported art. Feind, who was one of the first German writers to concern himself with the problems of creating a viable
art form combining drama and music, was troubled by the excesses that
were increasingly evident on the Hamburg stage, as well as by the
growing taste for implausible mixtures of high drama and low folk
humor. He discussed these and other matters relating to opera in his
*Gedancken* of 1708, and although this essay remained his only formal
statement on the subject, his deep and abiding interest in the relationship between drama and music is also evident in the series of prefaces for each of the nine librettos he wrote for Keiser and Graupner,
two of the most active Hamburg composers of the day. Prefaces of
this type were frequently published with librettos and were basically
designed to serve as plot summaries, but for Feind they also functioned as a platform from which he sought to enlighten the opera-
going public and to encourage appreciation for sound dramatic characterization. This is a significant point because such an approach to
opera criticism in Germany was to become common in the eighteenth
century and later in the writings of Weber and Wagner.

The chronology of Barthold Feind's most important librettos and
their relationship to the *Gedancken* is a matter of some interest, and
since these works are not generally known and the musical scores only
partly preserved, a list of titles and dates may be helpful to the reader.

*Die römische Unruhe, oder: Die edelmüthige Octavia.* Musicalisches Schauspiel. 5 August 1705.
Reinhard Keiser.

*Die kleinmüthige Selbst-Mörderinn Lucretia, oder: Die Staats-
Thorheit des Brutus.* Musicalisches Trauer-Spiel. 29 Novem-
ber 1705.
Reinhard Keiser.

*Masagniello furioso, oder: Die neapolitanische Fischer-Em-
pörung.* Musicalisches Schauspiel. June 1706.
Reinhard Keiser.

*La Costanza sforzata, die gezwungene Beständigkeit, oder:
Die listige Rache des Sueno.* Sing-Spiel. 11 October 1706.
Reinhard Keiser.

*L'Amore ammalato, die krankende Liebe, oder: Antiochus und*

*Stratonica.* Musicalisches Schauspiel. 1708.
Christoph Graupner.
*Bellerophon, oder: Das in die preussische Krone verwandelte Wagen-Gestirn.* Operetta. 28 November 1708.
Christoph Graupner.
*Desiderius, König der Longobarden.* Musicalisches Schauspiel.
26 July 1709.
Reinhard Keiser.
*Der Fall des grossen Richters in Israel, Simson, oder: Die abgekühlte Liebes-Rache der Debora.* Musicalisches Trauer-Spiel. November 1709.
Christoph Graupner.
*Der durch den Fall des Grossen Pompejus Erhöhete Julius Caesar.* Sing-Spiel.
Reinhard Keiser.[3]

Born in Hamburg in 1678, the same year that saw the establishment of the famous opera house "am Gänsemarkt," Feind was the son of a distinguished teacher of theology.[4] Educated in law, Feind completed his studies at Wittenberg and after several years of practice as a licentiate of law at Halle, the young man returned to Hamburg where he was active as a lawyer and writer. The period was a troubled one for the city. Economic uncertainty and political unrest resulted in bitter controversies between the liberal and conservative factions. Feind, soon drawn into the melee, was branded a radical because of the caustic tone of the religious and political satires he wrote in 1704 and the equally offensive attitudes he expressed in a series of articles that appeared in his weekly journal, *Relationes curiosae,* in the following year. He so provoked the powerful conservative members of the Senate and the Lutheran clergy that he found himself constantly under attack. These activities culminated in the burning of his books on 18 March 1707, in the Rathaus Square by order of the Senate, and his banishment from the city. Although the ban was rescinded in 1709 when the political climate in Hamburg grew less rigid, Feind spent much of the next decade away from the city, frequently involved in political skirmishes between Denmark and Sweden and writ-

---

[3]Modern editions of *Octavia* and *Masagniello furioso* are available; the other scores are either lost or extant only in part. Feind included the librettos with the prefaces of *Octavia, Lucretia, Masagniello furioso, Sueno,* and *Antiochus und Stratonica* in his *Deutsche Gedichte.*

[4]Biographical information about Barthold Feind is limited. The best source is *Lexikon der hamburgischen Schriftsteller bis zur Gegenwart,* ed. Hans Schröder (Hamburg, 1857), 3:281-89. See also Friedrich Baake, "Barthold Feind," *Die Musik in Geschichte und Gegenwart* 4 (1955): 7-11.

ing tracts in behalf of the latter country. In 1717, his fervor subdued by a period of imprisonment, he returned to Hamburg where he served for a short time as a curate at the cathedral. Little else is known of him; he wrote comparatively few works after 1719 and, according to Johann Mattheson, died in the night of 14 October 1721, presumably from a fall down a flight of stairs.

To this biographical sketch, which contains the basic facts that have been preserved about Feind, must be added the bits of information we can piece together concerning his activities as a librettist. Some time in 1702, after his stay at Halle, he was called back to Hamburg and he seems to have immediately begun taking an active part in the theatrical life of the city. Two scripts, dating from the 1702-1703 period, are extant: *Carneval der Liebe* and *Das verwirrte Haus Jakob.* Little is known about these works, but they were probably intended for one or another of the many fairs that took place there each year. No trace of accompanying musical scores exists; however, local composers regularly provided music for these occasions. How and when Feind met Keiser is unknown; their first collaboration, *Octavia,* took place in 1705.

At that time Keiser was at the height of his colorful career as the principal figure in the musical life of Hamburg. Having arrived there in 1696 or 1697, he rapidly assumed a position of leadership at the Theater am Gänsemarkt. He composed as many as five operas a season for the stage, and by 1703 was not only the musical director and chief conductor, but also joint owner and manager of the entire enterprise. However, bankruptcy overtook him in 1707, reflecting both his well-known taste for luxurious living and the general decline in the prosperity of the local merchants. This financial crisis was not a unique event for the opera; the house was periodically darkened throughout the sixty years of its existence, but until its final demise in 1738, it always managed to reopen, though with increasing difficulty after the 1720s when Keiser focused his attention on sacred music.

Feind was, of course, only one of many librettists active during the period of Keiser's directorship of the opera. The names of most of the others are all but forgotten and those that are not—Postel, König, Bostel, Hinsch, Feustking, and Hunold—were poets of largely local reputation whose general mediocrity and heavy-handed style have frequently been cited as one of the chief causes of the decline of German opera in the first third of the eighteenth century.[5] There

---

[5]Friedrich Chrysander, *Händel* (Leipzig, 1858), 1:105-10, 126-27. See also his series of articles on the history of the opera in Hamburg in the *Allgemeine musikalische Zeitung,* 1877-1880. Especially interesting are the five installments of 1880 in which Chrysander discusses the period during which Reinhard Keiser served as director of the

can be no doubt that the limited capacity of most of the librettists did not discourage the growing taste among the public for bizarre and vulgar subjects and crude language and hastened the process of deterioration.

Several factors may be noted that distinguish Feind from his contemporaries and perhaps account for the broadness of his perspective and his concern with plausible dramatic characterizations. First of all, he traveled far more widely than did most of his contemporaries in Hamburg. Between 1705 and 1707 he made at least two extensive journeys; one to Italy, the other to Paris. Explicit details about these trips are nonexistent, but his *Gedancken* and librettos provide ample evidence of the impact of his exposure to the Italian and French musical theater. At the very outset he took a position that clearly links him with the French critics of Baroque theater: opera, *dramma per musica,* or musical theater must be considered an unnatural or contrived kind of juggling of poetry and music, singing and acting. Obviously, excellence in opera demands the balanced combination of every aspect of the production, both musical and theatrical. Feind observed that operatic tradition and practice varies from country to country; strengths and weaknesses are everywhere apparent. Excessive artificiality he associated with the French, naive realism with the Italians, and an artless kind of buffoonery with the Germans. Against these tendencies, all of which he recognized as exerting an influence to a greater or lesser extent on the Hamburg stage, he proposed certain recommendations. They are elaborately detailed in his essay and skillfully applied in his librettos in a manner that displays a fine balance between theory and practice.

To encourage the development of what he called a strong operatic tradition he advocated clear-cut guidelines intended to improve theatrical conditions. At long last, librettists should abandon their use of both classical and biblical subject matter, such as he himself employed in works like *Octavia, Lucretia,* and *Simson,* and which were the standard themes among German poets of the time, and turn to topics of more timely significance. Though he never consistently followed his own advice in this regard, he did point the way in at least two of his librettos of 1706: *Masagniello furioso* and *Sueno.* The first of these works, the story of a mid-seventeenth-century uprising of

---

opera. H. M. Schletterer, *Das deutsche Singspiel von seinen ersten Anfängen* (Leipzig, 1863), pp. 78-79, 99; and H. Kretzschmar, *Geschichte der Oper* (Leipzig, 1919), pp. 143-45, are early authorities who include Feind among the ranks of inferior poets. More recently, however, his position has been reassessed and his contributions more fully recognized. See H. Ch. Wolff, *Die Barockoper in Hamburg 1678-1738* (Wolfenbüttel, 1957).

Neapolitan fishermen against colonial Spanish tyrants,[6] had pointed contemporary implications for Feind. Not only was he searching here for "a change from the inevitable materials of antiquity,"[7] but also he yearned for a text that would speak to his own day. Involved as he was in local politics, he relished the opportunity of jabbing the powerful demagogues among the clergy and the Senate who were unyielding in their attempt to wield absolute authority over the cultural as well as the spiritual life of the city. The issue as presented by Feind, though cloaked in another setting, had long been in the forefront of interest among the citizens of Hamburg and could only serve to focus attention upon the vital dramatic potential of the theater, and this was precisely Feind's purpose.

In *Sueno* Feind again turned to subject matter of regional concern, and at the same time used the story as a vehicle to illustrate one of his most progressive ideas. Sueno, a king of Denmark in bygone ages, was a man of cunning and treachery who despite the crimes he had perpetrated was not a "totally evil character," but rather an individual who combined good traits as well as bad. This attempt to avoid black and white characterization in opera librettos represented a crucial part of Feind's thinking on dramatic truth. He considered opera as an entirely independent art form in which drama must stand on equal footing with music and the decorative arts. And if sung dialogue must of necessity involve some distortion of reality, then all the more reason for the poet to avoid the stereotyped characterizations so often associated with the seventeenth-century operatic stage. Only if the main characters of the drama are convincing in their motivation could the *Sing-Spiel* assume its place as a genuine art form. For Feind two factors were essential in this regard and both were, in his opinion, badly neglected by the poets who were supplying the librettos for the Hamburg stage. Stated briefly these elements are (1) the need for as much *action* as possible in each scene of the play, and (2) character development based on clearly drawn and *psychologically* believable traits. When he speaks of action in his *Gedancken,* Feind leaves little doubt as to its importance for opera. The greatest emotional impact is achieved when the "Affectus" is suppressed and kept well under the surface, to be manifested in "heroic deeds" rather than tedious and static verbal descriptions. If emotions are not expressed in this manner, there can be no action; and if there is no action, everything in the theater freezes.

---

[6]Auber's *La Muette de Portici* (1828) is based on the same subject. Telemann prepared a setting of Masagniello in 1727.

[7]*Encyclopädie der deutschen Nationalliteratur,* 2:319.

Concern with the human temperaments and psychological characteristics was not new to eighteenth-century writers, but Feind was surely among the first librettists to try to make his characters emerge as authentic individuals rather than stereotyped figures by allowing their action to arise from clearly delineated temperamental inclinations and psychological states of mind. That he was intensely interested and well read in the subject is evidenced by the essay that precedes the *Gedancken* in his *Deutsche Gedichte, Eine Vorrede von dem Temperament und Gemühts-Beschaffenheit eines Poeten,* which is a thoughtful analysis of the application to the writing of drama of the various theories dealing with the relationship between types of temperament and behavior. In the prefaces to several of his librettos he illustrates his own interpretation of these theories as a means of strengthening the characterizations. One of the finest examples may be found in his *Lucretia* of 1705. Eschewing the cliché of Venetian opera that demanded the death of the villain but never of the valiant hero or heroine, Feind rejected the conventional but dramatically weak happy ending in favor of the tragic as the aesthetically satisfying way of intensifying audience compassion. Here he cited Aristotle as his mentor.[8] Lucretia, a woman of complex emotions—more ambitious than sensual, quick to anger and vengeance, by temperament both melancholic and choleric—must inevitably take her own life when her honor is violated. Despondent and fearful, she is capable of arousing sympathy and emerges as neither a model of virtue nor a figure of scorn. When the poet takes care to delineate a character in this manner and then allows the action to follow its predestined course, the result, Feind contended, is a powerful drama, and only such a drama can provide the basis for a successful opera. *Octavia,* too, shows similar preoccupation with character motivation. Nero and Octavia do not present a pattern of stark contrast between evil and good, but rather interact upon each other psychologically so that Nero's decision to restore Octavia as his wife after she has been sentenced to death is the result of his sensitive response to her willing self-sacrifice. Feind accounts for this magnanimous act by assigning to Nero a "sanguine-phlegmatic humor, to some extent blended with the choleric."[9] This may seem to be rather primitive psychology, but for its day it gave him a unique place among librettists.

As one reads through the pages of the *Gedancken,* one cannot fail to observe how deeply impressed Feind was by the ideals of French and English tragedy. It is this factor more than any other that ac-

---

[8]In his Preface to *Lucretia. Deutsche Gedichte,* p. 186.
[9]In his Preface to *Octavia. Deutsche Gedichte,* pp. 119-20.

counts for his ideas on the dramaturgy of the opera. He cited readings of Shakespeare and performances of French tragedies as examples of dramatic works that can arouse genuine emotional response from the audience, and thus he became one of the first German poets of his time to comment on the importance of Shakespearian drama. He was undoubtedly familiar with the performances of the troups of English actors who began traveling in Germany even before the turn of the century.[10] These influences could only have sharpened his dramatic instincts and led him to pursue similar achievements in his own works, to cry out against the carnival atmosphere and buffoonery of the Hamburg fairs on the one hand and the blind imitation of Italian models on the other. That he was forced to make concessions to the tastes of his time cannot be denied, but that he strove to raise the standards was equally true. When he wrote that poetry (not to be confused with mere versification) is an intrinsic part of the *Sing-Spiel* and that the aria must function as an interpretation of the recitative —the ultimate ornamentation of the poetry and the soul of the drama[11]—, he came close to describing the ultimate but elusive goal of all opera.

Dolores M. Hsu

---

[10]Wolff, p. 48.
[11]*Encyclopädie der deutschen Nationalliteratur,* 2:321.

# An Eighteenth-Century
# Parisian *Turandot*

Diamantine was a cold and haughty Princess of China who fired the imagination of Parisian theatregoers during the summer of 1729. Lesage and D'Orneval's opéra-comique about her, *La Princesse de Chine,* with some original music by Jean-Claude Gilliers, warmed the ailing coffers of the eighteenth-century Fair Theatres in Paris, as the first offering of that season at the Saint-Laurent Fair.[1]

This play with music opened June 15 and so successfully held the boards that when the bill was changed on August 20, a few lines in one of the new plays referred to it. The prologue that evening, *Les Spectacles Malades,* was concerned with a visit to the doctor by the Opéra, the Comédie-Française, the Comédie-Italienne, and the Opéra-Comique, each trying to find a cure for its ills.

The Opéra-Comique confessed that her problem was all the bad "food" she had been given during the Saint-Germain Fair's theatre season earlier that year, i.e., plays by many different authors. (This was Lesage's way of stressing the fact that he had not been well represented at that fair, whereas this new opéra-comique had put the players back on their feet.) The Opéra-Comique tells the doctor's assistant (Pierrot in disguise) that she took a certain medicine made of Chinese herbs that cured her, in spite of stiff-necked critics who complained that too many cold seeds were in the mixture.[2]

The tale of an obstinately virgin princess who condemns her unsuccessful wooers to death has been popular with storytellers of many countries throughout the centuries. It seems to have entered Western Europe through a French translation of Persian tales that appeared toward the end of the seventeenth century. This version also included the trial for life or death based on answers to three enigmas and the arrival of an unknown prince who poses an enigma of his own.[3]

---

[1]Lesage et D'Orneval, *Le théâtre de la foire ou l'opéra-comique* (Paris, 1731), 7:123-212.
[2]Ibid., pp. 236-37.
[3]Ernest Newman, *More Stories of Famous Operas* (New York, 1943), p. 4.

Carlo Gozzi's Italian play *Turandot,* written in 1762, and Schiller's German version of 1802 are well-known theatrical versions of this tale. Weber, Busoni, and Puccini have used music to enhance the colorful plot with its curious blend of commedia dell'arte and serious drama. The earliest music-theatre version of *Turandot* seems to have been the collaboration of Lesage, D'Orneval, and Gilliers, *La Princesse de Chine,* which has remained hidden in the volumes of Lesage opéra-comiques since the mid-eighteenth century.

The first act is set in front of the palace of the King of China, in the capital city of Peking. Elmasie, favorite slave of the Princess of China, is spending a few hours away from the palace visiting with her mother. As they talk, we learn that they fled Visapour seeking refuge from a war.

Prince Noureddin, son of the King of Visapour, enters with his riding companion, Pierrot. They are now seeking refuge because the Mongols conquered Visapour, killing the King. Pierrot immediately sets himself off from the others by his repartee.

> *Noureddin*: Here then is Peking. Have courage, Pierrot.
> *Pierrot*: I have it by becoming enraged.
> *Noureddin*: We are at the end of our journey.
> *Pierrot*: We are at the end of our money.

This is delivered by means of a rhyming dialogue song, using the *vaudeville* tune "Que je suis à plaindre." Each character sings one line.

The entire opening scene is sung to tunes like this, one generally following the other, though sometimes brief dialogue intervenes. This necessitated that the tunes be in the same or closely related keys, enabling the singers and instrumental accompanists to move easily from one to the next. Furthermore, the tunes were in the popular repertoire of the day, and most people knew the tunes as well as the original lyrics. Throughout this opéra-comique, Pierrot's tunes often have refrain lines of nonsense syllables.

The four characters on stage are surprised and happy to see each other, but the two ladies are upset at the news of the fall of Visapour and the death of the King. Repsima, mother of Elmasie, is the widow of Noureddin's former riding companion. This young Prince has come to ask the King of China, Altoun-Can, if he might fight in China's army to earn a living. Elmasie promises to speak to the King about the possibility—which is very strong since China is on the brink of going to war with Japan. The two men are promptly invited to lodge with Repsima, who leaves to prepare supper for them.

The sound of little bells and Chinese drums introduces a procession for which the orchestra plays a *marche triste*. Unfortunately, the instrumental music for this opéra-comique has not been found, but the stage directions are explicit about the local color evoked. A soldier enters carrying a dragon's head on the end of a pike. He is followed by two drummers and two town criers, each playing little bells. Next come four men carrying varnished tables, followed by four banner bearers. Then four mandarins precede Great Colao, the judge, who is leading the Prince of Basra to his death. The procession ends with the executioner, who carries an unsheathed sabre on his shoulder, and his two valets with hatchets on their belts.

A brief judgment scene is held during which the Prince of Basra takes the blame for daring to hope for the hand of the Princess of China, especially since the King of China had urged him not to risk his life. Admitting his error, he is led to the execution place with the same martial music. Elmasie rejoins Noureddin and Pierrot, who press her for an explanation of what they just saw.

Princess Diamantine is nineteen years old, the King's only child, and heir to the Chinese empire. Two years earlier, the King of Thébet sent an ambassador asking for her hand in marriage to his son, the Prince, who had fallen in love with a portrait of her. King Altoun-Can was delighted with the prospect, but his daughter was so upset that she cried incessantly, took sick, and was about to die.

A refusal was sent back to Thébet, but the haughty Princess insisted that her father swear by the prophet Jacmouni the solemn oath: Diamantine would only marry the prince who could answer three enigmas she would ask, and failure to answer correctly would bring death by decapitation. The King was horrified by such a request.

The Princess got her wish by stroking her father's chin, saying that she wanted to keep her freedom, live in retreat, and remain a virgin since marriage offended her pride. The tune used to sing these lines has interesting implications: "Gardons nos moutons, lirette, liron" (Let's keep watch over our sheep, tra la la).

The King and his daughter at first thought that no prince would accept this challenge, but many tried and all failed. To the tune "Pour passer doucement la vie" (In order to quietly live life), Noureddin comments "That barbarity is new, but we can admit to ourselves that the Princess is no less cruel than all those princes are crazy."

Elmasie explains that Diamantine is a "well of science," putting the most skilled mandarins to shame. It is almost impossible to make any sense out of her enigmas. For that reason, the King tries in every way he can to dissuade any prince from trying to answer them. In addition, he forbids any further portrait or sketch to be made of his daughter, because these seem to be the cause of the problem. The King offers one thousand gold *sequins* for every portrait returned to him. Pierrot replies with this wisecrack: "I wish I had half a dozen portraits of her."

So, here is a princess more beautiful and gentle than any painter can capture, with an inhuman hatred of men. Pierrot quips: "The morsel is tempting, but the price takes away my taste for it." In bidding Elmasie goodbye, he reminds her of their previous friendship to the tune "N'y a pas d' mal à ça" (There's no harm in that): "For you, my sweet, Pierrot will sigh. If you want, lovable rascal, he'll continue to." She responds with the refrain: "There's no harm in that!" upon which she promptly exits.

Noureddin and Pierrot discuss the strange Princess, declaring that those princes should be put in a crazy house rather than be killed. Zerbin, friend of the recently executed Prince, enters mourning the unfortunate death to the tune "Paris est en grand deuil" (Paris is in great mourning): "This was the young Prince's first love, and he was happy to die for it." Staring in disbelief at the portrait of Diamantine that he took from the Prince, Zerbin refuses to return to Basra with news of the death. He throws the portrait on the ground and steps on it.

Pierrot quickly picks it up, anxious to get the promised reward from the King during the appointed "job interview" set for the next morning. Noureddin takes it from Pierrot and decides to give it to the King himself, hoping to have a better chance of being hired for the army. Just as they leave to go and eat at Repsima's house, a procession of bonzes begins to fill the stage, preparing to make a sacrifice to the prophet Jacmouni. This is in response to an order from the King who hopes the sacrifice will bring an end to the misfortunes brought on by the Princess. The ceremony is performed after the death of each prince.

Here occurs the first original music in this opéra-comique, composed by the most prolific composer of the Fair Theatres, Jean-Claude Gilliers. He also wrote original music to close Acts II and III of this work and possibly wrote the other instrumental music mentioned throughout the play. In any case, he certainly collaborated with Lesage and D'Orneval in the selection of the *vaudeville* tunes in addition to arranging the music for the orchestra; he probably played and conducted as well.

The final scene of Act I begins with a *burlesque* march played by the orchestra. Eight bonzes enter, followed by two young bonzes carrying a small altar covered with flowers and heads of young pigs.

The High Priest enters, then four guards armed with pikes and hatchets. The High Priest, a baritone, opens the ceremony with a sung prayer to Jacmouni in three sections: a section in G minor and duple meter, a triple meter section cadencing on D, and a repeat of the first section. Stage and musical directions do not clarify whether the chorus joins on the repeat or just one line, or whether it sings all of the prayer alone.

The bonzes dance while the High Priest burns perfumes with gold and silver papers on the altar. After this "sacrifice," the High Priest sings another prayer in G minor, asking that no more princes come to seek the Princess's hand, or if they do, that a happier turn of events be the result. This air changes meter during the first two lines ( $\frac{3}{2}$ , $\frac{2}{2}$ , $\frac{3}{4}$ ) according to word accents—a subtlety ignored by necessity in adapting new texts to *vaudeville* tunes throughout this opéra-comique. A dance closes this colorful Act I finale. The music is neither given nor specified.

Act II takes place the next day in the gardens outside the palace. As the King and his judge Colao await the arrival of Noureddin for the appointment set up through Elmasie, they discuss the young Prince's reputation for bravery in battle. When they all meet, the King takes an immediate liking to Noureddin, naming him commander of the Chinese army to fight against Japan. Furthermore, the King expresses a wish that he were Noureddin's father, whereupon the young Prince declares his wish to marry the Princess of China that very day.

Noureddin admits he has fallen in love through looking at Diamantine's portrait. The King and Colao are horrified and try their best to dissuade him from pressing this awful suit. But they do not succeed.

Pierrot enters, singing to the tune "Je suis un bon soldat, Ti, ta, ta": "China will have in us, ti, ta, ta, two brave captains. Off I go to Japan, patapan, to break porcelain" (Japanese figurines). He is quite disgusted to learn that his friend intends to seek the hand of the Princess rather than go off to battle. He curses the fact that he did not personally return the Princess's portrait to the King as he had originally planned.

Elmasie enters in the same unhappy mood, surprised that Noureddin has changed so quickly. (A three-part song, originally titled "Quel caprice, quelle injustice," serves to carry this discussion.) Noureddin replies by singing of the beauty of the cruel Princess and how he is willing to die for her. Elmasie, in the middle section of this song, tries to change his mind, but Noureddin's answer is a return to the beginning of the song with the same text. They then divide another song, with the original refrain lines retained: "Je le crois bien, je n'en crois rien" (I believe it, I don't believe it at all).

> Elmasie: Don't you know that she is more learned than all the learned men of China?
> Noureddin: I believe it, but she can't confound me. I'll know how to answer her well.
> Elmasie: I don't believe it at all!

There seems to be no way to change Noureddin's mind.

Colao enters to announce that the King is determined to stop this folly at all costs. He is sending his most beautiful slaves in the hope that Noureddin will choose one rather than try for Princess Diamantine. The dialogue song between these two retains its original refrain lines: "oh, que si! oh, que nenni!"

> Noureddin: I don't believe, my friend, that any beauty can light a new flame in my heart.
> Colao: Oh, but yes!
> Noureddin: Even though ten thousand might come, it would be useless.
> Colao: Oh, but no!

Pierrot's attempt to change his Prince's mind is sung to the tune "L'appétit vient en mangeant" (Appetite comes while eating): "You will see that little girl indifferently at first. Then you will look at the little chickadee up and down less coldly. Finally you'll release the chain to your inclination. Appetite comes while eating."

Two slave girls, Dilara and Amine, enter, and Pierrot is immediately hopping all around them. Each girl tries to sell herself or the other to Noureddin, pointing out their fine qualities. A further plea is that they will both be freed from slavery if either of them is chosen. Noureddin turns them both down but promises to free them that very day, as soon as he wins the hand of the Princess of China.

With that decision, the two girls decide to dance for him, still hoping to sway his mind. Pierrot's comment satirizes the eighteenth-century Paris Opéra to the tune "O reguingué, o lonlanla": "In truth, you often see that happen at the Opéra, o reguingué, o lonlanla. He who resists the opera singer doesn't get away from the ballerina!"

Elmasie brings in male and female slave dancers for the finale. No music is given for the dances, but Gilliers wrote two short airs for Elmasie and Dilara to sing between the dancing. Both are in G major, and both repeat the last phrase. Their ranges are for mezzo voices, and Dilara's is a little higher.

The third act opens on the same set—gardens outside the palace— and the time sequence continues the preceding action. The King tries one more time to get Noureddin to stop the course he is determined to follow. The Prince prefers either to possess the Princess or die. The King leaves to find the judge Colao who will lead Noureddin to the *divan* (court of judgement). Left alone, he experiences a loss of courage for a brief moment and asks Mohammed for inspiration.

Scaramouche, a painter, strolls by, drawing Noureddin's portrait for the gallery of all princes who have lost their heads. He asks Noureddin if he would rather be shown proud and unafraid, reading the King's edict about his death, or be shown tenderly looking at the portrait of Diamantine. He dances off, remarking that somehow he feels this Prince will succeed.

The dancing master Arlequin enters next, preparing a ballet to celebrate the hoped-for marriage of the Princess, but he is discouraged because they have been rehearsing for the last two years without ever being able to perform. The plot includes the characters Cupid and Marriage with their courtiers representing all nations. These two dancers applaud the victory they obtained over a beauty who fought against their laws.

Arlequin, too, senses that Noureddin somehow might succeed, so he goes to get his dancers ready. He even refers to the maiden of Greek mythology who challenged her suitors to a race, death being the penalty of defeat, her hand the prize: "Come now, handsome Hippomenes, you will wed your Atalanta." Arlequin's ballet is to close the wedding ceremony, and he will even add a "fantasie" for the occasion. (A footnote in the Lesage play notes that the Opéra had just announced a special ballet entitled *Fantasie.* Thus, the opéra-comique at the Saint-Laurent Fair was continuing its practice of satirizing the Opéra.)

Pierrot begins to encourage Noureddin, but the Prince gives his friend back the Princess's portrait in case he does not win. To cheer him, Pierrot says, "You know that two heads are better than one. I want to give you a hand to help you succeed in this project. I'll whisper the right answers, to help out." Noureddin smiles at this offer.

Colao comes to lead them to the *divan,* and here the scene changes to the great judgment hall. The King is seated on a gold throne at the back of the stage with his daughter beside him on a silver throne. Six mandarins of science are seated on each side. Two guards stand next to the throne along with two handmaidens of the Princess.

Noureddin and Pierrot enter, the latter singing to the refrain of the *vaudeville* "J'entends le moulin taqueter" (I hear the mill go tic tac): "Oh, I feel my heart go tic tac." Once again Lesage crafted a natural line change just right for that spot in the opéra-comique.

Another appropriate use of *vaudeville* follows when a mandarin sings to the tune "Je ne veux point troubler votre ignorance" (I don't want to trouble your ignorance at all): "Do you agree that your intense love holds a deadly blindfold over your eyes?"

The Princess asks Noureddin if he wants to stop now. He answers using the popular tune "Quand le péril est agréable" (When danger is pleasing): "When danger is pleasing, the means of getting alarmed over it, the powerful god who makes me love, makes me incapable of change."

Diamantine sings the first enigma. The tune "Nouveau Joconde" is in four four-measure phrases: *aa'ba''*. The enigma occupies three phrases, ending on a half cadence at which point Pierrot whispers a wrong answer. Noureddin hesitates, rubs his forehead, and the crowd becomes alarmed. Suddenly he breaks in with the last phrase. Colao, the judge, repeats the final two measures to say the answer is correct, and then the chorus of mandarins, joined by Pierrot, repeat the same two measures, emphasizing the right answer.

> *Diamantine*: What girl, while being born, kills the one who gave her life? And who, when dying, quickly returns to her first estate? That girl has obtained a place in my heart.
> *Noureddin*: Beautiful Princess, my ardor wants to melt that ice ("la glace": ice—feminine noun).
> *Colao*: That's correct, it is ice.
> *Chorus*: Yes, indeed it is ice.

The King applauds this success by Noureddin, as he does after each of the two enigmas which follow.

> *Diamantine*: Who are two brothers who, without voice, have a language all their own, who can harm kings without being punished, who without a sound make great destruction, and who without leaving go everywhere?
> *Noureddin*: They are, Princess, your lovely eyes.
> *Colao*: He's right, they are the eyes.
> *Chorus*: "Bene, bene," they are the eyes ("les yeux": eyes—masculine plural noun).

Pierrot does not bother to give a wrong answer this time. The same musical procedure is followed: Noureddin finishes a tune and the others repeat the last few bars.

*Diamantine*: For the third time, tell me, I pray, that which you have not and which you have never had in your lifetime, which you can never have and which however I could receive from you.

*Pierrot* (whispers): It's a visionary animal.

*Noureddin* (to a new tune this time): It's a husband that I have never had, nor will have in my lifetime. It's a husband which I can give you.

*Pierrot* (finishing this new tune): He caught the magpie in its nest. So what says the chorus?

*Colao*: It's a husband.

*Chorus*: It's a husband.

*Pierrot* (hugging his friend, sings to the refrain of the tune "Mon Père je viens devant vous"): Embrace me, brave Jason, for you have won your golden fleece.

(This second reference by Lesage to classical mythology in this opéra-comique is again given to one of the comic characters.)

The King is delighted that heaven has granted him a son-in-law and that no more blood will be spilt. The Princess concedes defeat with a tune that allows for a hesitation at the end. She also admits that her enigmas were easier than usual because this time her heart, rather than her mind, dictated them.

Pierrot and the King divide a tune, "Je passe la nuit et le jour" (I spend night and day):

*King*: My daughter, after so many misfortunes, I conceive the sweet hope of having a successor to the throne from you.

*Pierrot*: In all conscience, she should replace the gallant dead princes by an equal number of children.

Then Pierrot asks Elmasie if she will not give him some successors too. "Yes," she says, "but I must ask an enigma first." Pierrot replies, "And if I don't guess it?" motioning as though his head were cut off. She tells him he could get by with just losing an ear.

*Elmasie*: Tell me, my beloved, what animal under heaven is comparable to a woman and resembles her best?

*Pierrot*: That animal is called—wait, no—yes, in faith, that animal is man.

*Elmasie*: You said it. I'm yours.

The final scene, presented by Arlequin and his dancers, consists of *vaudeville* songs and unspecified dances. Gilliers did write a tune for the *vaudeville final,* of six verses, the last one always being a moral addressed to the public. No verse is specified for any character in the play. The first verse praises the god of Cythère for intervening in Diamantine's enigmas this time. The last verse addresses the public: "If your delicate nature judges harshly this play, kind sirs, we are not responsible. May it be your indulgence that pronounces this sentence: a little help does a lot of good."

That last verse seems to belong to Pierrot—a last "plug" for the help he thought he gave Noureddin in winning Little Diamond (Diamantine). It is doubtful Pierrot ever thought her unattainable— just another hard-to-get Diamond Lil'.

Clifford R. Barnes

# The Dedications to Algarotti's
## *Saggio sopra l'opera in musica*
## (1754, 1762)

Dedications of a composer's or writer's works are most often explicable in terms of patronage (acknowledged or sought), gratitude, or friendship. Seldom does one have to search for the connection between the dedicator and the dedicatee. Usually an obvious relationship exists between the subject matter and the person or persons to whom the work is dedicated. Such is the case with the first version of Count Francesco Algarotti's well-known *Saggio sopra l'opera in musica*, first published in Venice in 1755 with a dedication to Baron von Schwerts, Director of Theatrical Entertainments at the court of Frederick the Great in Berlin.[1]

The dedication, dated Mirabello 6 October 1754, reads:

Who more than you can decide if in these my thoughts on the true form of Opera I have hit the mark? since to you was entrusted the direction of the Theatre in a land that has become in almost everything a model which other countries study by imitating. In fact, the reader will see that a good part of what I say ought to be done is yet that which is being done in the Theatre of Berlin: Thanks to that superior intellect which informs not only the more vital parts of the State, but coordinates all his staff, moving and animating everything. So it is that the Italians cannot today see their own arts perfected under

---

[1]The essay appears initially in Algarotti's *Discorsi sopra differenti soggetti* (Venice, 1755), pp. 1-112. It also appears as a separate print of ninety pages in 1755 with the title page giving the date but not the printer or place of publication. It is printed again in Algarotti's *Opere varie,* 2 vols. (Venice, 1757), 2: 277-365. All three contain the same dedication to Baron von Schwerts. Only the second print is listed in *Écrits imprimée concernant la musique, RISM* (Munich, 1971), 1: 80. For a recent edition and study of Algarotti's numerous essays, see Giovanni da Pozzo, *Saggi [di] Francesco Algarotti* (Bari, 1963). Baron von Schwerts [von Swerts, di Svertz] was *Intendant* of the Opera in Berlin from 1741 to 1756.

a sky so different from their own, as the ancient Romans were able to see examples of their virtues renewed.[2]

Algarotti (1712-1764), youngest son of a wealthy Venetian merchant and art lover, was associated with the court of Frederick the Great from 1740 when Frederick conferred on him the title of *Count*.[3] He added to the luster of Frederick's court until 1742, leaving to accept an invitation from August III, King of Poland and Elector of Saxony, to advise on paintings for the Dresden art gallery. His activities at August's court also included the staging of opera at the small Hubertusburg Theatre.[4] His correspondence with Frederick continued, although Frederick was at first peeved at Algarotti's departure, which may have been due in part to Frederick's increasing military activities.[5]

---

[2]The Italian text reads:
    Al Signor Barone di Svertz/Direttore de'Divertimenti Teatrali nella Corte di Berlino.
    Chi meglio di lei porterà decidere se in questi mei pensamenti sopra la vera forma dell'Opera io abbia dato nel segno? poichè a lei su già commessa la direzione del Teatro in un paese divenuto quasi in ogni cosa un modello che gli altri paesi si studiano d'imitare. In fatti ella vedrà che buona parte di quanto io dico doversi fare, è pur quello che si fa nel Teatro di Berlino: Mercè di quella mente superiore che informa con solo le parti più vitali dello Stato, ma mescolandosi per tutto il corpo di esso, muove ed anima ogni cosa. Talchè gli'Italiani possono oggimai vedere sotto un cielo tanto diverso dal loro perfezionate le proprie arti, come gli antiche Romani vi potrebbono vedere rinovellati gli esempj delle proprie virtù.                    Mirabello 6. Ottobre 1754.
Mirabello is identified in Letter IV (Padua, June 19th, 1782) of William Beckford in his *Italy; with Sketches of Spain and Portugal* (London, 1834), 1: 294, as "a country house, which Algarotti had inhabited, situate[d] amongst the Euganean hills, eight or nine miles from Padua."
[3]The two met at Frederick's court at Rheinsberg in 1739 before Frederick became King of Prussia and as Algarotti was returning from a trip to Russia and Poland. Frederick was charmed by the polish and learning of the young friend of Voltaire and Maupertuis who was already the author of a book on Newton's theories of optics as well as two books of poetry. See Ettore Bonora, "Francesco Algarotti" *Dizionario biographico degli Italiani* (Rome, 1960), 2: 356-60.
    Their first letters are filled with poetry, Frederick referring to Algarotti as the "Swan of Padua." See *Correspondance de Frédérick Second Roi de Prusse avec le Comte Algarotti* (Berlin, 1837). (Hereafter referred to as *Correspondance*.) In Letter IV, "à Berlin ce 26 de Fevrier 1740," Frederick writes: "J'ai reçu le paquet d'Italie, les sermons, et la musique dont je vous fais mes remerciments. . . . Vous êtes un excellent commissionaire, mon cher Algarotti: j'admire votre exactitude, et vos infatigables."
    In Letter VII, "à Charlottenbourg ce 2. de Juin 1740," Frederick writes tersely concerning his accession to the throne two days before, imploring Algarotti to join him: "Mon cher Algarotti, mon sort a changé. Je vous attends avec impatience; ne me faites point languir." And again in Letter VIII on 21 June 1740: "Mon cher Cygne de Padoue, . . . j'avoue que j'ai encore dix fois plus d'empressement à vous voir vous-même."
[4]See Werner Bollert, "Francesco Algarotti," *Die Musik in Geschichte und Gegenwart* 1 (1949-51): 318-20; and Heinz Becker, "Friedrich II," ibid., 4 (1955): 955-62. Hubertusburg, an elaborate baroque hunting lodge, was four days' journey from Dresden. With more frequent visits by the court between 1736 and 1747, the entire personnel of the Dresden opera were ordered there.
[5]"Cygne le plus inconstant . . . Adieu encore une fois, aimable, mais trop léger Algarotti." (*Correspondance*, Letter XXIII.)
    Writing from Dresden on 23 June 1742, Algarotti states his creed and obliquely

After the Treaty of Dresden, which ended the second phase of the War of the Austrian Succession, cultural life in Berlin again flourished. Returning to Berlin in 1747, Algarotti was appointed chamberlain to the court and "chevalier de l'ordre pour le merité." He advised Frederick on opera libretti and productions and occasionally accompanied Frederick's flute playing on the Silbermann pianofortes.[6] J. S. Bach visited the court and performed at Potsdam on 7 May 1747, an event which Algarotti may have attended as chamberlain.

In 1753 Algarotti again left Frederick's court, returning to Italy for reasons of health. Settling first in his native Italy for three years, he produced a variety of essays, drawing on his practical experiences as well as his wide theoretical knowledge of the arts and sciences. In Venice were written the first versions of the essays on opera and painting.[7]

From 1757 to 1762 Algarotti resided mostly in Bologna where he hoped to establish an academy to train the young. He continued his writing on a wide range of subjects and carried on a large correspondence with the intelligentsia of all Europe. In 1759 he was invited to the court at Parma, in consequence of his *Saggio sopra l'opera in musica*, to consult on the plans there for the "reform" of Italian opera.[8] The last two years of his life were spent in Pisa where he shared a villa with a painter friend, Mauro Tesi, reflecting and writing. It was at Pisa that the second and enlarged version of his *Saggio*

chides Frederick's bellicose activities: "Je félicite les beaux arts, la musique, et la philosophie, de ce qu'elles vont à la fin posséder V[otre] M[ajesté]. Elles regagneront aisément le tems perdu, si V.M. se prend pendant la paix, comme elle a fait à la guerre." (*Correspondance,* Letter XXXIII.)

[6]See Richard Northcott's forty-eight-page *Francesco Algarotti* [:] *A Reprint of his Essay on Opera and a Sketch of his Life* (London, 1917), p. 11.

[7]These were included in his *Discorsi sopra differenti soggetti* (Venice, 1755), a copy of which Algarotti sent to Frederick from Venice on 26 April 1755 with an accompanying letter: "Sire, Le livre que j'ai l'honneur de présenter à V.M. ne contient qu'une esquisse des sentimens d'admirations envers V.M. qui seront toujours présens à mon esprit comme ceux de la reconnaissance seront toujours gravés dans mon coeur: et si ce livre avoit le bonheur d'être approuvé par V.M. j'oserois me flatter que non seulement il rendoit témoignage de mes sentimens au public, mais même à la posterité." (*Correspondance,* Letter XCII.) Frederick answered in November, seven months later, that he had received the book but had not had time to read it. (Ibid., Letter XCIII.)

[8]Algarotti explains the invitation to Frederick in a letter from Bologna on 20 February 1759: "Sire, Tandis que V.M. ouvre le plus grand théâtre militaire, on ne songe dans cette partie de l'Italie qu'au théâtre de la comédie et de l'opéra. On a projeté à Parme de prendre ce qu'il y a de bon dans l'opéra françois, de le mêler au chant italien, et de donner des spectacles dans le goût de ceux qui fait tant de plaisir dans le théâtre de Berlin. Comme j'ai publié il y a quelques années maintes réflexions là dessus, l'on a souhaité que je visse le plan qu'ils se proposoient de suivre. L'Infant D. Philippe m'a fait inviter, et j'ai passé quelques jours à la cour de Parme." (*Correspondance,* Letter CXVI.)

The reform opera created in Parma in 1759 was Tommaso Traetta's *Ippolito ed Aricia* and in 1760 Traetta's *I Tindaridi.* (See Henry Bloch's excellent article on Traetta in *Die Musik in Geschichte und Gegenwart* 13 (1966):613-19.)

*sopra l'opera in musica* was written, with a new dedication signed "Pisa 18 December 1762." It is this second dedication to William Pitt, English political leader, that seems most curious, a fact Algarotti recognizes. The dedication reads:

### To William Pitt

That to you, immortal man, who knew how to rekindle in your nation, her native valor, to provide for her perpetual defence, and caused her to triumph, in one year, in the four quarters of the globe, a treatise on Poetry, Music, and Theatrical Subjects, should be addressed, will to some appear strange.

But, these, it should seem, are not apprized, that the restorer of England, the Friend of the Great Frederic, knows also to invigorate his leisure with the powers of literature; and that that victorious eloquence, with which he thunders in the senate, proceeds not less from the elevation of his mind, than from his studies in Tully and Demosthenes, his predecessors.

May this treatise even find place in the leisure of such a man, and obtain the suffrage of one, who, in the highest offices of the state, has deserved the admiration and applause of all Europe![9]

The dedication to Pitt might be explained in terms of Algarotti's interest in and associations with England. He had visited England three times in the 1730s, had studied English, and frequently quotes Pope and other English poets and writers in his essays and letters. He

---

[9]Translation from *An Essay on the opera written in Italian by Count Algarotti F.R.S.* [Fellow of the Royal Society] *F.S.A.* [Fellow of the Society of Antiquaries] *etc.* (London, 1767). Name of translator not given. The Henry E. Huntington Library copy has a notation on the title page by a contemporary hand that reads: "Miserably translated. Or rather, DONE into English"! The London translation was reprinted in Glasgow by R. Urie the following year, 1768, and it is part of this edition that is reprinted in Oliver Strunk's *Source Readings in Music History* (New York, 1950), pp. 657-72. Strunk mistakenly assumes that the 1768 reprint was the original English edition and that the translation was of the 1755 version rather than that of 1763. He also gives the incorrect title for the *Saggio sopra la pittura.* (See his introductory remarks on p. 657.)
The Italian dedication reads:

A Guglielmo Pitt.

Sembrerà ad alcuni assai strano, che a Voi, Uomo immortale, che nella vostra nazione sapeste riaccendere il nativo valore, sapeste provvedere per sempre alla sua difesa, e la faceste in un medesimo anno trionfare nelle quattro parti del Mondo, venga intitolato uno scritto, che ragiona di Poesia, di Musica, di cose di Teatro. Ma pare che ignorino costoro, come il Restitutore dell'Inghilterra, l'amico del gran **FEDERIGO** sa ancora munire il suo ozio co'presidj delle Lettere, e come quella sua vittoriosa eloquenza, colla quale egli tuona in Senato, non è meno l'affetto della elevatezza del suo animo, che dello studio da lui posto nei Tullj, e nei Demosteni antecessori suoi. Possa solamente questo mio Scritto esser da tanto, che trovi anch'esso un luogo nell'ozio erudito di un tal Uomo, e giunga ad ottenere il suffragio di Colui, che ne'più alti uffizj dello Stato ha meritato l'ammirazione e l'applauso di tutta Europa.

Pisa 18. Dicemb. 1762.

had been elected to membership in two English intellectual societies[10] and had written a discourse in praise of Pitt's military and political successes.[11] All of these, however, do not explain satisfactorily his curious choice of Pitt for his expanded ideas on the reform of opera, a subject that had elicited his thought, taste, and knowledge in three royal courts.

The key to the dedication appears in a letter to the Right Honourable William Pitt from Thomas Hollis, Esq.,[12] dated Pall Mall [London], 21 December 1762:

Sir,

I have been much embarrassed by the receipt of the inclosed letter and papers, which were wholly unexpected. At length I resolved to send them to you as I received them: forgive their liberty who wrote them, for they are *ingenuous;* and mine who send them, for I mean well. Retain the dedication, I request; and bestow on me beneficently, such an answer as I wish to send, and they to receive. For the sincerity of the dedication, I appeal to the suffrages of the English people in Runnymead, in general assembly convened, or any such hallowed spot; or to Foreigners, everywhere. Sir, you have surprized, astonished us all, on a late remarkable occasion; it brought honest Lucan to my mind:

VICTRIX.CAVSA.DIIS.PLACVIT.SED
VICTA.CATONI.

I am, with unfeigned and deepest respect and reverence, your most obedient and most humble servant,

Thomas Hollis[13]

---

[10]Algarotti was elected a Fellow of the Royal Society in 1736 "on account of his great knowledge in all parts of philosophical and mathematical learning." (Quoted in Northcott, p. 8.) In the same year he was elected an Honorary Member of the Society of Antiquaries. See Joan Evans's detailed *A History of the Society of Antiquaries* (Oxford, 1956), p. 87.

[11]*Discorso XVII: Sopra la condotta militare e politica del ministro Pitt* (1761) in *Opere del Conte Algarotti,* 17 vols. (Venice, 1791-94), vol. 5. That discourse, however, is dedicated to Signor Francesco Maria Zanotti, Segretario dell'Accademia dello Instituto di Bologna, Algarotti's mentor and friend.

[12]Thomas Hollis, Esq. (1720-1774), Dr. Johnson's "strenuous Whig," was a supporter of radical causes and a generous bibliophile, who sought to spread the ideals of liberty and *virtù* through the publication and dissemination of books. ("*Virtù* signifies a superiority of genius and talents," according to the glossary of terms at the end of *Essay on the Opera Written in Italian by Count Algarotti F.R.S. F.S.A. etc.* [London, 1767], p. 191.) Harvard College and the Public Library of Bern, Switzerland, were the main recipients. See Prof. Caroline Robbins, "The Strenuous Whig, Thomas Hollis of Lincoln's Inn," *William and Mary Quarterly,* 3d ser., 7 (1950): 406-53; idem, "Library of Liberty—Assembled for Harvard College by Thomas Hollis of Lincoln's Inn," *Harvard Library Bulletin* 5 (1951): 5-23, 181-96; and Hans Utz, *Die Hollis-Sammlung in Bern* (Bern, 1959).

[13]Hollis became friends with Pitt in 1757. The letter is contained in the Chatham

Pitt replied to Hollis's letter accepting the dedication on December 27, "employing another's pen" because of illness:

> With regard to the great honor destined to him from Pisa, Mr. Pitt blushes while he reads, and while he answers; and, standing as an example of human vanity, accepts with pride what he too well knows he has not the least title to receive. Little did he dream that his name was to live to posterity, before Count Algarotti, by joining it with his own, forbid it to die till Literature shall be no more; thus giving him to be indeed *immortal*.
>
> Mr. Pitt desires the favour of Mr. Hollis to convey to Count Algarotti as soon as may be these sentiments of respect and gratitude; at the same time offering Mr. How his best acknowledgments, with the assurance of great esteem and consideration.[14]

Thomas Hollis had been in correspondence with William Taylor Howe,[15] a young Englishman traveling in Italy, and through Howe's offices commissioned dedications to new editions of both Algarotti's *Saggio sopra la pittura* and *Saggio sopra l'opera in musica*.[16] The first was dedicated to the Society for the Encouragement of Arts, Manufactures and Commerce, now called the Royal Society of Arts, of which Hollis was a very active member.[17]

Following his usual practice of anonymity, Hollis planned to keep his part in the dedications unknown. This is shown in his letter to Howe the day after receiving Pitt's acceptance.

---

Papers at the Public Records Office, [London] 30/8/40. (Hereafter referred to as Chatham Papers.) A copy of it is also included in London, British Museum, *Add.* 26889 with Hollis's note explaining "the remarkable occasion" on which Pitt spoke in the House of Commons for three hours and twenty minutes on the "rise and progress of the [French and Indian] war" while seated, due to an attack of gout, sustaining himself with cordials from time to time. The letter was published in the *Gentleman's Magazine* 75 (1805): 106, in a series of "Original Letters to and from the Right Hon. William Pitt; afterwards Earl of Chatham."

[14]London, British Museum, *Add.* 26889; and *Gentleman's Magazine,* 75: 106-7.

[15]Fourteen letters and one fragment undated (four pages of advice on traveling in Italy) from Hollis to Howe are in London, British Museum, *Add.* 26889, a collection of letters to William Taylor Howe ( =How).

[16]Both published in Livorno by Marco Coltellini in the spring of 1763. The dedication to the essay on painting is dated Bologna 17 March 1762.

[17]See Prof. John Abbott, "Thomas Hollis and the Society 1756-1774," *Journal of the Royal Society of Arts* 119 (1971); 711-15, 803-7, 874-78.
Algarotti was elected a Corresponding Member of the Society on 29 December 1762. See *Minutes of the Society for the Encouragement of Arts, Manufactures and Commerce* 8 (1762-1763): 61-63. See my "Count Francesco Algarotti and the Society for the Encouragement of Arts, Manufactures and Commerce," *Journal of the Royal Society of Arts* 123 (1975): 605-8, 668-71, 728-30.

Pall Mall, dec. 28, 1762

Dear Sir,

By the inclosed paper you will see how far I have proceeded in the commission [to deliver Algarotti's dedication to Pitt] with which you have honoured me.

The Copy of the letter [to Pitt] is sent, as it explains the transaction of the affair; and the answer to it, *the original,* in the handwriting of a singularly accomplished & excellent English Lady [Mrs. Pitt?] is parted with, without reluctance, tho' the writer [Hollis] would have been *unfeignedly* glad at least to have kept back part of it [a paragraph of very flattering remarks to Hollis, omitted above].

You will see the propriety, I imagine, of not suffering copies to be taken of either of these letters.

On Friday, or this day Sixnight, you shall hear from me again, concerning the remaining part of your Commission.

My compliments being presented, respectfully to the Count, & affectionately to yourself, I bid you heartily farewell,

Thomas Hollis[18]

A month later Hollis writes happily to Howe concerning the dedication Algarotti had written to the Society for the Encouragement of Arts, Manufactures and Commerce and Algarotti's election as a Corresponding Member of the Society. He concludes:

My Commissions are now ended. Both of them were delicate, the first especially. They have been conducted in the best manner I could imagine and with the greatest dispatch; and if the Count & You should be satisfied with the proceedings, I shall rejoice.[19]

Six months later a parcel arrived from Italy and on 22 July 1763 Hollis delivered it to Pitt.[20] Pitt responded in a note:

Mr. Pitt begs Mr. Hollis will accept many sincere acknowledgements for the very obliging expeditious gratification of his anxious wishes about the precious parcel he has been so good to send him.

The Essay on the Opera in Musick is indeed a master-piece in its kind. What order, light, and interest, thrown into a confused, dark, and, till now, but little affecting matter![21]

---

[18]London, British Museum, *Add.* 26889.
[19]Ibid., letter dated 28 January 1763.
[20]Chatham Papers.
[21]London, British Museum, *Add.* 26889; and *Gentleman's Magazine,* 75: 107.

On 9 August 1763 Hollis writes to Algarotti acknowledging receipt of copies of the essays on opera, painting, and a third, *Saggio sopra l'Accademia di Francia che è in Roma,*[22] dedicated to "Signor Tommaso Hollis," "the only Dedication and that against his consent and knowledge."[23] The letter reads:

> Sir,
>
> The parcels containing the copies of the *Essay on the Opera in music* were immediately distributed on their coming to hand, according to the directions which had been given me and my best judgement. [One copy to the British Museum and one to Dr. Akenside, "physician to the queen, an accomplished gentleman, and a very fine poet." Copies of the essay on the French Academy to the British Museum, the Bodleian and Radcliffe Libraries at Oxford, the University Library at Cambridge, the public library of the University of Glasgow, the Advocate Library at Edinburgh, and the public library of the University of Dublin.] The eighth copy of that Essay, and two copies of the other Essays, master-productions, ALLOWED, of ability, elegance and beneficence, remain by your bounty with me, and claim my highest thanks.
>
> But, Sir, what can I write concerning the Dedication? You have heaped honors on a man without mark & without Likelyhood; from the biased representations of his friends, and a too hasty opinion formed of him from a few plain transactions which had somehow, fallen within your knowledge.[24]

In writing to Howe, his friend and intermediary, on 13 September 1763, Hollis suggests that the proposed new edition of Algarotti's complete works be carried on jointly in England and that the Count

---

[22]Livorno: Marco Coltellini, 1763. Dedication dated Pisa 2 February 1763.

[23]Archdeacon Francis Blackburne, ed. and comp., *Memoirs of Thomas Hollis, Esq. F.R. and A.S.S.* [Fellow of the Royal and Antiquaries Societies] (London, 1780), 2: 710. (Hereafter referred to as *Memoirs.*)

[24]London, British Museum, *Add.* 26889. He admits to Howe in a letter dated 2 August 1763 that he tore out the dedication to him before giving copies of the essay on the French Academy to the British Museum and to the Society for the Encouragement of Arts, Manufactures and Commerce!

Hollis's modus operandi is best explained by his letter to Rev. Jonathan Mayhew, pastor of West Church, Boston, on 28 July 1762:

"Know then that I have long declined all public business, or the taking charges or leads of any kind.

That my whole time is filled up, as an uncharged, undistinguished individual of large societies, or in certain more private studies and pursuits.

Likewise, that I am more and more resolved to avoid all public business; and am thinking seriously in what manner, by degrees, to withdraw into the country, so as to settle there." (Quoted in *Memoirs,* 1:162).

visit England.[25] The latter proposal was shattered by the news of Algarotti's death in Pisa on 24 June 1764 at age fifty-two of phthisis. Hollis writes to a friend:

> I am in great affliction at present on the news just received of the death of Count Algarotti, which happened lately at Pisa, with whom I have been united for some time in an entire friendship, and whose great abilities, knowledge of the world, and good mind, I was just going to have employed, on a subject he had desired of me, to which he of all others, it is probable, was most equal. But we must submit, I hope most humbly.[26]

Hollis sent an anonymous letter to the *London Chronicle,* 5 July 1764, calling attention to Algarotti's dedication to William Pitt, signing it "Diapason":

> Without having recourse to any of your foreign correspondents, behold one curious anecdote concerning the late accomplished and beneficent Algarotti. The last year he published a dissertation in twelves in Leghorn, intituled [*sic*], *Saggio sopra l'opera in musica,* the completest that has hitherto appeared on so refined and complicated a subject, and dedicated to William Pitt. The dedication itself is a beauty. As it is little known in Britain, and declares the sense of foreigners in general relating to that man, forerunning the sense of all posterity; you will do well, I apprehend, to find a place for it in your paper. I am, Sir, your humble Servant, Diapason.[27]

*     *     *

One wonders what "subject" Thomas Hollis had in mind for Algarotti "to which he of all others, it is probable, was most equal." Could it have been related to "The Treatise on the Arts of Peace" for which the Society for the Encouragement of Arts, Manufactures and Commerce had offered a prize in 1761, but which had proved unsuccessful?

Thomas Hollis was on the committee to judge the entries in the contest, and he personally had undertaken, through an intermediary

---

[25]London, British Museum, *Add.* 26889. "The Count is a Citizen of the World, is not tied, it may be, to any spot, is in highest esteem, I apprehend, amongst our ingenuous & first People; and, by a change of climate & nation for a time, might, it is possible, better his Health, & pass that time in a new & yet not unacceptable manner."

That Algarotti seriously considered the visit is shown by Hollis's letter to Howe on 20 December 1763: "I rejoice exceedingly that Count Algarotti is so well established & as his thoughts of visiting this Country."

[26]*Memoirs,* 1: 201. Algarotti's letter to Hollis offering to be of service, dated Pisa 5 November 1763, is printed in *Opere del Conte Algarotti,* 10: 177-78.

[27]*Memoirs,* 1: 201.

of course, to engage Samuel Johnson, who was also on the committee, to write the treatise. Johnson had declined because he was "not sufficiently informed of the several matters to which it must relate." Hollis then, through the offices of the same intermediary, engaged John Hawkesworth to write it. But Hawkesworth, Hollis says in his diary, "unhappily did not succeed in it." The editor of Hollis's *Memoirs* adds: "After that we may presume the design was dropped."[28]

But was it dropped in Hollis's mind? After securing Algarotti's membership in the Society for the Encouragement of Arts, Manufactures and Commerce, procuring the dedications to two of Algarotti's treatises on painting and opera, and inviting Algarotti to England, perhaps he was going to "employ" Algarotti to write on just such a "subject" as the "arts of peace." In his diary entry for 17 December 1761, Hollis elaborates on what he thinks "The Treatise on the Arts of Peace" should include.

> . . . a Dissertation on the polite & liberal arts; their use & benefit, to civil life & manners, & to commerce; the State of them in this Nation; the views of the Society, the noble Society for promoting arts & commerce in respect to them; the success of those views already, & the future expectations for them.[29]

Algarotti was certainly equal to the task of the first two requirements of the dissertation, as perhaps no other writer was. Had he lived to write it, it might well have been his magnum opus, encompassing all of Europe, supported by his personal observations and experiences. Even if this did not materialize, we can be grateful to all concerned in 1762 for a major aesthetic treatise on opera, the dominating art form of the eighteenth century, by "one of the beaux esprits of this age."[30]

George Truett Hollis

---

[28]Ibid., 1: 123. The summary of the affair in the *Memoirs* is based on entries in Hollis's diary (6 vols., now in The Houghton Library at Harvard University). Also see John Abbott, "John Hawkesworth and 'The Treatise on the Arts of Peace,'" *Journal of the Royal Society of Arts* 115 (1967): 645-49.

[29]Quoted in Abbot, "John Hawkesworth," p. 647, with the date incorrectly given.

[30]Epitaph of Wilhelmina, Margräfin von Bayreuth, Frederick the Great's musical sister, describing Algarotti. Quoted in Northcott, p. 11.

# Goldoni's *La Putta Onorata,* Some Parallels with Beaumarchais's *Le Mariage de Figaro*

Edward J. Dent, in his valuable volume *Mozart's Operas,* says that "the libretto of *I due Litiganti* . . . by Goldoni . . . bears a certain resemblance to that of *Figaro* and da Ponte probably found it a useful guide. There is a Countess who wishes to marry her maid Dorina to a certain Mingone, and a Count who wishes to marry her to his own servant Titta. The Countess, who thinks that her husband no longer loves her, and is arranging Dorina's marriage with a certain ulterior object of his own in view, calls to her aid the *soubrette* Livia and the bailiff Masotto; Masotto manages everybody and everything, and eventually obtains the hand of Dorina for himself. Beaumarchais' play was written in 1776, but not performed until 1784 and first printed in 1785; Sarti's opera came out in 1782. Obviously neither Goldoni nor Beaumarchais could have been indebted to each other; the skeleton of the plot probably goes back to the Comedy of Masks."[1]

Dent is probably correct in assuming that the skeleton of the plot and the ideas for individual scenes in Beaumarchais's *Figaro* ultimately derive from the commedia dell'arte. And, as has been recognized, Goldoni's reform of the eighteenth-century Italian comedy consists of the transformation of the improvised commedia dell'arte into a completely written drama. Whether Beaumarchais could have been directly indebted to Goldoni is less clear. It may be noted, however, that Dent overlooks an important point with respect to the libretto for Sarti's opera.

Goldoni's libretto *Le Nozze* or *Le Nozze di Dorina*—other titles used at the time for *I due Litiganti*—was first set by Baldassare Galuppi and premiered at Bologna, 14 September 1755.[2] It was, to-

---

[1] *Mozart's Operas,* 2d ed. (London, 1947), p. 105.
[2] August Buck, "Carlo Goldoni," *Die Musik in Geschichte und Gegenwart* 5 (1956): 486.

gether with *Il Filosofo di Campagna* (on another libretto by Goldoni) and *La Diavolessa,* one of Galuppi's three most successful and widely performed operas.[3] Consequently, Beaumarchais, who had originally written *Le Barbier de Seville* as a comic opera and who was something of a musician himself, could easily have known the original version of this libretto well before he began writing *Le Mariage de Figaro.* There is, however, another work by Goldoni, the play *La Putta Onorata,* that is even closer in overall plot and specific detail to Beaumarchais's masterpiece.[4] In essence, the plot of *La Putta Onorata* reads as follows.

Ottavio, the Marchese di Ripa Verde, and his wife, Beatrice, are no longer, if in fact they ever were, in love. Each has had affairs. Within moments of the opening of the play, it is clear that the Marchese is interested in the young Venetian orphan Bettina and has approached her through his servant Brighella, the shrewder of the two *zanni* of the commedia dell'arte in this play. Brighella has been rebuffed.

Bettina lives with her older sister, the washerwoman Catte and Catte's husband, Arlecchino Batocchio. Arlecchino, the other well-known servant of the commedia, is louder, lazier, more selfish, and usually more entertaining than Brighella. Bettina loves Pasqualino, a rather anemic young man who is presumably the son of a burly, outspoken gondolier named Menego Cainello, who is in the employ of the Marchese. Pasqualino, however, is actually the son of Pantalone de Bisognosi. Pantalone, another of the Venetian mask characters frequently to be found in Goldoni's plays, is traditionally a wealthy older merchant susceptible to attractive younger women. In *La Putta Onorata,* Pantalone has adopted the role of protector for Bettina. He provides financial assistance regularly and has promised a substantial dowry for her marriage. He is opposed, however, to Bettina's marrying Pasqualino, ostensibly because the latter has no trade. Actually Pantalone, true to his mask character, has designs on Bettina himself and proposes to her. He is rebuffed.

The Marchese, aware of Pantalone's interest in Bettina, quarrels with him, and to achieve his aim of seducing Bettina, proposes the following: Pasqualino should marry Bettina, for whom he, the Marchese, would furnish a dowry in place of the one promised by Pantalone. Furthermore, he suggests that Pasqualino become his valet and consequently that the young couple come to live with him.

---

[3]Werner Bollert, "Baldassare Galuppi," *Die Musik in Geschichte und Gegenwart* 4 (1955): 1346.
[4]First performance, Carnival season 1748-49, Venice. H. C. Chatfield Taylor, "Catalogue of Goldoni's Works," *Goldoni* (New York, 1913), p. 604 (appendix A).

The Marchesa Beatrice joins Pasqualino and Bettina to foil her husband's plot. After many adventures, Pasqualino is discovered to be Pantalone's son and receives Bettina's hand as well as all the promised dowries. In the final scene, the Marchese, found out and thoroughly discomfited, begs forgiveness of the Marchesa and seeks the assistance of the others present in achieving this forgiveness.

From the foregoing, it is clear that the essential outline of Beaumarchais's plot is to be found in Goldoni's work. A remarkable number of specific details are there as well.

1. The nobleman's servant, Brighella (Bazile), conveys messages of the nobleman's amorous intent to the virtuous heroine, Bettina (Suzanne), who refuses to accept or acknowledge them.

2. Bettina (Suzanne) is an orphan who lives with relatives, Catte and Arlecchino (Antonio, Fanchette-Barbarina), of a barely reputable character. These relatives, who must consent to the orphan's marriage, have little respect for Pasqualino. Recall the ill will borne by Suzanne's uncle, the gardner Antonio, towards Figaro.

3. In the final act, Pasqualino (Figaro) fears that Bettina (Suzanne) is unfaithful to him.

4. There are scenes to be played in the dark and some involving the exchange of clothing. Particularly noteworthy is the scene in which the Marchesa (Countess) takes Bettina's (Suzanne's) place to await the Marchese (Count). In another scene, Bettina (Suzanne) wears the Marchesa's (Countess's) clothing, and finally there is a scene in which Pasqualino and the Marchesa are paired off momentarily as are Figaro and the Countess in the last act of Beaumarchais's play.

5. Late in the play there is a short solo scene for Catte (Fanchette-Barbarina) set at night. She has lost her way in the side streets of Venice and becomes, momentarily, quite a pathetic figure. Recall Fanchette-Barbarina's monologue at the beginning of the last act of *Figaro.*

6. Much of the story of *La Putta Onorata* hinges on the discovery that Pasqualino (Figaro), supposedly a member of the lowest class, is in reality the son of the wealthy Pantalone (Dr. Bartholo).

7. An especially striking similarity of plot detail occurs near the close of both second acts. Pasqualino leaps from Bettina's balcony to avoid being found there by her protector, Pantalone.

8. Following the leap from the balcony, a masterly confrontation scene takes place between Pantalone on the one hand and Bettina together with Catte on the other. Recall the final scenes of Beau-

marchais's Act II. Again and again Pantalone seems to have scored with the truth about the youth's leap from the balcony only to have the truth confounded by the clever women.

9. All of the promised dowries end in Pasqualino's (Figaro's) hands.

10. There is an additional item of interest. Goldoni's *La Putta Onorata* has a sequel, *La Buona Moglie,* and Beaumarchais's *Le Mariage de Figaro* has both a predecessor, *Le Barbier de Seville,* and a sequel, *La Mère Coupable.*

Did Beaumarchais know or even intentionally model *Le Mariage de Figaro* on Goldoni's *La Putta Onorata?* Certainly the Frenchman could have known the Goldoni play. Between 1751 and 1771 there were at least eight separate editions of Goldoni's play.[5] Furthermore, it appears to have been one of Goldoni's more significant plays, at least in his own eyes. See the extensive discussion of its origin in Goldoni's *Memoires.*[6] Goldoni's plays were extensively performed in Paris in the decades before the writing of *Le Mariage de Figaro* and before the Italian had moved to Paris in 1762. Of particular significance is the fact that Goldoni and Beaumarchais moved in the same French court circles in the 1760s and 1770s. Both men were favorites of Louis XV's daughters. Princess Adelaide, for example, studied music with Beaumarchais from 1759 to 1763 and began Italian lessons with Goldoni in 1764 or 1765. Goldoni was, in fact, formally in the employ of the royal family and resided in Versailles almost from his arrival in Paris until his retirement in 1780.

Beaumarchais himself and numerous scholars point to other works as sources for the plot and detail of Figaro.[7] But were *La Putta Onorata* to be in fact the principal source, would Beaumarchais have wished to admit it? He might have considered the similarities too numerous and perhaps too close for comfort.

What may seem more surprising is the fact that Goldoni, who discusses *Figaro* near the close of his *Memoires,* does not notice the resemblances. It should be remembered, however, that Goldoni's

---

[5]In the following collected editions: Venice: Bettinelli, 1751, v. 2 (first edition); Bologna: Pisari, 1752, v. 2; Bologna: dal Corciolani, 1753, v. 2; Florence: Paperini, 1755, v. 9; Turin: Fantino, 1757, v. 11; Turin: Guibert, 1764, v. 15; Venice: Savioli, 1771, v. 10. Listed in *Commedie di Carlo Goldoni* (Venice, 1908), 2: 512.

[6]*Memoires of Carlo Goldoni,* trans. John Black, edited and introduction by William A. Drake (New York, 1926), pp. 241-45.

[7]See Pierre Augustin Caron de Beaumarchais, *Essai sur le genre dramatique: Le Barbier de Seville et Le Mariage de Figaro* (Paris, 191—) and, among others, Janice B. Rutermanis and W. R. Irwin, *The Comic Style of Beaumarchais* (Seattle, 1961) and Jacque Vier, "*Le Mariage de Figaro*: miroir d'une siècle," *Archives des lettres modernes* 6 (November 1957).

*Memoires* postdate *La Putta Onorata* by almost forty years. Furthermore the play was one of his earliest, and he wrote an incredible number of stage works, particularly in that phase of his career.[8]

Another point remains to be made. Goldoni was born and raised in the oldest republic in Europe, Venice, and in his writing he consistently depicted the nobility as less honorable than the commoners with whom they come into contact. Beaumarchais's own democratic leanings are well known. To cite one example, he effectively provided arms for the American colonists during their war of independence. These leanings have their literary outlet during the scintillating dialogues between Figaro and Almaviva in his two great comedies.

Goldoni was by all odds the most successful and certainly one of the most prolific comic playwrights and librettists of Europe in the generation before Beaumarchais. In view of their similar outlook and the parallels mentioned between *La Putta Onorata* and *Le Mariage de Figaro*, it is tempting to hypothesize a stronger and more direct influence by Goldoni on Beaumarchais than has previously been suggested.

A final comment: although *La Putta Onorata* is a vigorous play, rich in incident, and well worth modern revival, it does not match the rapid pace and brilliantly cutting dialogue of Beaumarchais's masterpiece. It is undoubtedly posterity's good fortune that da Ponte based his libretto on the Frenchman's work rather than on *La Putta Onorata* by his fellow Italian, Goldoni.[9]

Martin Chusid

---

[8]*La Putta Onorata* is no. 23 of 173 "Improvised Comedies, Comedies, Tragedies and Tragi-Comedies" in the catalogue cited in fn. 4. There are also listed 94 librettos ("Books for Operas, Light Operas, and Interludes") most of which were written after *La Putta Onorata*. Ibid., pp. 601-32.

[9]According to Anna Amalie Abert, "Lorenzo da Ponte," *Die Musik in Geschichte und Gegenwart* 2 (1952): 1917-18, da Ponte did in fact base a number of his other librettos on works by Goldoni: *Il Burbero di Buon Cuore*, set by Vicente Martin y Soler (perf. 4 Jan. 1786, Vienna), is based on *Le Bourru Bienfaisant; Il Talismano*, set by Antonio Salieri (perf. 10 Sept. 1788, Vienna), derives from a libretto with the same name by Goldoni; *Il Consiglio Imprudente*, set by F. Bianchi (perf. 20 Dec. 1796, London), is based on *Un Curioso Accidente;* and *I Contadini Bizzarri*, set by Giuseppe Sarti (perf. 1 Feb. 1794, London), is based on a libretto by T. Grandi, *Le Gelosie Villane*, set earlier by Sarti (perf. Nov. 1776, Vienna), which in turn is derived from Goldoni's *Il Feudatorio*. Another libretto by da Ponte, *Axur, Ré d'Ormus*, set by Salieri (perf. 8 Jan. 1788, Vienna), is based on Beaumarchais's *Tarare*.

# Opera: A Morphological Approach

An opera is a vocal work sung by characters who also use words and act their parts. Both ear and eye are involved, and the appeal to the ear by word and tone moves, moreover, on two different channels. The law governing the development of the passions and the symphonic law are not identical. Schopenhauer drew the merciless conclusion: "Strictly speaking, one might define opera as an unmusical invention for the pleasure of unmusical minds."[1] At all times, opera has caused difficulties because of a profound incompatibility between the laws of the various participating arts. The relationship of text and plot to music varies and accordingly produces different results.

Ideally, one likes to think of a complete amalgamation of the different arts so that their inherent morphological forces will cooperate rather than compete. This ideal may have existed in the *musiké* of the ancient Greeks of which Plato already speaks with the regretful melancholy attached to a lost accomplishment.[2] The recovery of the ideal has guided the ambitions of every opera reformer; of these, Wagner's *Gesamtkunstwerk* may be the most articulate formulation. The continuous struggle for a union of the arts takes on the meaning of a longing to restore an aboriginal state of affairs. From the viewpoint of an opera composer, what is artificial is the separation of the arts, not their reunion. Since the era of *musiké*, however, the conditions of the partners have radically changed. Poetry and music have developed away from each other. In the process, both have suffered a loss of their inherent magical essence and now find themselves relegated to a place apart from what modern man deems to be reality.

In relation to this separation, we can examine the problem of opera by proceeding downward from postulates, from ideals. For man on the magical level, art is reality—a higher kind of reality than ordinary life. On this level, the distinction between creator, performer, and public is minimal and irrelevant. The member of the audience at one moment may be the creator, and the performer at the next. The unity

---

[1]*Parerga und Paralipomena,* vol. 2, chap. 19, par. 224.
[2]*Republic* 2-4; also *Laws* 2.

of experience is perfect. Furthermore, all modes of expression—word, tone, gesture—are intimately tied to each other. To think of such a state in other than theoretic terms is difficult because we have no experience of it. The nearest approximations available today might be dances of so-called primitive tribes, some song-plays of children, and religious ritual. The common quality of such manifestations is the creation of a community experience. There is no distinction between performers and audience. Words, music, and gestures all contribute jointly. Opera on this ideal level has two characteristics. First, the work is known to everybody. As a practical outcome, there is no problem of text that must be clearly understood. Second, realism in the vulgar sense does not exist. Nor does any of its consequences, above all "dramatic speed." Whenever this ideal primary state is abandoned, operatic difficulties arise, which become increasingly insoluble as the various elements draw farther apart.

Opera has been criticized for being unnatural. People do not sing arias when they are about to die. Such criticism misinterprets the meaning of art. Realism is the doom of art. If anything, life ought to be viewed in terms of art and not inversely. A source of profound misunderstandings has been the use by poetry of words and phrases shared with ordinary speech. They do not mean the same thing in poetry and in daily life. The portion of realism in a Shakespeare drama is artistically the least important part of it. Modern movies have compounded the misunderstanding. The concert hall is somewhat protected because the setting and the music itself are removed from any realistic interpretation. Opera, however, contains all the prerequisites for nourishing the misconception. The development of opera has done everything to feed it.

Granting that the operatic work should not be judged on the level of ordinary reality, we still encounter dilemmas built into the situation. The separation of the original community into a performing and a receiving portion is complete. The public is not inside the performance but outside. Hence dramatic speed is measured in terms not of inner time production, but of clock time; the public brings to the performance a reaction speed taken from ordinary life. The theme is unknown to the public. Therefore the text ought to be clearly heard and understood; but poetry and music have developed away from each other, with divergent form tendencies.

Constrained by these facts, the composer has to do his work. The separation of the community into a performing and a receiving sector entails the necessity of a sort of rape of the audience: it has to be forced into participation. The immediate result is a striving toward effect, toward excessive tensions and climaxes. Opera has to become dramatic in the more vulgar sense of a "thriller." Because drama is conveyed mainly through dialogue, the words ought to be clearly perceived by the public. But musical forms, being essentially architectural, use musical means—repetition, recapitulation, polyphony, and the like —which are in opposition to dramatic speech, still more to ordinary speech. Hence they are fundamentally incompatible with the postulates of both realistic dramatism and intelligibility of the text.

All these dilemmas can essentially be reduced to the difficulty of reconciling dramatic speed and literary clarity with a musical unfolding of forms. Because these two sets of postulates are incompatible, all operatic solutions have to be based on some sort of compromise. The history of opera reveals three compromise solutions. Either the music is subservient to the text, or the text is subservient to the music, or the two divide the field between themselves.

The first two categories contain the lesser compromise and have therefore remained the most problematic. Text rules in the operas of the Florentine Camerata. Recitative from beginning to end generates little musical interest. Later examples of similar literary concern are some works by Gluck and Wagner, at least according to their own writings on the subject. Here also belong such operas of the twentieth century as Debussy's *Pelléas et Mélisande* and probably Berg's *Wozzeck,* although the latter shows a trend to revert to closed musical forms—not arias, but rather purely instrumental structures like passacaglia, variation, et al. The other extreme, which sacrifices text and dramatism to the exigencies of music, is heard in those operas of which the librettos have been maligned, be it *Euryanthe* or *Il Trovatore.* Carried through consistently, this extreme would be the end of music drama in any current sense and could exist only on a magical level. Nearest to this type comes the madrigal comedy. Exactly contemporaneous with the antipodal effort of the Camerata composers, Orazio Vecchi's *L'Amfiparnaso* spells out the attitude in the prologue: "This spectacle appeals to the imagination through the ear, not the eye."[3]

In a much-quoted letter (13 October 1781), Mozart wrote to his father: "In an opera the poetry must be altogether the obedient handmaiden of the music." Yet the solution Mozart followed in all his operas, which he inherited partly from the Neapolitans and partly from popular comedy, can be best described as a "division of labor." The text leads in the recitatives or dialogues between the music numbers; during the numbers, in turn, it becomes ancillary. Repetitions of

---

[3]"Spettacolo, si mira con la mente,
Dov'entra per l'orecchie, e non per gl'occhi."

words and phrases in arias make no literary sense but supply material
for the musical form. The alternation of musical pieces and literary
stretches is obvious in all eighteenth-century operas and modern
Broadway shows. It may be less distinct in the through-composed
operas characteristic of most of the nineteenth century; but Wagner's
attestations to the contrary, it exists as much in his works as in Meyer-
beer's and Verdi's. The literary stretches are all those where the music
is not developed and structured according to purely musical laws. On
the other hand, purely musical units recur, either in the form of arias
and ensembles (Gralserzählung, *Meistersinger* Quintet and others), or
tonally unified "periods" (Tristan's Awakening and Yearning),[4] or
pseudo-symphonic pieces in which the voices are part of an instrumental web (Wotan's Farewell). The technique is recognizable in
most post-Wagner operas, be they by Richard Strauss, Alban Berg,
Britten, or Menotti. The result can be viewed as a "number opera"
on the symphonic level.

Do these operatic numbers—the result of a compromise that has
lasted three centuries—make a particular contribution of their own
to musical morphology? The da capo aria has done so; for in addition to serving the purely musical needs of an operatic situation, it has
doubtless contributed to all instrumental compositions that contain
a recapitulation. C.P.E. Bach's concept of a *veränderte Reprise* (recapitulation with changes) stems in some way from the opera aria.

Otherwise the forms of numbers in operas seem to have followed
general musical, rather than specific operatic, principles. One need
not consider the overture which, lying outside the opera itself, has always reflected the instrumental conviction of the day. The pieces
within the opera are as conventional or as free as the composer cares
to shape them. There are open and closed forms, strophes and ron-
dos, variations and fugues. The employment of a form for characterization is an ingenious practice of Mozart's. In the opening duet of
*Le nozze di Figaro,* for example, the expectation of strophes generated
by the initial recurrent alternation of two distinct melodies associated,
respectively, with Figaro and Susanna soon yields to the recognition
that the disappearance of the Figaro theme halfway through the piece
is producing a rondo based on the musical (and personal) superiority
of Susanna—a superiority that the remainder of the opera amply
demonstrates. For a morphological inquiry, however, only the opposite practice would be important; but the employment of dramatic
characterization to create a musical form does not, to our knowledge,
exist.

---

[4] In Alfred Lorenz's terminology.

Closest to it come key relationships. The tonal organization of the whole of *Le nozze di Figaro* hinges upon subtle interplays of sharp and flat keys.[5] Tonal interactions also govern the structures of finales. The first *Figaro* finale parallels the increasing imbroglio of Figaro by a steady drop across five keys through the circle of fifths. In the first *Don Giovanni* finale, the huge C major structure gains cadential articulation from the most noticeable recurrence of the minuet, first in F major and then in G major.

Although questioned and attacked more than any other type of art, opera has proved its vitality again and again, in one guise or another, surviving onslaughts of aesthetic theory and practical sarcasm alike. Often declared dead and gone, it has kept alive on all levels from sheer entertainment to religious contemplation. This phoenix-like nature of opera has repeatedly puzzled observers, but one need not look far for an explanation. Human endeavors firmly anchored in the world of ideas are not jeopardized by imperfections and vices of temporal realization. Though opera as a magical communion does not and cannot actually exist in the present state of society, the original quality of magic has not left opera altogether. The fascination with opera, we submit, is like a faint remembrance of its magical essence and of the pristine togetherness of language, gesture, and tone.

Siegmund Levarie
Ernst Levy

---

[5] For detailed analyses, see Hermann Abert's foreword to the miniature score (New York, n.d., pp. vii-xx) and Siegmund Levarie, *Mozart's Le Nozze di Figaro: A Critical Analysis* (Chicago, 1952).

# PART IV

# Five Settings of Goethe's "Mailied" in Relation to His Concept of the German Lied

The central position Goethe occupies in the history of the German lied, in its poetic as well as musical sense, derives in part from the nature of his lyric poetry and in part from the very timing of his appearance. When Goethe was born (1749) J. S. Bach was still alive, and when he died (1832) Mozart, Beethoven, Schubert, and Weber had come and gone. His musical views were formed in the era of Rationalism and did not change as fast and as much as the musical world around him. According to Goethe a lied is a poem to be sung; it necessitates music but in a subordinate role.[1] There is nothing surprising about this view. It was basically that of the two Berlin Schools and was shared by Goethe's earliest composers such as Breitkopf, von Seckendorff, Schröter, Kayser, Zelter, and Reichardt. It agrees with the definition of the form in Koch's *Musiklexikon* (1802):

> Mit diesem Namen bezeichnet man überhaupt jedes lyrische Gedicht von mehreren Strophen welche zum Gesang bestimmt, und mit einer solchen Melodie verbunden ist, die bey jeder Strophe wiederholt wird, und die zugleich die Eigenschaft hat, dass sie von jedem Menschen, der gesunde und nicht ganz unbiegsame Gesangorgane besitzt, ohne Rücksicht auf künstliche Ausbildung derselben, vorgetragen werden kann.[2]

Goethe's conservative attitude has often been blamed on Zelter, whose musical advice he enjoyed for thirty years, especially since it was responsible for his lack of recognition of Schubert's genius and to some extent of Beethoven's.[3] But Hermann Abert has shown that Goethe's attitude was clearly established before he met Zelter, who merely reinforced it.[4]

---

[1]Samuel Fisch, *Goethe und die Musik* (Frauenfeld, 1949), p. 96.
[2]Definition of *Lied*, col. 901.
[3]Romain Rolland, *Goethe and Beethoven*, trans. G. A. Pfister and E. S. Kemp (New York, 1931), pp. 89-93.
[4]Hermann Abert, *Goethe und die Musik* (Stuttgart, 1922), pp. 15-16.

Goethe came to his concept of the lied during his Strassburg years (1770-71). His early friendship with Herder had opened his eyes to the beauty of folk poetry, which he collected and studied. Goethe adopted the folk song as a model for his lyric poetry.[5] Folksongs inspired him to write new words to known tunes, which he tried out with his Wednesday evening club in informal group singing.[6] Many of these parodies were published in an Almanach, edited by Goethe and Wieland.[7] When he saw one of his lieder set to music, he expected its character to remain unchanged: simple, straightforward, and sincere. The poet developed a lied style that seems completely natural and inevitable in language, form, and mood.[8] These three elements must be respected by the composer; he must find the basic mood—the *Stimmung*—it expresses and enhance it through the melody; he must leave the strophic structure intact since that is part of the very definition of the lied, as a poem or as a song. Hence Goethe's outspoken antagonism against the two musical techniques most inimical to the lied character: tone-painting and through-composition.[9] The former calls attention to details of description or characterization so as to distract from the basic, pervasive *Stimmung;* the latter so transforms or dismembers the structure of the poem that it becomes unrecognizable. On 2 May 1820 Goethe wrote to Zelter:

> Die reinste und höchste Malerey in der Musik ist die, welche Du auch ausübst; es kommt darauf an, den Hörer in die Stimmung zu versetzen, welche das Gedicht angiebt, in der Einbildungskraft bilden sich alsdann die Gestalten nach Anlass des Textes, sie weiss nicht, wie sie dazu kommt. Muster hast Du gegeben in der „Johanna Sebus", „Mitternacht", „Über allen Gipfeln ist Ruh", und wo nicht überall? Deute mir an, wer ausser Dir dergleichen geleistet hat. Töne durch Töne zu malen: zu donnern, zu schmettern, zu plätschern und zu patschen ist detestabel. Das Minimum wird davon als Tüpfchen aufs i in obigen Fällen weislich benutzt, wie Du auch tust.[10]

---

[5]Edgar Istel, "Goethe and Music," *The Musical Quarterly* 14 (1928): 218.

[6]For an extensive discussion of Goethe's parodies, see Frederick W. Sternfeld, *Goethe and Music* (New York, 1954), pp. 7-130.

[7]Ibid., p. 8.

[8]Günther Müller, *Geschichte des deutschen Liedes vom Zeitalter des Barock bis zur Gegenwart* (Munich, 1925; reprint ed., Bad Homburg, 1959), p. 243.

[9]Goethe's famous criticism of Beethoven's and Spohr's "Kennst du das Land" indicates that he included extensively modified strophic structure in this category and that he considered through-composition the domain of the aria. For Goethe's opinions on dramatic music see Abert, p. 82.

[10]*Briefwechsel zwischen Goethe und Zelter in den Jahren 1799 bis 1832,* 3 vols., ed. by Ludwig Geiger (Leipzig, n.d.), 2: 56.

It is important to note that Goethe's disdain concerns specifically the realistic imitation of auditory effects (thunder, crashing, splashing, etc.) because they stay on the surface of specific word-images rather than expressing, suggesting, or symbolizing the mood-content of the poem. Goethe's verdict against through-composition was also very specific; thus we should note that he praises Zelter's "Über allen Gipfeln," which is a through-composed song.[11] Characteristically, Zelter selects poems of a single stanza such as this for through-composition, apparently with the poet's approval. Since there is no story or action, no refrain, no stanzaic analogy or repetition, the musical freedom does not interfere with the poetry. Characteristically also, Zelter never through-composed a ballad: a narrative poem in which action is central and strophic form essential.[12] It is therefore not just a poet's selfishness when Goethe prefers Zelter's strophic ballad compositions. The fact that most ballads occur in a play or Singspiel ("König in Thule" in *Faust,* "Erlkönig" in *Die Fischerin*) illustrates the genre; it is a long-familiar song that a character sings and that is not necessarily related to the action of the play.[13]

The irony in Goethe's position is apparent: his lied concept is of the eighteenth century while his own poetry helped transform the lied into the nineteenth-century art form, the Romantic Kunstlied. It is not the present purpose to trace the Romantic conception from Schubert's early Goethe songs[14] to Hugo Wolf's. Goethe's poems continued to inspire composers after Schubert in amazing numbers,[15] although less frequently than during the poet's lifetime.[16] Schumann, Franz, Brahms, and Liszt set Goethe poems occasionally, but the younger Romantic poets such as Heine and Eichendorff reflected more closely the emotional intensity of Romantic composers. Goethe's *Wilhelm Meister* songs, which retained their attractiveness to composers until Hugo Wolf, were interpreted along increasingly Romantic lines, in spite of the element of classic understatement in the lyrics.[17]

At this point several interesting questions arise: 1. What happened to the German lied after Hugo Wolf? 2. Is Goethe's poetry still a

---

[11]In length and form very similar to Schubert's setting. For a comparison see Thrasybulos G. Georgiades, *Schubert. Musik und Lyrik* (Göttingen, 1967), pp. 17-34.

[12]Gertraud Wittmann, *Das Klavierbegleitete Sololied Karl Friedrich Zelters* (Berlin, 1936), p. 37.

[13]See Goethe's letter to Kayser (1779), quoted in Fritz Egon Pamer, "Das deutsche Lied im 19. Jahrhundert," *Handbuch der Musikgeschichte,* 2 vols., ed. Guido Adler (Berlin, 1930; reprint ed., Tutzing, 1961), 2: 940.

[14]See Edith Schnapper, *Die Gesänge des jungen Schubert vor dem Durchbruch des romantischen Liedprinzips* (Bern, 1937), p. 7.

[15]See Willi Schuh, *Goethe-Vertonungen. Ein Verzeichnis* (Zürich, 1952).

[16]Hugo Holle, *Goethes Lyrik in Weisen deutscher Tonsetzer bis zur Gegenwart* (Munich, 1914), p. 6.

[17]Donald Ivey, *Song Anatomy, Imagery and Styles* (New York, 1970), pp. 215-16.

source of inspiration to song composers of the twentieth century?
3. Did the anti-Romantic reaction bring a reemergence of Goethe's
lied concept?

1. H. J. Moser has shown that the veritable flood of post-Romantic songs did not come to an ebb until the end of World War I.[18]
But modern music was moving in directions that seemed to spell
defeat to the lied: atonality, dodecaphonic technique, *Sprechstimme*,
instrumental formalism, microtonalism, and electronic music, while
not inherently exclusive of vocal writing, tended to supersede or by-
pass lied composition.[19] Clearly the leading composers in the German-
speaking world pushed the song into a position of marginal importance. After his early songs of 1908 (op. 15), Arnold Schoenberg
wrote relatively few songs. *Pierrot Lunaire* (1912) had reached and
gone beyond the limits of vocal melody or *Sangbarkeit*.[20] Paul Hindemith's important songcycle *Das Marienleben* (1922) exemplifies
the new instrumental formalism in vocal music.[21]

Meanwhile modern German poetry rejected nineteenth-century
lyricism and its established patterns.[22] Gottfried Benn's advocacy of
the "absolute poem" (1951) illustrates further the crisis of the lied.[23]
Even without the above developments the contemporary spirit shunned
the subjectivity associated with the Romantic solo song; younger composers in the vocal field tended to favor choral and dramatic music,
as apparent from the works of Carl Orff, Werner Egk, and Boris
Blacher.[24]

2. It was Moser, too, who asked the second question.[25] The avant-
garde composers hardly draw on Goethe texts.[26] However, a real
Goethe-connoisseur like Ernest Křenek can find completely new
Goethe sources that allow modern expressive possibilities, as he did
in the *Konzertarie*, op. 57.[27] Othmar Schoeck went beyond the usual

---

[18]Hans Joachim Moser, *Das deutsche Lied seit Mozart* (Berlin, 1937), 2: chapter 12.

[19]Walter Wiora, *Das deutsche Lied* (Wolfenbüttel, 1971), p. 103.

[20]Hans Mersmann, *Die Moderne Musik seit der Romantik* (Potsdam, 1928), pp. 141-42.

[21]Rudolf Schäfke, "Das Liedschaffen der Gegenwart," *Melos* 4 (1925): 539.

[22]Ivey, p. 233.

[23]August Closs, *The Genius of the German Lyric* (London, 1962), p. 351.

[24]Phillip Radcliffe, "Germany and Austria," *A History of Song*, ed. Denis Stevens
(New York, 1960), p. 264.

[25]H. J. Moser, "Goethes Dichtung in der neueren Musik," *Goethe-Jahrbuch* 17
(1931): 266.

[26]However, Winfried Zillig (1905-1963), a student of Schoenberg, set such Goethe-
poems as "Ich denke dein" and "Trocknet nicht" in *Zehn Lieder nach Gedichten von
Goethe*, Bärenreiter-Edition No. 3864.

[27]Moser, "Goethes Dichtung," p. 277.

Goethe texts in "Haben sie von deinen Fehlen" in his op. 19b.[28]
Giselher Klebe set the *Roman Elegies* for speaker, piano, harpsichord,
and double bass (op. 15, 1957).[29] Among traditional Goethe texts
there is a preference for the lightness of Singspiele (Schoeck's *Erwin
und Elmire*, 1916) and for the serene objectivity of the proverbs, as
in the *Lieder und Sprüche nach Worten von Goethe* by Karl Marx
(op. 49, 1949).[30] The first song "Kommt Zeit, kommt Rat" runs
thus:

> Wer will denn alles gleich ergründen!
> Sobald der Schnee schmilzt, wird sich's finden.

Predictably twentieth-century composers seem to avoid the ballad of
dramatic action such as "Erlkönig."[31] One might reason that the burden of history, in this case Schubert's and Loewe's all-too-famous settings, deters composers from setting this text anew, but it certainly had
no such effect on the nineteenth century. Likewise, emotion-charged
lyrics that contrast extremes such as "Freudvoll und leidvoll," epi-
tomizing the Romantic gamut from "himmelhoch jauchzend" to "zu
Tode betrübt," no longer attract composers. On the other hand, the
delicate understatement of "März" ("Es ist ein Schnee gefallen"), with
its somewhat dry and calmly flowing style denoting the later Goethe
(1807), inspired contemporary composers like Edgar Istel, Robert
Kahn, Kurt Pfister, Ernst Pepping, Armin Knab, Karl Marx, and
others.[32] Today the supernatural, fantastic, and mystical elements in
nature may have lost interest, but joyful love of nature or longing
for its solace and peace have survived the Romantic era. Thus "Über
allen Gipfeln" was set by Nicholai Medtner[33] and Ernst Pepping,[34]
and "Fetter grüne, du Laub" by Othmar Schoeck[35] and Wilhelm
Petersen.[36]

  In the following section a few settings of a Goethe poem, three
from the eighteenth and two from the twentieth century, will be
compared in order to answer question 3: did Goethe's lied-concept
reemerge in the twentieth century?

---

[28]Hans Corrodi, "Othmar Schoeck's Songs," *Music and Letters* 29 (1948): 132.
[29]Franz A. Stein, *Verzeichnis deutscher Lieder seit Haydn* (Bern, 1967), p. 46.
[30]Bärenreiter-Edition No. 2421.
[31]Among the exceptions is Arnold Mendelssohn's *Der getreue Eckart*. See Moser,
"Goethes Dichtung," p. 268.
[32]Schuh, p. 30.
[33]Op. 6, no. 1.
[34]*Haus- und Trostbuch für eine Singstimme und Klavier* (1946), Bärenreiter-Edition No. 2251.
[35]Op. 19a, no. 1.
[36]Op. 40, no. 3.

## "MAILIED" BY GOETHE

### THE POEM

Goethe wrote "Mailied" in May of 1771, when he was twenty-two years old.[37] It was the period of his love for Friederike Brion of Sesenheim. In his case it is not futile to link his creative work with contemporary experiences in his life, at least not in the case of a love lyric. As he said himself: "Liebesgedichte habe ich nur gemacht, wenn ich liebte."[38] The poem follows:

Wie herrlich leuchtet
Mir die Natur!
Wie glänzt die Sonne!
Wie lacht die Flur!

Es dringen Blüten
Aus jedem Zweig
Und tausend Stimmen
Aus dem Gesträuch.

Und Freud' und Wonne
Aus jeder Brust.
O Erd', o Sonne!
O Glück, o Lust!

O Lieb', o Liebe!
So golden schön,
Wie Morgenwolken
Auf jenen Höhn!

Du segnest herrlich
Das frische Feld,

Im Blütendampfe
Die volle Welt.

O Mädchen, Mädchen,
Wie lieb' ich dich!
Wie blickt dein Auge!
Wie liebst du mich!

So liebt die Lerche
Gesang und Luft,
Und Morgenblumen
Den Himmelsduft,

Wie ich dich liebe
Mit warmen Blut,
Die du mir Jugend
Und Freud' und Mut

Zu neuen Liedern
Und Tänzen gibst.
Sei ewig glücklich,
Wie du mich liebst!

The exuberant spirit of these lines reminds one of "Rastlose Liebe," another poem of the same period in which the flow of the words is accelerated to a breathless pace.[39] What accounts for such spirit and pace? In both poems the lines are very short; both begin with a series of exclamations. Each line strives toward its end where the most important (or the only) noun is placed. Analogous beginnings ("Wie herrlich . . . wie glänzt . . . wie lacht . . .") create a pattern of successive spurts of energy. This drive comes to a climax in the

---

[37] J. A. O. L. Lehmann, *Goethes Liebe und Liebesgedichte* (Berlin, 1852), p. 87.

[38] Ibid., p. 9.

[39] Such restless motion elicited very similar reactions (continuous sixteenth-notes in the piano part, r. h.) from Zelter, Reichardt, Schubert, and Schoeck. Georgiades, pp. 63-69, compares the first three.

third stanza ("O Erd, o Sonne! O Glück, o Lust!") where these
spurts follow each other so closely as to form a kind of rhythmic stretto effect. Thus far the poem is a hymn to nature, but the ecstatic
exclamations overflow into the next stanza as "O Lieb', o Liebe . . . ."
The transition to the theme of love is imperceptible: at this point in
the poem we feel that the earlier rapture ("O Glück, o Lust!") included both nature and love inseparably. The poet continues linking
up new images in nature with love which, in the end, is the reason for
new songs (lieder!) like this one.[40] The last three stanzas have a
slightly quieter effect due to the greater continuity of the phrases (or
more frequent enjambements), which flow smoothly into the last
stanza. The poem ends serenely with a sort of grateful blessing of
the beloved.

"Mailied" has nine stanzas of four lines each, Goethe's preferred
form for strophic poems.[41] There are few deviations from the
iambic meter, but sometimes they prove troublesome to composers.[42]
In each quatrain masculine and feminine endings alternate. Except for
the third stanza (*abab*) only the second and fourth verses rhyme
(*abcb*), a fact that counteracts the abrupt brevity of verses with only
two stresses.

THE MUSIC

Willi Schuh lists fifty-eight composers who set the poem as a solo
song.[43] As Max Friedlaender has pointed out, all German-speaking
areas are represented by the composers.[44] Beethoven is the best known
among them. Our comparison concerns the settings by Reichardt,
Gabler, and Beethoven from the eighteenth century and by Schoeck
and Knab from the twentieth century.

Reichardt (C major; ⅔ time)

A setting of "Mailied" appeared in *Lieder geselliger Freude,* published in 1796. Later the composer published three volumes of
Goethe songs.[45] In general, Reichardt's style includes a wide range
of expression and forms, but this piece is so simple, it is primitive.
However, it serves the purposes of this discussion because it shows
the pitfalls of Goethe's lied-concept, if taken to the extreme. Anal-

---

[40]Both the title and stanza 9 identify the poem as a lied.
[41]Müller, p. 242.
[42]Stanza 1, verse 2; stanza 2, verse 4.
[43]Schuh, p. 69.
[44]Max Friedlaender, "Goethes Gedichte in der Musik," *Goethe-Jahrbuch* 17 (1896):
179.
[45]Vol. 3 was republished in *Das Erbe deutscher Musik,* 58, 59, ed. Walter Salmen.
"Mailied" is no. 50.

ogous to the form of the poem is the eight-measure melody in which
the number of notes equals that of the syllables exactly. In order to
reflect the *b*-rhyme, the melody is divided into two four-measure
phrases with corresponding cadences (see table 1). The main problem with this song is its extreme monotony: to repeat the colorless
melody nine times would challenge any singer's interpretive powers
beyond reasonable bounds. It is well known that Goethe demanded
a varied interpretation from the singer of strophic songs.[46] This is

Table 1
Reichardt's "Mailied"

|  | I |  | stanza |
|---|---|---|---|
| Text: | 1   2   3   4 |  | verses |
|  | *a*        *b* |  | phrases |
| Music: | (4)       (4) |  | no. of measures |
|  | I |  | strophe |

a problem when contrasting moods have to be expressed by the same
music, but here we have the opposite problem: nine repetitions in
a poem of one sustained *Stimmung* indicated as "herzlich froh." Since
the setting doubles as a four-part song[47] there is no accompaniment.
The melody consists of two arpeggiated chords (I and V[7]). The
rhythm follows the iambic pattern closely, but a few glaring instances of faulty accentuation result where Goethe deviates from the
iambic meter[48] (Ex. 1).

Ex. 1

Wie  herr - lich  leuch - tet  mir  die  Na - tur!

## Gabler (A major: ¾ time)

Christian August Gabler was a German composer who lived and
taught in Russia.[49] His setting of "Mailied," written in 1798, was
published by Reichardt in *Neue Lieder geselliger Freude* (Leipzig,
1799).[50] Friedlaender praises Gabler's "pleasant talent for melody"

[46]See Abert, p. 73; and Sternfeld, p. 20.
[47]As a choral piece it is equally inadequate, especially the bass part.
[48]Cf. footnote 42.
[49]Max Friedlaender, *Konzert im Stile von Goethes Hausmusik* (Weimar, 1914),
p. 11.
[50]Reprinted as no. 6 in *Gedichte von Goethe in Compositionen seiner Zeitgenossen*,
ed. Max Friedlaender (Weimar, 1896), p. 132.

even though it sometimes descends to the trivial.[51] The melody of his "Mailied" has been included in folksong collections without the composer's name.[52] Gabler wrote a strophic song but he combined three stanzas of the poem into one musical strophe (see table 2). The

Table 2

Gabler's "Mailied"

| Text: | I | | II | | III | | stanzas |
|---|---|---|---|---|---|---|---|
| | 1 2 3 4 | | 1 2 3 4 | | 1 2 3 4 | | verses |
| | a | b | a | b | c | d | phrases |
| Music: | (2) | (2) | (2) | (2) | (2) | (2) | no. of measures |
| | | | I | | | | strophe |

melodic phrases share the same rhythmic pattern. Taken separately it gives the impression of § time, especially with the upbeat pattern of three eighth notes. Accentuation in § time would fit the first measure in free meter ("mir die Natur") but not the remainder of the strophe. The uniformity of the musical rhythm has a more insistent effect than the poetic meter because it never varies. The musical meter constrains the poetry: too many important words go by too quickly in the pattern of three eighth notes (herrlich, glänzt, lacht, tausend, Freud') (Ex. 2). It is important that the singer provide a flowing, rather than a heavily accented, performance in order to veil the flawed prosody. The melody is quite independent of the modest accompaniment (except in phrase c),[53] which forms a rhythmic and harmonic underpinning up to the melodic highpoint (phrase c). Here the bass joins the movement in eighth notes creating a sense of climax on a modest scale. The harmonic movement is equally simple (T-D-T-D-T-SD-T).

Ex. 2

Wie herr - lich leuch - tet mir die Na - tur!

It is quite possible that Goethe might have been pleased with Gabler's composition, for it has a certain naive charm. But the song

---

[51]Max Friedlaender, *Das deutsche Lied im 18. Jahrhundert,* 2 vols. (Stuttgart, 1902), 1: 347.

[52]Ibid.

[53]Loewe set the same song thirty-eight years later with the melody doubled in the accompaniment (op. 79, no. 4). Curiously, he begins with almost the same rhythmic pattern as Gabler.

does not fulfill Goethe's own requirement "den Hörer in die Stimmung zu versetzen, welche das Gedicht angibt":[54] its pedestrian pace ("wenig geschwind") and its monotonous rhythm and cadencing leave almost nothing of the magnificent exuberance of the poem.

Beethoven (E♭ major; $\frac{2}{4}$ time), op. 52, no. 4

In comparison with the settings discussed so far, Beethoven's "Mailied" seems even more of a masterpiece than usually acknowledged, especially if we remember that even this composer could write such modest examples as Goethe's "Marmotte" in the same year (1792).[55] "Mailied" was his first Goethe song[56] in the midst of minor poems that gave way to a series of Goethe compositions (ca. 1800) extending to *Egmont* in 1810.[57]

Like Gabler, Beethoven combined the nine stanzas in three groups of three each, in a strophic setting with a few modifications (see table 3). The modifications are few but telling. In phase *d* of the first strophe the melody ascends to the scale third in line with the enjambement between the second and third stanzas of the poem. At the corresponding point ($d^1$) in the second strophe the melody turns back to the tonic in line with the period after the word "Welt." This slight change was definitely made for the sake of the words; it functions like a caesura at the point where the poet turns to address the beloved directly ("O Mädchen, Mädchen . . ."). The changes in the third strophe bespeak the musician, his desire for a climactic feeling at

Table 3
Beethoven's "Mailied"

| | I | II | III | IV | V | VI | stanzas |
|---|---|---|---|---|---|---|---|
| Text: | 1 2 3 4 | 1 2 3 4 | 1 2 3 4 | 1 2 3 4 | 1 2 3 4 | 1 2 3 4 | verses |
| Music: | *a*    *b* | *c*    *d* | *c¹*    *d¹* | *a*    *b* | *c*    *d¹* | *c*    *d¹* | phrases |
| | (4) (4) | (4) (4) | (4) (4) | (4) (4) | (4) (4) | (4) (4) | no. of measures |
| | A    B | | B1 | A | B2 | B2 | periods |
| Intro. (14) | I | | Interlude (14) | II | | | strophes piano part |

[54]See p. 170.
[55]Op. 52, no. 7. The melody is doubled in the r. h. of the piano part throughout the song.
[56]Joseph Müller-Blattau, *Goethe und die Meister der Musik* (Stuttgart, 1969), p. 47.
[57]Hans Boettcher, *Beethoven als Liederkomponist* (Augsburg, 1928), p. 41; and Appendix (chronological table of songs).

|  | VII | VIII | IX |  | stanzas |
|---|---|---|---|---|---|

Text:

| 1 2 3 4 | 1 2 3 4 | 1 2 3 4 3 4 3 4 | verses |
|---|---|---|---|

Music:

| $a$ | $b$ | $c$ | $d$ | $d^2$ | $e$ | $e^1$ | $e^2$ | phrases |
|---|---|---|---|---|---|---|---|---|
| (4) | (4) | (4) | (4) | (4) | (4) | (4) | (4) | no. of measures |
|  | A |  | B | (B3) |  | Coda |  | periods |

| Interlude (14) | III | Postlude (6) | strophes piano part |
|---|---|---|---|

the end of the song and his instrumental coda-technique. Beethoven foreshortens the third strophe, omitting the expected second $c$-phrase, arriving at the end of $d^2$ when a thought in the poem is completed.[58] The last new thought ("Sei ewig glücklich . . ."), set to a new melodic phrase, is repeated twice and worked out with increasing excitement and dynamics in a true miniature "Beethoven coda."[59] Significantly it is the only portion of the song ($e$, $e^1$, and $e^2$) where eighth-note movement in the accompaniment is added to that of the voice rather than alternating with it. The accumulated energy plays itself out in the sixteenth-note arpeggii of the little postlude or codetta. Finally a setting that equals the youthful enthusiasm of Goethe's poem, perhaps because poet and composer were at the same age when they wrote their respective "Mailied"!

Beethoven's melody belongs to an eighteenth-century type derived from dances, used by Sperontes and contemporaries as well as in Singspiel-songs of the later decades.[60] Beethoven was fond of its even notes (Choral Fantasy, op. 80; "Ode to Joy" in Symphony No. 9) or two-note motives of even eighth notes ("Mit einem gemalten Band," solo quartet-variation "Freude trinken alle Wesen" in "Ode to Joy"). In fact the melody of "Mailied" also served for a tenor aria in a Singspiel by Umlauf.[61] Surprisingly this melody fits the word accents of Goethe's poem excellently while at the same time flowing smoothly. The adaptation to a strict musical meter is more successful than Gabler's because it is not strictly syllabic.[62] It is true that many unaccented syllables receive a two-note motive, but invariably a

---

[58]This change is analogous to the one at $d^1$ in strophe II.
[59]For musical reasons Beethoven heightens the thrust of the song where Goethe relaxes it.
[60]Schnapper, pp. 19-21.
[61]Boettcher, Appendix, Table II.
[62]See ibid., p. 79, for a comparison of Beethoven's with Tomašek's and Scherzer's rhythms in the same song.

metric accent follows, strengthened by a longer note, so that it over-
shadows the unaccented syllable. A meter of $\frac{2}{4}$ coupled with the
two-note motive can accommodate the regular and irregular verses
of the poem (Ex. 3).

Ex. 3

Du   seg - nest ___   herr - lich das   fri ___ - sche ___   Feld, ___

The role of the accompaniment is significant. Arialike, the prelude anticipates the voice part. But the *b*-phrase continues upward
avoiding the dominant key and returning to a slightly extended variant of *a*. The constant eighth-note movement (tempo allegro) immediately sets the pervading mood with modest means. During the
singing the piano retreats to supporting chords in slower note values
doubling the essential notes of the melody. The interludes feature
a two-note motive ( ♪♪ ) resembling a cuckoo call that may be con-
strued as an instance of tone-painting, the only one in the song.[63] But
the derivation from the two-note motive in the melody integrates it
so well into the musical texture that it can be heard as a natural outgrowth of the musical material, especially since it reappears in the coda
increasing the excitement in the climactic last phrase ($e^2$).

We do not know Goethe's reaction to Beethoven's "Mailied" or if
he knew the composition. The poet might have objected to the two-
fold repetition of the last two lines although he took similar changes
from Zelter without criticism;[64] he might have disliked the importance
of the accompaniment and its tone-painting if he heard it as such.
But basically, Goethe should have approved this song, because it respects the form and prosody of the poetry[65] and expresses the totality
of its mood.

Schoeck (D major; $\frac{4}{4}$ time) op. 19a, no. 3

The Swiss composer Othmar Schoeck set the same poem in 1911
as part of a set of eight Goethe songs.[66] While some composers today
seem to avoid the favorite poets of the past,[67] Schoeck thrives on them,
especially Heine, Eichendorff, and Uhland. Among the recent poets,

[63]H. J. Moser, "Historical Introduction," *The German Solo Song and the Ballad,*
Anthology of Music, 14 (Cologne, 1958), p. 7.
[64]Wittman, p. 25.
[65]Jack Stein calls it "Beethoven's finest fusion of poem and music" in *Poem and
Music in the German Lied from Gluck to Hugo Wolf* (Cambridge, Mass., 1971), p. 52.
[66]Edition Breitkopf No. 5025a.
[67]Mario Castelnuovo-Tedesco, "Music and Poetry: Problems of a Song-Writer,"
*The Musical Quarterly* 30 (1944): 104-5.

he favors Hermann Hesse, his personal friend.[68] In Goethe's poetry Schoeck admired the singular fusion of beauty with substance.[69] He expressed his respect for the integrity of the poem: "Musik und Sprache sind gleich wichtig. Sie durchdringen sich und zeugen ein drittes neues Phänomen. . . ."[70] A "third phenomenon," needless to say, goes beyond what Goethe envisioned the lied with music to be. Corrodi calls Schoeck's lied-style of the period (ca. 1909-1916) a synthesis of Wolf and Schubert.[71] "Mailied" bears this out: the melody dominates, but in a rich, expressive accompaniment. The triadic melody, the spacing in the piano part, the repeated chords in gently syncopated rhythm remind one of Brahms's song technique (as in "Feldeinsamkeit"). "Melodie und Harmonie entstehen bei mir immer gleichzeitig," says Schoeck, "die erste Taktgruppe [bildet] gleichsam die 'Urzelle' des Liedes. . . ."[72] In this song the *Urzelle* is a wavelike pattern of eighth notes in both hands of the piano part, an arpeggiated dominant seventh chord that never resolves but fades out eventually on the same two notes with which it started (E and G). This *Urzelle* forms the binding material for the through-composed song: through constantly changing harmonies its rhythmic impulse drives on. The pattern also helps define the form: in each section it disappears just before a climax (or earlier) and then sets in again at the beginning of the next one (see table 4). Schoeck's sections correspond to Gab-

Table 4

Schoeck's "Mailied"

| Text: | I | | | II | | | III | | | IV | | | V | | | VI | | | stanzas |
|---|---|---|---|---|---|---|---|---|---|---|---|---|---|---|---|---|---|---|---|
| | 1 2 3 4 | | | 1 2 3 4 | | | 1 2 3 4 | | | 1 2 3 4 | | | 1 2 3 4 | | | 1 2 3 4 | | | verses |
| Music: | a | a¹ | a² | b | | c | | d | | e | | f | | g | | h | e² | i | phrases |
| | (2) | (2) | (2) | (2) | | (2) | | (2) | | (2) | | (2) | | (2) | | (2) | (2) | (2) | no. of measures |
| | A | | | | | | | | | | B | | | | | | | | sections |
| | U U U1 U2 U3 U4 | | | | | | U5 | | | | | | | | | | | | *Urzelle* in piano part |

---

[68]Hans Corrodi, *Othmar Schoeck*, 3rd. ed. (Frauenfeld, 1956), p. 35.

[69]Werner Vogel, *Othmar Schoeck im Gespräch* (Zürich, 1965), p. 157.

[70]Ibid., p. 53. Joseph Marx expressed a similar concept of lied-composition in "Schuberts Lied," *Bericht über den internationalen Kongress für Schubertforschung* (Vienna, 1928), p. 116.

[71]Corrodi, p. 44.

[72]Ibid. The concept is also part of Hans Pfitzner's song composition. See Heinrich Lindlar, *Hans Pfitzners Klavierlied* (Würzburg, 1940), pp. 31-32. Pfitzner also set "Mailied" (op. 26, no. 5).

| Text: | VII | | | | VIII | | | | IX | | | | (I) | | | | stanzas |
|---|---|---|---|---|---|---|---|---|---|---|---|---|---|---|---|---|---|
| | 1 | 2 | 3 | 4 | 1 | 2 | 3 | 4 | 1 | 2 | 3 | 4 | 1 | 2 | | | verses |
| Music: | $a^2$ | | $f^1$ | | $j$ | | $k$ | | $g^1$ | | $l$ | | $a$ | | | | phrases |
| | (2) | | (2) | | (2) | | (2) | | (2) | | (3) | | (3) | | | | no. of measures |
| | A1 or C | | | | | | | | | | | Coda ($A^2$) | | | | | sections |
| | U6 | | U7 | | U8 | | | | | | | | U U extended | | | | *Urzelle* in piano part |

ler's and Beethoven's strophes, but each has an individualized treatment. Schoeck's melodic style defies diagrammatic representation: all melodic phrases are closely interrelated, yet no two are exactly the same, except in the deliberate recurrence of *a* in the coda. The declamation is largely syllabic. Many dotted rhythms reflect the iambic poetic meter, but the musical rhythm is so flexible that it never becomes monotonous or restrictive. At climactic points the syllables are stretched for emphasis, but the pace is kept by preceding or following the longer note values with short ones in a rubato-like effect (Ex. 4). The melody of phrase *a* and its variants is triadic but, as the first section approaches its ecstatic end, the melody reaches upward on the important words ("*Wonne, Erd', Lust*"). Similarly at the beginning of the B section phrase *e* reaches for successive highpoints (Ex. 5).

Ex. 4
(a)

Ex. 5

Harmonically the song passes from one key to another without establishing them, not even the tonic. The basic harmonic movement leads from D to B major and back to D. The return to the implied tonic occurs so late in section C (or $A^2$) that Schoeck repeats the opening as a coda.

Schoeck's "Mailied" is firmly rooted in the Romantic tradition; Goethe would not have accepted it with all its fluctuations of harmony, tempo, and dynamics (from *ppp* to *f*). But the amazing thing about this setting is its freshness, energy, and truth to the spirit of Goethe's poem. Schoeck's song career, which continued to at least 1950 (*Mörike Songs,* op. 62), seems to belie the opinion that the era of lied-composition was brief and is now over.[73]

## Knab (G major; ⅜ time)

Armin Knab's Goethe songs, a set of twelve, were published in 1949.[74] "Mailied" is the second song. At first sight we seem to be back in the days of Gabler: a strophic setting, again three stanzas to a strophe,[75] a simple accompaniment, and a simple, largely diatonic harmonic vocabulary (except for a few diminished-seventh chords). But here the similarity ends, for Knab, although clearly limiting his technical means to the capabilities of amateurs or *Hausmusik,* has none of the monotony of Gabler. The melody, the most important element,[76] changes throughout the musical strophe; one might say the song is through-composed for the first three stanzas of the poem. The phrase structure changes, too, sometimes keeping a normal four-measure length (*a*), sometimes observing the caesura between verses ("Wie glänzt die Sonne!/Wie lacht die Flur") by creating two phrase members of three measures each (*b*), sometimes extending the phrase to five (see table 5). Knab repeats the last verse of the third, sixth, and ninth stanzas in coda-like extension. The melodic phrases are interrelated without exactly repeating, growing more melismatic toward the end of the song. Knab often extends a phrase by sustaining the last note, which usually falls on the most important word. There is a simple but delightful interplay between the voice and accompaniment: when the melody is held, one or more parts in the piano part move constantly, keeping the lilting motion going. For the accompaniment is polyphonically conceived: the introduction begins in two parts and grows to four; it anticipates the melody, as in Beethoven's setting. The identity of the four parts is clear throughout, even when they form only chordal support.[77] Partly doubling the

---

[73]Elaine Brody and Robert A. Fowkes, *The German Lied and Its Poetry* (New York, 1971), p. 299.

[74]*Zwölf Lieder für eine hohe Stimme mit Klavier nach Gedichten von Johann Wolfgang von Goethe.* Edition Schott No. 3931.

[75]Bernhard Klein divides the poem into four strophes of two stanzas each. He leaves out stanza 5 and separates 7 from 8 although they form one sentence. His setting (1827) is no. 64 in *Gedichte von Goethe,* ed. Friedlaender.

[76]Edith Weiss-Mann, "Ein Zeitloser," *Musica* 5 (1951): 54, quotes Knab: "Man muss einfach singen, man muss alles Wesentliche in der Melodie ausdrücken."

[77]This polyphonic piano accompaniment also characterizes the songs in Jens Rohwer's *Das Wunschlied* (Wolfenbüttel, 1951).

Table 5
Knab's "Mailied"

| | I | | II | | III | | | | |
|---|---|---|---|---|---|---|---|---|---|
| Text: | | | | | | | | | stanzas |

| | 1 2 | 3 4 | 1 2 | 3 4 | 1 2 | 3 | 4 | 4 | verses |
|---|---|---|---|---|---|---|---|---|---|

| Music: | a | b | c | d | c¹ | e | f | g | phrases |
|---|---|---|---|---|---|---|---|---|---|

| | (4) | (3+3) | (3+3) | (5) | (3+3) | (5) | (5) | (4) | no. of measures |
|---|---|---|---|---|---|---|---|---|---|
| | | A | | B | | C | | | sections |

| | Intro.<br>(8) | | | I | | | | | strophe |
|---|---|---|---|---|---|---|---|---|---|

melody, the upper part elsewhere moves in contrary or oblique motion to the voice (Ex. 6). Knab's song, marked *beschwingt,* carries a quietly happy mood rather than one of passionate energy. Even this points back to the eighteenth century in its contained, reserved expression.

Ex. 6

aus  dem  Ge - sträuch,_____  und

## CONCLUSION

The many different stylistic directions of our century include the post-Romantic (Schoeck) and the anti-Romantic but conservative (Knab). The latter trend was inspired in part by the *Jugendmusik-* or *Singbewegung,* which at first reflected a broad based reaction against the post-Romantic solo song, its emotionalism, subjectivity, and refined virtuosity. Fritz Jöde's *Musikmanifest* (1921) verbalizes the antipathy toward the *Klavierlied* in drastic terms.[78] It is interesting to note that one of the earliest milestones on the road of this movement was the songbook *Zupfgeigenhansl* (1909), the result of Hans Breuer's search for old folksongs and the beginning of a wave of enthusiasm and collecting activity.[79] Like Goethe in Strassburg? The *Singbewegung* culti-

---

[78]Quoted in Moser, *Das deutsche Lied seit Mozart,* 1: 264.
[79]Otto Haase, "Hans Breuer und der Zupfgeigenhansl," *Pro Musica* (1969): 25.

vated the group ideal and found its realization in the polyphonic repertoire of the Renaissance and Baroque, including the instrumental chamber music of the *Spielmusik*-variety, both old and new.[80]

But what about the solo song, the lied? In view of the Romantic associations of the form, of the inevitable piano as accompanying vehicle—to say nothing of the symphony orchestra—the chamber song (*Kammerlied*) emerged as a new alternative in which the lied became a group form.[81] And when the solo song as such was recognized again, it tended to reflect the simplicity of the folksong with simple accompaniment or the group ideal in a nonpianistic style of polyphony or quasi-polyphony. Thus the lied was pulled back from the realm of "professionals only" and reentered the home and the school. Some composers were central in this connection:

> Armin Knab . . . gebührt das Verdienst, das eigentlich Liedhafte, die geschlossene Liedweise „wiederentdeckt" zu haben, wie Karl Marx das Klavierlied mit einfacher Begleitung für die Hausmusik zurückgewann.[82]

In a sense it can be said that Goethe's concept of the lied reemerged here, if for different reasons than the poet's. But insofar as his concept is that of the so-called Second Berlin School, it is in accord with that of the twentieth-century *Jugendmusikbewegung*. Moser even likens one of its composers, Jens Rohwer (b. 1914), to a J.A.P. Schulz in mid-twentieth century.[83] Some of the parallels between the two song concepts are:

1. A reaction against the "music of yesteryear," the high-Baroque and post-Romantic styles, respectively

2. The conscious return to a folksong ideal[84] of simplicity, sincerity, and "singability"[85]

3. The objective to reach "the people," to infuse their life with song, to bridge the gap between the professional and the amateur musician

4. An aversion to virtuosity or technical display for its own sake

---

[80]For example, Hindmith's *Sing- und Spielmusiken für Liebhaber und Musikfreunde,* op. 45 (1929).

[81]Knab's contribution to this genre is discussed by Heinrich Lindlar in "Der Lyriker Armin Knab," *Zeitschrift für Musik* 112 (1951): 361.

[82]Kurt Gudewill, "Lied. Das Kunstlied im deutschen Sprachgebiet," *Die Musik in Geschichte und Gegenwart* 8 (1960): 771-72.

[83]Moser, "Goethes Dichtung," p. 271.

[84]Fritz Jöde, *Deutsche Jugendmusik* (Berlin, 1934), p. 17.

[85]*Sangbarkeit* was one of the requirements of eighteenth-century lied-aesthetics. See Heinrich Schwab, *Sangbarkeit, Popularität und Kunstlied* (Regensburg, 1965), p. 19.

5. Both imply the concept of word-tone relationship in the lied, so close to the heart of Goethe, as expressed by J.A.P. Schulz:

Denn nur durch eine frappante Ähnlichkeit des musikalischen mit dem poetischen Tone des Liedes; durch eine Melodie, deren Fortschreitung sich nie über den Gang des Textes erhebt, noch unter ihm sinkt, die, wie ein Kleid dem Körper, sich der Declamation und dem Metro der Worte anschmiegt . . . erhält das Lied den Schein . . . des Kunstlosen, des Bekannten, mit einem Wort, den Volkston. . . .[86]

Olga Termini

---

[86]J. A. P. Schulz, *Lieder im Volkston,* 2d ed. (1784), Preface quoted in Friedlaender, *Das deutsche Lied im 18. Jahhundert,* 1:257.

# Some Settings of Heine

It is ironic in a way that Heine, so much admired in Germany, should have spent the last twenty-five years of his life in France. He would have appreciated the irony. He was, in Berlioz's words, "l'inimitable ironiste," a "chat-tigre." The sharp tongue could make enemies. When Frau Wesendonck asked Liszt if he did not think Heine's name as a poet would be inscribed in the temple of immortality, the answer was: "Yes, but in mud." Heine, like Berlioz, was not a Romantic; if anything he was anti-Romantic. The Romantic poets were concerned in the main with simple emotions; with Heine there is apt to be a worm in the bud, a sting in the tail. He was aware of suffering. He wrote:

Aus meinen grossen Schmerzen
Mach' ich die kleinen Lieder

but his suffering was not the *Weltschmerz* in which so many nineteenth-century poets indulged.

The Romantic composers were not always aware of this. They tended to see him as one of themselves and often failed to realize that though there is sentiment in his poetry, there is no sentimentality. Schumann knew Heine, but being himself incapable of irony he rarely understood him. There are obvious examples in *Dichterliebe*. "Ich grolle nicht" has long been admired for its passionate declamation, but it bears little relation to Heine's text. The music suggests a proud and noble resignation in the face of unrequited love, whereas the words express a bitter and contemptuous rejection. "I am not angry," says the poet. He says it twice; Schumann makes him say it six times. The bitterness is perhaps most marked in the line "Wie du auch strahlst in Diamantenpracht," which singers, encouraged by Schumann's setting, often deliver in a pompous style suggesting triumph, whereas the text says exactly the opposite: "You may be covered in diamonds [i.e., you may marry a rich husband] but there is darkness in your soul." This is the end of the first verse of the poem, which continues in the same vein: "I knew it all along: I saw the darkness, I saw how wretched you are." There is no hint of compassion here: the poet is stating bare, ugly facts. Schumann distorts the picture by tacking "das weiss ich längst" onto the end of his first verse, repeating "Ich grolle nicht, und wenn das Herz auch bricht" at the beginning of his second, and repeating "Ich grolle nicht" twice at the end.

Schumann was more successful with "Das ist ein Flöten und Geigen." He pays little attention to the text, which is set in a curiously noncommittal style (the words "dazwischen schluchzen and stöhnen die lieblichen Engelein" go for nothing), but the melancholy, insistent waltz-tune in the accompaniment does suggest that this is not a happy occasion. On the other hand in "Ein Jüngling liebt ein Mädchen" he misses the point completely. This folky jingle has nothing to do with the theme of the poem: "It's always been the same: off with the old, on with the new." Eric Sams writes: "In the postlude . . . we can hear the coarse and angry emphasis of jealous despair,"[1] but this is true only if we want to hear it—there is nothing in the music to suggest it. "Im Rhein, im heiligen Strome" is another example of misunderstanding. Schumann was so impressed by the image of Cologne Cathedral towering over the Rhine that he failed to appreciate the vulgarity of the comparison between the statue of the Virgin and the beloved: Heine does not say that his loved one is like the Virgin, but the other way about. The austerity of Schumann's accompaniment is no preparation for the irony in the final lines. He did better, however, than Franz, who provided merely amiable music for this poem, and so far misunderstood it that he marked his setting "Im Legendton" (Ex. 1). Liszt saw the poem differently. His setting, of which he wrote two versions, begins with the rippling movement of the waters of the Rhine, breaks off for a triumphant declamation of the contemptuous words "das grosse, das heil'ge Cöln," and dissolves into a delicate ecstasy at the thought of the beloved's eyes, lips, and cheeks. It is a sentimental setting, beautiful in its own right, but even further away from Heine than Schumann's.

"Im wunderschönen Monat Mai" seems on the surface to present no problems. It appears to be simply a declaration of love in springtime. This was how Franz saw it in his very charming setting (Ex. 2). But Schumann, with more perception than he showed in some of his other Heine songs, realized that the poem was not quite so simple as it appeared. The concluding lines,

Da hab' ich ihr gestanden
Mein Sehnen und Verlangen

---

[1]Eric Sams, *Songs of Robert Schumann* (London, 1969), p. 118.

Ex. 1 Robert Franz, "Im Rhein, im heiligen Strome," mm. 1-8.

Ex. 2 Robert Franz, "Im wunderschönen Monat Mai," mm. 1-5.

suggest that the awakening of love was not pure happiness. The key-
words are *Sehnen* and *Verlangen*. The whole of Schumann's setting
is infused with the conception of longing, from the hesitant dissonance
at the beginning to the inconclusive ending. The music is in fact in
no definite key: it begins and ends in F# minor, but the setting of
the words is in A major and each verse ends in D major.

Here the strophic setting fits perfectly, since Heine's two verses
are parallel. This is not always the case. In "Berg und Burgen schaun
herunter" (op. 24, no. 7) all four verses are set to the same exquisite
melody, with the same harmonic twists in the tranquil accompaniment.
This music is ideal for the first two verses, which picture the boat sail-
ing on the Rhine and the reflections in the water. But as so often in
Heine, the tranquility is deceptive. In verse 3 he points to the dangers
that lurk beneath the calm waters, and in verse 4 comes the savage
comparison with the loved one: she smiles happily but in her heart is
malice and deceit. "Schöne Wiege meiner Leiden" (op. 24, no. 5) presents a variant of the same problem. Here Schumann, recognizing
that there is passion and suffering in the text, has recourse to a rondo
structure; but the result is as artificial as the strophic setting of "Berg
und Burgen." He seems to have been seduced by the adjective *schöne*
(*schöne Wiege* and *schöne Stadt*) into composing a sort of lullaby
for his rondo theme. But this is not a peaceful leave-taking. The
town to which the poet is saying goodbye is the cradle of his sorrows,
the tombstone of his peace; and the poem ends, where Schumann does
not allow it to end, with the words

> Und die Glieder matt und träge
> Schlepp ich fort am Wanderstab,
> Bis mein müdes Haupt ich lege
> Ferne in ein kühles Grab.

Needless to say, there are poems where the contrast between happiness and bitter despair is less marked. Schumann is tolerably successful with "Es treibt mich hin," where the whole of his setting
represents the lover's impatience, though he takes no account of the
fact that the hours move slowly ("schleppen sich behaglich träge,
schleichend gähnend ihre Wege"). Franz's setting, with its sudden
outburst on "tummle dich, du faules Volk!" (Ex. 3) is even more effective than Schumann's. It might be objected that he breaks up the music
into sections, but he also observes the contrast between the lover's
impatience and the dragging hours. Liszt, too, had no difficulty with
"Vergiftet sind meine Lieder" (Ex. 4), where the whole poem breathes

Ex. 3 Robert Franz, "Es treibt mich hin."

Ex. 4 Franz Liszt, "Vergiftet sind meine Lieder," mm. 19-29.

hatred, though the setting, rather like an operatic *scena,* is probably more dramatic in expression than Heine would have expected.

"Du bist wie eine Blume" presents no problems. No doubt it is possible to read into it more than it actually says. "Ich schau dich an, und Wehmut schleicht mir ins Herz hinein" may be taken to suggest that the experience is not all happiness; and the prayer that God will keep the loved one "so rein und schön und hold" may imply that this is by no means a certainty. But on the whole it is simpler to take the text at its face value—as a genuine reaction to beauty. This at least is what Schumann does in his setting (op. 25, no. 24)—one of the most beautiful songs he ever wrote, rich in sentiment but without the sentimentality that mars some of his music for texts by lesser writers. Liszt's setting, which attempts to be simple and achieves nothing, is feeble by comparison.

Schumann could be simple on occasion, and in "Anfangs wollt ich fast verzagen" (op. 24, no. 8) simplicity hits the mark perfectly. It has often been pointed out that his opening phrase is identical with the first line of the chorale "Wer nur den lieben Gott lässt walten," though without the initial upbeat. This may be purely accidental. If it is intentional the implied association is inappropriate, since the text of the chorale urges Christians to leave everything to God, whereas Heine's verses speak of an intolerable burden that has somehow been borne—"but do not ask me how." But if we disregard the association, the austerity of the music, with its stony acceptance of tragedy and its final question mark, seems the perfect expression of the text: it adds nothing and lets the words make the maximum effect. Such restraint was foreign to Liszt's temperament. It is not that his setting is complicated: it is almost as simple in texture as Schumann's. But instead of the blunt defiance of the text it offers indulgence in self-pity and spoils the ending by a fortissimo cry on *wie*. In some respects it is curiously like what Wolf might have written had he set the poem.

The problem of setting words to music is not peculiar to Heine's poetry, though it is more acute there. The difficulty that faces any songwriter is that in poetry the emphasis tends to come at the end, whereas in music it is liable to come earlier. Only the most innocent texts are really suitable for a strophic setting: in fact any setting in which music is repeated runs the risk of being at odds with the words. In Schumann the musical impulse was often stronger than appreciation of the words—which is not to deny that the result may be enjoyable to sing and to listen to. He has been chosen for examination here because he seems to have set Heine more often than any of his contemporaries with the exception of Franz. It may well be that later nineteenth-century composers saw more clearly the problems that Heine's verses presented. Wolf certainly wrote a number of settings in his early years, but they are not characteristic, and once he was immersed in Mörike and Eichendorff he forgot all about Heine. The only Heine setting from the time of his maturity and the only one published in his lifetime was "Wo wird einst," which is best forgotten.

Brahms set only six poems by Heine, the earliest in 1877, at the age of forty-four. The most successful are "Sommerabend" and "Mondenschein" (op. 85, nos. 1 & 2), linked thematically though without any convincing justification. Both songs have a subtlety that is often lacking in Schumann. The innocent tranquility of the texts is matched by music that is both sensitive and faithful to the mood, suggesting in the second the undercurrent of unhappiness so frequent in Heine's poems. "Der Tod, das ist die kühle Nacht" (op. 96, no. 1) was a tougher nut to crack. There is so much here that is left unsaid and hence unexplained. Brahms makes no attempt to dig beneath the surface. The cool night of death, the sultry day of life are effectively contrasted, though in the latter case with a certain smugness that seems out of place. But what sets his ideas winging aloft is the song of the nightingale, which in fact is only incidental in the poem. The piece is a striking example of his harmonic invention in particular, but the poem is more than a nocturne. In "Meerfahrt" (op. 96, no. 4) on the other hand, so much admired by Elisabeth von Herzogenberg, the underlying sadness, which in the poem is not revealed until the end, is present in the music throughout: the gondolalike movement of the accompaniment suggests not only the boat on the water but the restlessness, the desolation in the soul.

It would seem that Brahms was cautious about setting Heine; he was also more subtle than Schumann when attempting it. But it was Schubert who came nearest to the spirit of Heine's poetry, not only in time (they were exact contemporaries), but in understanding. His six Heine songs were written only a few months after the *Buch der Lieder* was published.[2] It is easy to imagine that he may have felt a strange kinship between these poems and the vein of pessimism that runs through much of his later work—for instance, the G major quartet and *Die Winterreise*. It is sometimes said that he was too childlike a character to appreciate Heine. But he was not a childlike character at all. There are profound depths in his work that do not always yield their secrets at once and in some cases remain enigmatic. His simplicity can be deceptive. It is so in "Ihr Bild," which has been criticized because the third verse is set to the same music as the first, thus missing the sudden revelation of loss in Heine's final lines. In fact he has not missed it: it is there in the brief postlude for the piano. So far as the vocal setting is concerned there is much to be said for an almost laconic simplicity that allows the words to make their point without overemphasis. Even in "Das Fischermädchen," which is admittedly the least successful of the six settings, there is a hint of mockery that matches the cynical tone of Heine's apparently innocent verse.

---

[2]The poems had appeared in the first volume of Heine's *Reisebilder* in 1826; but it is known that Schubert had a copy of the *Buch der Lieder,* in which he had marked the pages on which the songs he wished to set occur (O. E. Deutsch, *Schubert: a Documentary Biography* [London, 1946], p. 709).

But whatever criticism may be leveled at these two songs, the remaining four are by any standard masterly. To say that "Der Atlas" dramatizes the poem is to ignore the fact that the poem itself is dramatic. It is difficult to imagine any setting that could represent more forcefully and more painfully the intolerable burden to which the poet refers. The recapitulation of the opening lines does nothing to weaken Heine's last words ("und jetzo bist du elend") and is justifiable on musical grounds. "Die Stadt" provides an impressionistic background to the misty scene and drives home the final line ("wo ich das Liebste verlor") with a brutal emphasis. It is not so much a scene-painting as the representation of a mood. So also in "Am Meer" the introductory chords repeated at the end tell the whole story, leaving the voice as in "Ihr Bild" to declaim the words. There is hardly any need to defend "Der Doppelgänger" against adverse criticism. But it needs to be stressed that in all these songs there is more than meets the eye, just as there is in Heine's poems. There is not complete unity of purpose: that would be impossible. But the evidence of suffering is as strong in the music as it is in the verse: the secrets are shared.

It is not the purpose of this article to deal with later composers. At first sight it might seem that Mahler would have been the ideal person to set Heine. He was a Jew, and his instrumental music in particular shows a marked capacity for irony. Instead he concentrated on Rückert and *Des Knaben Wunderhorn.* It may be that identity of race and similarity of temperament do not necessarily provide the best basis for the union of two minds. With Mahler the inclination to folk poetry was too strong and clearly influenced him more than any Romantic texts. Strauss was more catholic in his tastes, if indeed he had any pronounced literary taste at all. Of his few Heine settings, "Schlechtes Wetter" is still popular, though it is an extraordinary interpretation of a relatively simple poem. By the time the climax comes the modest background has disappeared into the world of *Der Rosenkavalier.* What the devil, one may ask, is Octavian doing in this galley? The song is delightful to sing and to play; but if Heine was capable of turning in his grave, this would have been a reasonable opportunity for doing so.

Jack Westrup

# E. T. Pound and Unorthodox
# Music Notation

The pragmatic approach seems to have been a trademark of the American artist from the early days of Colonial settlement. John Cotton in his Preface to the *Bay Psalm Book*—as the first book published in the English Colonies was popularly known—established this tone when he acknowledged that if

> the verses are not always so smooth and elegant as some may desire or expect; let them consider that Gods Altar needs not our pollishings: Ex. 20. for wee have respected rather a plaine translation, then to smooth our verses with the sweetnes of any paraphrase, and soe have attended Conscience rather then Elegance, fidelity rather then poetry, in translating the hebrew words into english language.[1]

Probably with no such intention, Cotton thus set the tone for subsequent American artistic endeavors. The frontier was to exact an aesthetic penalty, leaving a no-frill, no-nonsense, practical approach to the arts, which was far removed conceptually as well as geographically from its genesis in the glory of Elizabethan England and the High Renaissance of Europe.

This functional concept of art nowhere has been more evident than in the fields of music printing and pedagogy, especially as these relate to the numerous and diverse attempts at simplification of musical notation. These attempts began about 1720 and continue today in the schoolroom, home, and music store with the abundance of "instant performance" methods and instruments.[2]

During the nineteenth century there was a proliferation of these attempts. One of the men who advocated notational reforms seems

---

[1] All spellings are as in the original, p. [14] (verso of **3) of the Preface to *The Whole Book of Psalmes* . . . *Imprinted 1640*, as reprinted in facsimile by the University of Chicago Press, 1956.

[2] For a history of the first music publication in unorthodox notation see "John Tufts's *Introduction to the Singing of Psalm-Tunes*," Chapter 3 in Irving Lowens, *Music and Musicians in Early America* (New York, 1964).

to have been overlooked by other researchers in the fields of music notation and pedagogy. He is Edwin T. Pound of Barnesville, Georgia, who is unique both for his own unusual notational developments and for his publications in which he combined and utilized various unorthodox notations.[3]

Edwin T. Pound was born in 1833 in the Big Bethel Church community of Hancock County, Georgia. His youth was spent there and at the Pound family homestead in Talbot County, Georgia. In 1855 he was married to Miss Elizabeth Bloodworth (born 1838) of Lamar County, Georgia. They were the parents of four sons and two daughters. By 1867 he had settled his family in Barnesville, and in that year he was a cofounder of the first local newspaper, the weekly *Gazette*. He was the editor for many years and later became sole owner. In addition to his newspaper work, he was a merchant, farmer, extensive land owner, and an active participant in local and civic affairs. At one time he was Judge of the Inferior Court, and was known thereafter as Judge Pound. He died in 1919, his wife in 1913. Their bodies are in the Greenwood Street Cemetery, Barnesville, Georgia.[4]

Judge Pound began his lifelong study of music at age twelve and by the age of sixteen was teaching, presumably in singing schools of the period.[5] Apparently his love for and interest in music never wavered, for he wrote many articles and editorials on various aspects of music during his long tenure at the *Gazette*. He also published actual music in the paper, which is one of the reasons cited for its extraordinarily wide circulation throughout the deep South and as far west as Texas. It is claimed that at one time there were more subscribers to the Barnesville *Gazette* in the state of Texas than other weeklies had in their entirety.[6]

The publications of Pound remain almost as enigmatic as the man. From 1870 to 1903, he apparently published several tunebooks: *Vocal Triad, Golden Sheaves, Songs for All,* and *Gospel Voices,* each

[3]Pound is not mentioned in the two most comprehensive discussions of unorthodox musical notations: George P. Jackson, *White Spirituals in the Southern Uplands* (Chapel Hill, N. C., 1933); and Earl O. Loessel, "The Use of Character Notes and Other Unorthodox Notations in Teaching the Reading of Music in Northern United States During the Nineteenth Century," Ed.D. diss., University of Michigan, 1959).

[4]Biographical data in this paragraph were compiled from the sketch on Judge Pound and other locations in: Augusta Lambdin, ed., *History of Lamar County* [Georgia] (Barnesville, Georgia, 1932), passim. I wish to thank Mrs. John B. Hewitt, Librarian, and Mrs. J. E. Bush, Librarian Emeritus, of the Barnesville Carnegie Library for their assistance and kindnesses during my work there. This is reflected in all references to holdings of the Barnesville Carnegie Library.

[5]This information is compiled from the biographical sketch in Lambdin and from Pound's Preface to the *Vocal Triad*.

[6]Lambdin, p. 393.

of which may have appeared in more than one edition. These apparently enjoyed widespread sales, but copies of them seem to be extremely rare today. Only two copies of the *Vocal Triad* have been located, none of *Golden Sheaves,* one each of three editions of *Songs for All,* and one of *Gospel Voices Supplemented.* Each of these known copies was published by Pound and bears a Barnesville imprint.

Neither copies nor publication dates are known for *Golden Sheaves.* However, from limited information in an advertisement,[7] it is assumed that this was published between *Vocal Triad* and *Songs for All,* placing it between 1870 and 1882. *Golden Sheaves* was in standard notation, but was issued later with a *Supplement,* which was printed in Pound's Twelve Letter Staff. This notation, discussed below, received a copyright in 1884, which would indicate the *Supplement* was of that date or later.

*Gospel Voices* appeared in 1886, and *Gospel Voices Supplemented* received an 1890 copyright. Frank M. Davis is shown as coeditor with Pound.[8] No copy of *Gospel Voices* has been located, but the Barnesville Carnegie Library has a single copy of *Gospel Voices Supplemented.* The 1886 work is in standard notation, while the *Supplement* employs Pound's Twelve Letter Staff.

From the notational viewpoint, the two most important publications by Pound are his first and last works, respectively *Vocal Triad* and *Songs for All with Supplement.* His pragmatic approach to music publication is adequately reflected in these two books, especially the later one.

Although the *Vocal Triad* seems to have been printed in two editions, the two known copies seem to be identical.[9] As they have no number in the title and no secondary copyright date, it must be assumed that they both are copies of the 1870 edition. According to its title page, the *Vocal Triad* was published in "three systems of musical notation." In retrospect, this seems obviously another functional attempt to capitalize on then current notational trends.

However, to comprehend more fully what Pound was attempting, perhaps a brief historical survey would be helpful. One of the notations he uses is known today as "fasola" notation. This method uses geometric shapes for the heads of notes, was invented in the 1790s by John Connelley of Philadelphia, and subsequently was introduced in

---

[7]This advertisement is on p. 287 of *Gospel Voices Supplemented.*

[8]Frank M. Davis (1839-1896) was born in New York but lived in several states. He was a major contributor to Pound's publications.

[9]Lambdin mentions *Vocal Triad No. 1 and 2,* while several musical selections in *Songs for All* are taken from *Vocal Triad No. 2.* One copy is in the Library of Congress, the other is in the Barnesville Carnegie Library.

the long-lived *Easy Instructor.*[10]   Other publications with wide distribution were published in this four-shape notation, and it became extremely popular particularly in the less urban areas of the South and
West—the frontiers of the nation—where it fulfilled specific artistic
needs.  Literally hundreds of thousands of copies of tunebooks in
fasola notation were sold,[11] and it remains popular today with ad-
herents of *Sacred Harp* and *Southern Harmony* singing.[12]

Subsequent to the success of fasola notation, the four-note system
of solmization gradually was supplanted by the currently used seven-
note method.  Again, the practical music masters over the nation
scrambled to develop a seven-note notational system, however unorthodox, which would be as popular, functional, and economically rewarding as was fasola.  Most of these systems utilized geometric shapes for
note heads, as does fasola, although some systems used numerals,
standard printing symbols, or other devices.[13]  Because of their vogue
at the time, Pound used two of these latter systems and the most important seven-note method in his *Songs for All with Supplement.*  For
probably the same reason, he used fasola and the best available seven-
shape system in *Vocal Triad.*

Of course, the basic system in *Vocal Triad* was standard notation
in which numerous compositions were printed.  The second form was
fasola, which at the time was extremely popular.  The third notation
was the seven shapes, which William Walker recently had adopted for
his *Christian Harmony*, abandoning the fasola of his *Southern Harmony.*  Obviously Pound hoped to cash in on the popularity of Walker's books, both in fasola and seven-shape notation.[14]  Thus we see a
practical, economically oriented approach: give each purchaser a little

---

[10]For additional information on fasola notation, see Jackson, p. 3 passim, and Loessel,
p. 22 passim.  See also "A New Notation," Chapter 6 in Richard Crawford, *Andrew
Law, American Psalmodist* (Evanston, Ill., 1968); and "The Easy Instructor," Chapter 6
in Lowens.

[11]Arthur L. Stevenson, *The Story of Southern Hymnology* (Salem, Virginia, 1931),
p. 17 passim, cites amazing publication data which he compiled from southern publishers, most of whom were shape-note purveyors.

[12]For a discussion of these two types of singing, see Glenn C. Wilcox, "American
Musical Tradition: Kentucky's Unique 'Big Singing'," *Bluegrass Music News* (official
magazine of the Kentucky Music Educators Association) 23, no. 4 (April-May 1972),
pp. 4-7.

[13]In the development of these various systems of notation and in the attempts to
sell the public on their use, one can see parallels to the phonograph recording industry
struggles in this century over speeds, sizes of records, and systems of recording and
reproducing stereophonic and four-part sound.  In all cases, great economic benefits
were and are at stake, not only in the marketplace, but also in royalties, prestige, and
industry leadership and recognition.

[14]Walker's *Southern Harmony* sold over 600,000 copies, according to the introduction to his *Christian Harmony* of 1866.  With Walker obviously expecting his followers
to change to the seven shapes he introduced in *Christian Harmony,* Pound was attempting to have the best of both worlds: fasola and Walker's seven shapes.

of what he wanted, whether that was standard, fasola, or a seven-shape notation, and thus insure a wide distribution and large sale.

The *magnum opus* of Pound was his *Songs for All* in its various configurations. At this writing, only three copies have been located, and each is of a different edition.[15] The original edition with an 1882 copyright is simply entitled *Songs for All.* The two later copies both are named *Songs for All with Supplement,* and both bear an 1885 copyright, but the later of these two copies has an additional section with a 1903 copyright. Except for the covers and title pages, all three copies are identical through page 352, which ends the original book. The two later copies are identical through page 480, which ends the 1885 copy, and the 1903 edition continues through page 584. The paper covers on the two *Supplement* copies are different colors, but this was a commonplace even with the same edition.

The unique properties of these books are derived from their notation. Pound uses four separate systems, then combines these with his own unorthodox development. He uses standard notation, Aiken's seven shapes, Hood's notation, and a late notational development of the Fillmores.

Jesse Aiken was one of the music masters who attempted to develop a seven-shape system to supplant the four shapes of fasola. In this he was quite successful and finally succeeded through various means, which apparently included intimidation and threatened lawsuit, in having his seven shapes adopted by all publishers of seven-shape music as the standard of the industry.[16] Thus, in using Aiken's seven shapes, Pound was quick to accept the new industry standard, adopted shortly before his publication.[17]

From their first publication in 1846 in Aiken's *Christian Minstrel* until today, literally millions of hymnbooks and tunebooks have been printed in Aiken's seven shapes. The importance of this system, which continues to be overlooked by musical pedagogues, is that except for the shapes of the note heads, notation remains completely standard. Thus, a "trained" musician reads such music simply by ignoring the shapes. However, an "untrained" musician, i.e., one who reads only shapes, can likewise read the music and perform it acceptably.

[15]The known single copies of the original publication and the 1885 copy with *Supplement* are in the library of the writer. The 1903 copy is in the Barnesville Carnegie Library.

[16]Jackson, p. 352, relates an amusing incident relative to the adoption of Aiken's seven shapes by the famed Ruebush-Kieffer Press. For the latter's official story on the adoption, see the "Author's Preface" in Aldine S. Kieffer, *The Temple Star* (Singer's Glen, Virginia, 1877). See also monthly issues of *Musical Million,* published by Ruebush-Kieffer.

[17]See Example 1.

John J. Hood received a copyright in 1880 for his notational system. It was first published in the *Quiver of Sacred Song* by John R.
Sweney and William J. Kirkpatrick and actually varies but little from
standard notation.[18] The only differences are that Hood uses either
lines or dots inside the note head to indicate which degree of the scale
is represented. His concept, as explained in the theoretical introduction to the *Quiver,* not only shows the degree of the scale, but also
is designed to show "proper" resolution of each tone to the next chord.
Of course, after explaining this, Hood immediately lists several exceptions to his rules, a problem common to all unorthodox systems
except Aiken's. Hood was one of the major publishers of the day,
so it is easy to see why Pound would want to utilize his rather popular
notation.

Upon the untimely death of their father, James H. Fillmore and his
younger brothers developed a small family enterprise into a major
publishing house. They progressed through several unorthodox notations in their publications, all of them numerically oriented. When
earlier systems were not readily accepted by the public, the Fillmores
showed their own pragmatism by moving to still another notation,
which is the one used by Pound. This employs numbers, here printed
inside the note head, corresponding to the degree of the scale.[19] This
system indicates the preoccupation of the Fillmores with numeral systems as opposed to shaped systems, but shows their willingness to
adapt as each method proved fallible. Each of these notations was in
vogue for a short period of time and was an obvious attempt at
achieving economic success while avoiding copyright royalties by developing their own method of notation.

In themselves, each of these systems is unorthodox, though not to
the extreme. However, when each of these is combined with Pound's
own staff and letter system, for which he was granted a copyright in
1884, the resultant notations are quite unusual.

In an oversimplification of Pound's system, we may state that each
line of his expanded staff represents a black key on the piano keyboard, and each space represents a white key.[20] Thus, at the incidence
of the natural half steps, we find wider white spaces to accommodate
the two white keys. In these cases, the higher of the two notes, F
or C, rests against the upper line enclosing the space. Similarly, the
lower note, either E or B, rests against the lower line enclosing the
space. Theoretically, if we know the piano keyboard, Pound's staff
can be read with alacrity.

---

[18]See Example 2.
[19]See Example 3.
[20]See Example 4.

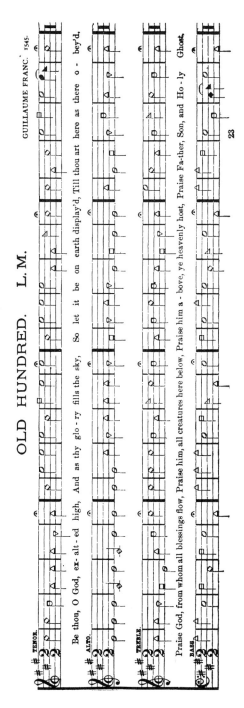

Ex. 1 Aiken's Notation, from Jesse B. Aiken, *The Imperial Harmony* (New York, 1876), p. 23.

Ex. 2 Diagram of Hood's Notation, from Edwin T. Pound, *Songs for All with Supplement* (Barnesville, Georgia, 1885), p. 401.

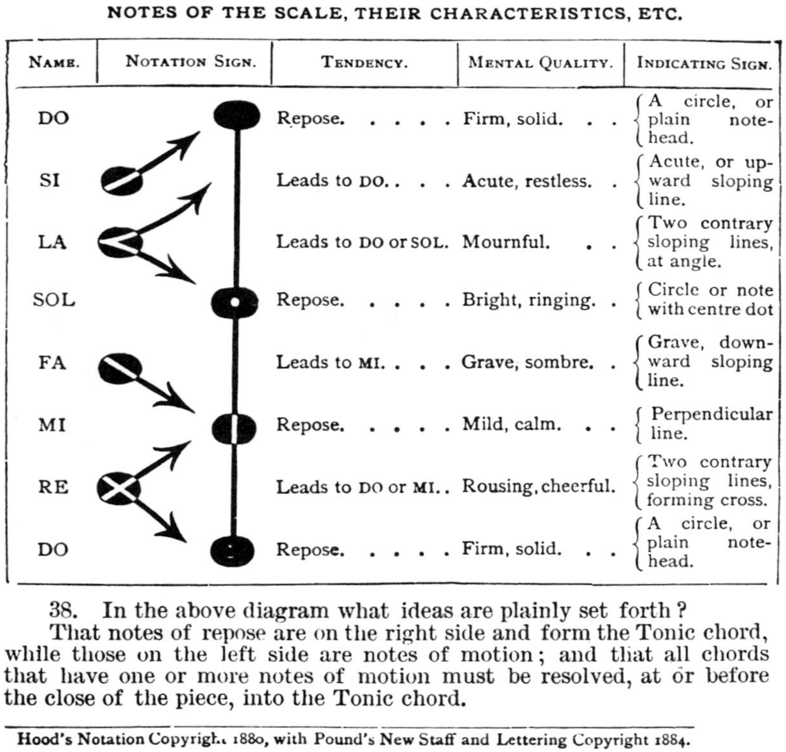

**NOTES OF THE SCALE, THEIR CHARACTERISTICS, ETC.**

| Name. | Notation Sign. | Tendency. | Mental Quality. | Indicating Sign. |
|---|---|---|---|---|
| DO | | Repose. . . . . | Firm, solid. . . | A circle, or plain note-head. |
| SI | | Leads to DO. . . . | Acute, restless. . | Acute, or upward sloping line. |
| LA | | Leads to DO or SOL. | Mournful. . . | Two contrary sloping lines, at angle. |
| SOL | | Repose. . . . . | Bright, ringing. . | Circle or note with centre dot |
| FA | | Leads to MI. . . . | Grave, sombre. . | Grave, downward sloping line. |
| MI | | Repose. . . . . | Mild, calm. . . | Perpendicular line. |
| RE | | Leads to DO or MI. . | Rousing, cheerful. | Two contrary sloping lines, forming cross. |
| DO | | Repose. . . . . | Firm, solid. . . | A circle, or plain note-head. |

38. In the above diagram what ideas are plainly set forth?

That notes of repose are on the right side and form the Tonic chord, while those on the left side are notes of motion; and that all chords that have one or more notes of motion must be resolved, at or before the close of the piece, into the Tonic chord.

**Hood's Notation Copyright 1880, with Pound's New Staff and Lettering Copyright 1884.**

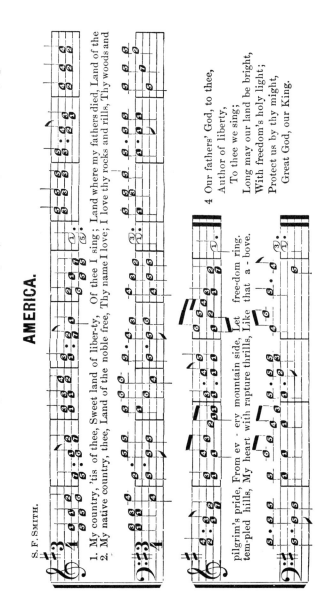

Ex. 3 Fillmores' Notation, from James H. Fillmore, *Songs of Gratitude* (Cincinnati, 1877), p. 23.

S. F. SMITH.

**AMERICA.**

1. My country, 'tis of thee, Sweet land of liber-ty, Of thee I sing; Land where my fathers died, Land of the
2. My native country, thee, Land of the noble free, Thy name I love; I love thy rocks and rills, Thy woods and

pilgrim's pride, From ev - ery mountain side, Let free-dom ring.
tem-pled hills, My heart with rapture thrills, Like that a - bove.

4 Our fathers' God, to thee,
Author of liberty,
To thee we sing;
Long may our land be bright,
With freedom's holy light;
Protect us by thy might,
Great God, our King.

Ex. 4 Plan of Pound's Twelve Letter Staff, from *Songs for All with Supplement*, title page.

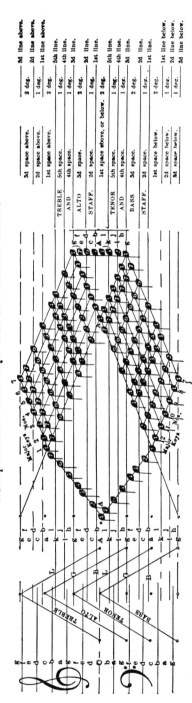

Ex. 5 Aiken's Notation with Pound's Staff and Lettering, from *Songs for All with Supplement*, p. 453.

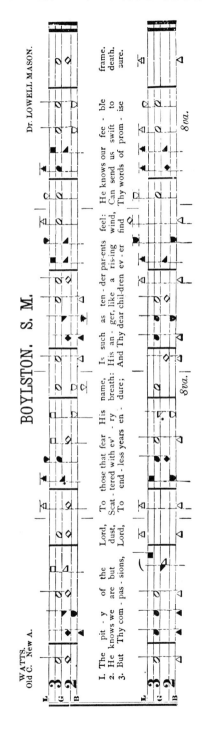

Ex. 6 Hood's Notation with Pound's Staff and Lettering, from *Songs for All with Supplement*, p. 427.

Ex. 7 Fillmores' Notation with Pound's Staff and Lettering, from *Songs for All with Supplement*, p. 476.

476

## IF FATHER WOULD ONLY COME SOBER.
### TEMPERANCE SONG.

MRS. E. C. ELLSWORTH.                                                                 CHAS. EDW. PRIOR.

1. If father would on-ly come so-ber, Poor mother no longer would cry; We'd watch till he came round the corner, But not from his presence to fly.
2. If father would on ly come so-ber, He'd see that we're hungry and cold, And that, to just keep us from starving, Most all that we had has been sold.
3. If father would on-ly come so-ber, I'd tell him how long mother sews; That pain in her side keeps her coughing, And paler and paler she grows.
4. If father would on-ly come so-ber, I think I could coax him to pray; Then Jesus would keep him from drinking, And we would be happy alway.

CHORUS.

O yes! if he'd on - ly come so - ber, How happy to-night we would be; My own dear pa - pa would be with us, Mam-ma, and wee Willie, and me.

Although Pound uses two staves in noting his tunes, a further refinement eliminates the F and G clef signs. Each of the two staves is identical, except that the lower is for male voices and the upper is for female voices. Hence, they are an octave apart. To help identify the lines and spaces, Pound places three of his "new" letter keys at the left of each staff.

These letters represent the final development of his system, that of key naming. No key signatures are used, as theoretically the position of the notes on the expanded staff shows whether a "white" or "black" key is to be sung, therefore obviating a key signature. Although he mentions the existence of minor keys and how to build them on his expanded staff, Pound does not illustrate them.

To "simplify" his notation, Pound replaced all "old" key letter names with "new" names, which are the letters from A through L. "Old" C major becomes "new" A, and each subsequent half-step receives the next letter in the alphabet, so that $C^\#/D^b$ becomes B, old D becomes new C, and so on to old B becoming new L. Consequently, in looking at the guide letters on each expanded staff, we find that they represent, in standard notation reading upward, $C^\#/D^b$, $G^\#/A^b$, and B. Pound makes no attempt to alter meter signatures or note values, which thus remain standard.

Even though he was a substantial citizen and apparently well-to-do economically, Pound seemingly was an opportunist who employed the hucksterism characteristic of so many of the itinerant singing masters of the nineteenth century. Thus, as a means of increasing his sales, he adapted his books to whatever was the current fashion in musical notation. Certainly he was willing to change and experiment as demands of his customers changed.

Summarizing, in the *Vocal Triad* we find standard and fasola notation and Walker's seven shapes. Twelve years later, with the publication of *Songs for All,* fasola and Walker's shapes were omitted—they were less popular then—but standard notation was joined by Aiken's seven shapes, just beginning to crest toward their ubiquitous popularity. With the subsequent appearance of *Songs for All with Supplement* we find the retention of the entire *Songs for All,* with its standard and Aiken's notations to which the *Supplement* adds music in Hood's, Fillmores', and Aiken's notations. These additions were not on standard staves, but were used on Pound's Twelve Letter Staff with his lettering and key system.[21] All three of these systems were well known and widely used, so that by using them to introduce his own system, which could be used as a complement to them, Pound

---

[21]See Examples 5-7.

was able to reach a much wider audience more quickly than he might otherwise do.

Additional comment might be made of the 1903 addition to *Songs for All with Supplement,* where none of the music is in Pound's, Hood's, or Fillmores' notational variants. Obviously these had not been well accepted, so Pound dropped them from this addition. However, all the music in the 1903 portion of the book is either in standard or Aiken's notation, indicating the industry-wide importance of the latter.

Thus, in the publishing career of one relatively obscure craftsman, a capsule summary of the publishing history of unorthodox musical notations may be traced.[22] From this cursory examination of Pound's largest work, with its eclecticism in authors and composers and its many notational systems in their varieties, it is apparent that Pound chose a literal title: truly it was a book of *Songs for All.*

Glenn C. Wilcox

---

[22]While our interest is primarily in his notation, Pound showed similar wide choices in the words and music for *Songs for All.* Approximately 123 different hymn sources are cited 255 times, and 87 composers are named 525 times. However, only five of these individuals appear in all sections of the three editions examined, exemplifying Pound's practical, commercial approach to publication.

# Henry Russell's
# American Experience*

Henry Russell (Levy), 1812-1900, was born in Sheepness, England, at a time when "Jews were [becoming] increasingly prominent in many callings besides that of financier which brought them into the public eye."[1] The stage and the concert hall increasingly constituted for them a sphere of successful activities. Yet it took another forty-six years to fully remove the so-called Jewish Disabilities, i.e., the barriers that excluded them from the complete exercise of civil and political rights—including membership in the House of Commons.[2]

As a boy singer Russell appeared in Christmas pantomimes and other musical show activities. He dedicated his vocal treatise L'Amico dei cantanti to young Princess Victoria. Italian maestros such as Donizetti and Rossini were his teachers. After his return from the continent, Russell found it difficult to apply his studies to professional activities in his home country. Thus he spent nine years almost continuously in the United States, and a few months in Canada, Central America, and Cuba. He started out as an organist and choir director in Rochester, New York, only to find his true inclination in the performance of popular songs, ballads, and descriptive songs (scenas, cantatas). These attained immediate recognition in America. Initial successes in Boston and New York helped to spread word of his fame to other large communities such as Philadelphia, Baltimore, New Orleans, Charleston, and Cincinnati. The lyrics of his compositions gained genuine popularity, too. Edgar Allan Poe considered "Woodman, Spare That Tree!" and "Near the Lakes" compositions of which any poet, living or dead, might justly be proud.[3] After a very successful career as a singer and entertainer, Russell retired from the concert

*Recognition must be given to Anna-Marie Ettel and to Peter Petzling for their assistance in this essay.
[1]Cecil Roth, A History of the Jews in England, 3rd ed. (Oxford, 1964), p. 243.
[2]Roth, pp. 241-66; and James Picciotto, Sketches of Anglo-Jewish History (London, 1875), pp. 394-401.
[3]Nelson F. Aekings, "George Pope Morris," Dictionary of American Biography (New York, 1937), 13: 207-8.

hall and settled in London as an opulent moneylender and broker.[4] The great popularity of Russell's songs is attested by the many public and private Russell collections in the country.[5]

\* \* \*

Russell managed to capture the American imagination. In looking at Russell's voluminous works, what stands out is his ability to capture the American musical imagination of the late 1830s. Partially this can be understood by looking at the types of songs Russell sang and composed. The basic taxonomy of his songs is: 1) emigration, 2) politics, 3) social climate and memory of heritage, and 4) lifestyle. In addition, one has to acknowledge the particular mode of presentation in which these songs were brought to the attention of the audience.

Following English and American, Dibdinian and Franklinian tradition, the overriding feature of Russell's songs was their simplicity, "when he gives the simple, fully round note, without any adornment excepting what it may receive from the pathos and feeling in which it is clad. His style is simple, chaste, unadulterated by modern fopperies —yet it is ornamental in the highest degree by its own peculiar attribute of simplicity."[6] Thus his simple, nonornamented, nonoperatic, ballad style of singing was hailed during his time as unrivaled by any English singer, Braham (another English-Jewish singer) alone excepted. Though some of the songs were narrative and descriptive poems of considerable length, they were delivered as clearly and intelligibly as if simply being recited. His enunciation was as distinct as if he were speaking.[7] The clearness, variety, and force of his musical declamation was entirely his own. It was coupled with his lifelong love of melody. In his autobiography he states:

> I can still give reasons which I think justify me in saying that melody has a power to the human heart in such a way as no other form of music can appeal. One stands awed in the presence of the mighty genius of Wagner, and one almost staggers at the profundity of a brain that could produce a "Tristan" or a "Parzifal," but on the other hand I have seen

[4]Goodman Lipkin, "Henry Russell," *The Jewish Encyclopedia* (New York and London, 1912), pp. 517-18.

[5]Some of these are the Lilly Library at Indiana University, Bloomington, Ind.; the Minnesota State Historical Society, St. Paul, Minn.; The Luther Thompson Collection, Forestville State Park, Wykoff, Minn.; and the Anna-Marie Ettel Collection, St. Paul, Minn.

[6]*New York Mirror and Ladies Literary Gazette* 20, no. 3 (January 1842): 14-15.

[7]Ibid.

a man, whose heart has been hardened by the influence of time and misfortune, melted to tears on hearing a melody which has recalled the associations of his youth, and reminded him, perchance, of the strength of a dead mother's love.[8]

Russell gave Americans music for the people. Part of Russell's popularity can be attributed to the fact that he loved audiences all his life, that he was always anxious to get at the multitudes, to address the crowds, and to be amongst the public, "who have loved me so well and treated me to far more kindness and generosity than I deserved."[9] He did give the audiences what they wanted:

We would suggest that a greater number of simple songs be included in the bills of fare. Much recitative is not generally pleasing, and a Boston audience will return home better satisfied with one simple ballad than with a dozen recitatives, decked out in ornament. This is the grand secret of Russell's success.[10]

It seems appropriate to infer that Russell gave Americans music for the people, music that answers simple and direct emotions, a "popular music which must be domestic, social music; in other words, 'music for the common heart.' "[11] The common heart beats in the breast of the common man, and it seems safe to say that the commoner was very much the preoccupation of Russell's social and musical imagination. How else should one understand his particular predilection for political campaign and the celebration of the central role that the commoner played in campaign. Russell's political songs were included in *The Log Cabin,* a Harrison songster (presidential campaign of 1840). For "The Brave Old Chief" (Ex. 1),[12] Russell uses the tune

Ex. 1 "The Brave Old Chief."

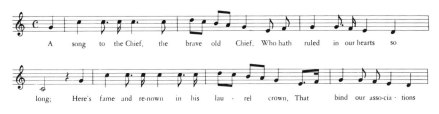

A song to the Chief, the brave old Chief, Who hath ruled in our hearts so long; Here's fame and re-nown in his lau - rel crown, That bind our asso-cia - tions

---

[8]Henry Russell, *Cheer! Boys, Cheer!* (London, 1895), pp. 253-54.
[9]Ibid., pp. 3-4.
[10]*Boston Morning Post,* 24 November 1840, p. 2.
[11]Henry Giles, "Music," *Graham's,* October, 1850, pp. 228-29.
[12]*The Log Cabin* was a weekly publication by Horace Greeley. This song appears in the issue of 26 June 1840, p. 4.

strong. There was strength in his blow, man-y years a - go. And Hon - or has long been his

due; For he show'd his might in the deep mid - night, On the field of old Tip - pe - ca -

noe! Then sing to the Chief, the brave old Chief, who stirs ev - ery bo - som a -

new; And hon - or'd be he, by the brave and free, Who con-quer'd at Tip - pe - ca - noe!

2. He ruled these fair climes, in the fearful times,
   When the Indian's fiendish howl
   Was heard in the wood, where the Log-Cabin stood,
   Exposed to his nightly prowl;
   On him we relied, our hope and our pride,
   And we banished our needless fear,
   Then hail him with cheers for hundreds of years,
   The Chief to our bosoms so dear
   Then sing to the Chief, the brave old Chief,
   Who fires every bosom anew.
   And honor'd be he, by the brave and free,
   Who conquer'd at 'Tippecanoe.'

of his own "The Brave Old Oak," published simultaneously in New York and Albany.

It may be asked if Russell's enthusiasm for politics, including presidential campaigns, bore any relationship to his feelings about the exclusion of Jews from the political process in England. Is it possible that his initial exposure to Henry Clay in Rochester, New York, was a particularly strong influence? That question can only be considered in a speculative manner, as Russell's own autobiography does not provide any clues as to his feelings about the yet unfinished Jewish emancipation in England. What might be said, however, is that the public sentiment of the late 1830s must have exercised a profound influence upon Russell, his political and social imagination. A short glimpse at Mrs. Sigourmey's text of "Washington's Tomb," set to music by Henry Russell, reveals the very conscious use of a Marseillaise-related theme in the final stanza of the song.

\*    \*    \*

Whether examining the aforementioned political songs or his emigration songs, unifying characteristics are to be seen in Russell's ability to trace and portray a sensibility that seems to be embedded in the prevailing social climate of post-Jacksonian American society. This is not to say that Russell necessarily understood and interpreted the public sensibility in all of its dimensions, but rather to assert that he excelled in catching and displaying the sentiment of an epoch. That epoch has been aptly characterized by Gilbert Chase with the metaphor of the cult of the fashionable.[13] Very clearly Russell was well endowed in this regard. The influence of the aforementioned Italian maestros allowed him to perform and create the kind of songs and ballads that could be grasped and consumed by the multitude of those "interested" in music—those who passively consume as listeners as well as actively participate in the experience of a sentiment, in short, those who engage in the act of *Mitvollzug*.[14] From this perspective it may in fact be possible to explain a somewhat unusual event that occurred during a recital of Russell's well-known "Woodman, Spare That Tree!" At the close of the concert, a gentleman got up and said excitedly, "Was the tree spared, sir?" "It was," said Russell. "Thank God for that!" the other answered with a sigh of heartfelt relief as he sat down again.[15] *Mitvollzug* may be a helpful concept in understanding the act of musical communication of which Russell was so capable.

"To the West," "Far, Far upon the Sea," and "Cheer! Boys, Cheer!" were songs that "induced many who were starving in their native land to turn their attention to emigration and to the bright promises held out by a new land, where flesh and blood were not so cheap and bread was not so dear."[16] The *ne plus ultra* of emigratory folklore is laid out in Russell's vocal and pictorial entertainment, entitled *The Far West, or the Emigrant's Progress from the Old World to the New*.[17] In it Russell shows his great affection of all things American. "In the States were spent the best years of my early man-

---

[13]Gilbert Chase, *America's Music from the Pilgrims to the Present*, 2d ed., (New York, 1966), p. 165.

[14]Carl Dahlhaus, "Trivialmusik und ästhetisches Urteil" in *Studien zur Trivialmusik des 19. Jahrhunderts*, ed. Carl Dahlhaus (Regensburg, 1967), p. 15.

[15]Harold Simpson, *A Century of Ballads 1810-1910* (London, [1910]), p. 131.

[16]Russell, p. 144.

[17]*Songs in Henry Russell's Vocal and Pictorial Entertainment entitled The Far West or The Emigrant's Progress from the Old World to the New* (London, [185–]).

hood and from the warmhearted Americans I have received many kindnesses, which my nature does not allow me readily to forget."[18] This publication consists of detailed accounts of the poor emigrants' adieu from their native land, with an exact list of provisions to be taken along; the ship's departure, with a description of the interactive assistance poor emigrants give to each other while crowded together amid all the inevitable discomfort of the vessel; and the activities of the emigrants while aboard the ship, including fiddle or flute music, dancing, and story telling: "many a bulletin of the great 'battle of life' has undoubtedly been communicated in these confidences of the Emigrant ship—the reminiscences rebound over a wide field, thus there are recollections of the lanes and alleys, and low suburbs of London—of the dreary and unenlightened life of the agricultural labourer, dwelling in a hovel not half so good as the wigwam of the Indian."[19] Russell quotes from Charles Dickens's *Martin Chuzzlewit*:

> There were English people—Irish people—Welsh people and Scotch people there, all with their little store of coarse food and shabby clothes, and nearly all with their families of children; there were children of all ages, from the baby at the breast to the slattern girl who was as much a grown woman as her mother. Every kind of domestic suffering that is bred in poverty, illness, banishment, sorrow and long travel in bad weather, were crammed into this little space, and yet was there infinitely less of complaint and querulousness, and infinitely more of mutual assistance and general kindness to be found in that unwholesome ark than in many brilliant ball rooms.[20]

"The eyes of the emigrant, at the arrival to New York have been regaled by a panoramic view of a bold and romantic, yet rich and highly cultivated country, wooded with trees equal in girth and massiveness to the finest of our park timber, and dotted alternately with comfortable farm-houses and the white villas of New York merchants and citizens."[21] Special discussions are devoted to New York, the North River, the Erie Canal, the rapids in the Niagara, the sublime peace-inspiring spectacle of the Falls of Niagara, the settlement in Ohio, the backwoods, the inundation, the rolling prairies, the sleigh, and letters from home. These accounts are interrupted by fitting songs such as "Farewell, A Last Farewell," "Cheer! Boys, Cheer!" "Far, Far upon the Sea," "Land! Land! Ho for the West!" "Niagara," and

---

[18]Russell, *Cheer!*, pp. 4-5
[19]Russell, *The Far West*, p. 11.
[20]Ibid., p. 12.
[21]Ibid., p. 14.

"Long Parted Have We Been." Two all-time favorites, "The Gambler's Wife" and "The Ship on Fire," conclude this musico-poetic-pictorial entertainment.

The preceding may in fact allow us to find a key to the understanding of Russell's creative talent and success, his musical rapport with a given audience that one might call the dialogical evocation of an experience or sentiment. He was a "pugilistic" performer delighted by individuals in the audience who responded directly to him, during or after a concert. The man who was driven to ask the fate of the tree is a dramatic underscoring of a communicative ability rare in the history of musical performers.

* * *

Russell composed around 800 songs, ballads, and descriptive songs (scenas, cantatas). The texts of the songs were provided by famous writers of the day. Among them were George Pope Morris, editor of the *New York Mirror and Ladies Literary Gazette* and of a collection of popular songs (texts only, called *American Melodies* [1841]); Epes Sargent, a popular American poet; Charles Mackay, an English poet and journalist; Eliza Cook, a prolific English poetess and editor of *Eliza Cook's Journal* (1849-1854); and others including Robert Burns, Charles Dickens, Henry Wadsworth Longfellow, Alfred Lord Tennyson, and William Thackeray.[22] Most of his songs were dedicated to prominent people. "Washington's Tomb" was dedicated to the Honorable Daniel Webster; "A Life on the Ocean Wave" to Fenimore Cooper; "The Free, The Free" to fellow singer Mr. Seguin. Vanity is constant, and his dedications could only result in increased interest in his music among the recipient's circle of friends.

Russell's songs were published in sheet-music form. Many of them were published with pictorial title pages. Lithography of music titles may have been considered a fleeting by-product of the commercialism of the period, an enticement used by publishers to enlarge their markets, but the pictorial record it left deserves a place in the history of

---

[22]Eliza Cook's poems as set to music by Russell include: The Old Arm Chair; The Heart That's True; I'm Afloat, I'm Afloat; The Old Clock; The Farm Gate; The Old Water Mill; I Love, I Love the Free; The Poor Man's Friend; The Indian Hunter; The Fisher Boy Merrily Lives. Charles Mackay's contributions to Russell's repertoire are: O' Sadly, Ye Dark Rolling Waves; Old Tubal Cain; Resignation; Rouse! Brothers, Rouse!; The Sea King's Burial; To the West! To the West! The Land of the Free!; The Founding of the Bell; Wind of the Night, Whence Comest; Our Way across the Mountains, Ho!; Some Love to Roam o'er the Dark Sea Foam; The Ship on Fire; Far, Far upon the Sea!; Come, Maidens, Come (Tyrolien); Cheer! Boys, Cheer!; *The Far West or The Emigrant's Progress from the Old World to the New*. George Pope Morris's poems set to music by Russell are: I Love the Night; Oh, This Love; The Chieftain's Daughter; Woodman! Spare That Tree!; Will Nobody Marry Me; Not Married Yet!; Old King Time; My Mother's Bible; The Soldier and His Bride; The Dismissed.

RIEDEL

American graphic art and today provides a remarkable insight to the scenes of over a century and a quarter ago. The Russell pictorial title pages are a part of this genre. John and William Pendleton of Boston, the first commercially successful lithographers in the United States, published the first pictorial music title cover with this new process in 1826. It was Anthony Philip Heinrich's "The Log House," and it initiated the era of lithographed pictorial titles which flourished for the succeeding five decades. Lithography provided an economic process for illustration in a prephotographic era, and music publishers were quick to realize the advantage of selling pictures with their music. It was a lure for the buying public, just as is today's visual advertising.

One of Russell's most enduring and popular songs, "Woodman! Spare That Tree!" copyrighted by Firth & Hall, 1837, was lithographed by Endicott of New York City. The vignette title page depicts a farmer, ax in hand, admonished by a gentleman to save that tree and includes a modest home and barn, open well, chickens, and a boat on a river. The thirteenth edition appeared with a variant illustration by Endicott, the vignette being replaced by an ornamental scrolled border.

The Pendletons and their successors, Thomas Moore, Benjamin W. Thayer, and John H. Bufford, are important in the history of American lithography not only for their prints, but also because they provided training and employment for aspiring young artists. The famous painter Winslow Homer (1836-1910) apprenticed with Bufford in the 1850s and drew a number of music covers highly prized today. Fitz Hugh Lane (1804-1865), renowned for his marine paintings, worked for the Pendletons in 1832 and in 1840 provided the cover of Russell's "The Mad Girl Song," published by Oakes & Swan and lithographed by Thayer, as well as the pictorial title for "The Maniac" published by Parker & Ditson.

Benjamin Champney began his apprenticeship in 1834 with the Pendletons and worked in Boston from 1838 to 1841 as a lithographic artist. Later, he became a portrait and landscape artist, known as the dean of the White Mountain landscapists. His drawing for Russell's "Rockaway" (1840) appeared in two variations printed by Thayer. Early attempts to use color in lithography employed a single tinted stone upon which the artist's drawing was printed from a second stone. The George P. Reed edition appeared with a rectangular pale yellow background, the William H. Oakes edition with the same scene printed on a beige octagonal background. Champey also drew the pictorial titles for Russell's "Old Farm Gate" (1840), "Old Sex-

ton" (1841), "Old Water Mill" (1841), and "We Were Boys Together" (1841). Both he and Fitz Hugh Lane, as well as anonymous
artists, drew pictorial covers for "The Old Arm Chair." It was an
immensely popular song, printed in at least twenty-three editions, but
the cover remained essentially unchanged, with Eliza Cooke, the poetess, gazing sadly on a vacant arm chair. A later London edition
lithographed by Stannard & Son replaced the poetess with an English
mother-and-daughter scene. Another popular song with poetry by Eliza
Cooke was the "Indian Hunter" with Thayer's lithograph of a wary
Indian, tomahawk in hand.

Robert Cooke was the chief draughtsman at Pendletons' in 1834,
an original and prolific artist. In 1840 he drew the cover for Russell's
"Fisher Boy Merrily Lives." Attaining success as a painter, he and his
friend Benjamin Champney left in 1841 to study in France, where he
died in 1843.

Russell's songs of the sea inspired dramatic title pages. "The Newfoundland Dog" (1843), copyrighted by J. L. Hewitt, was published
by Firth & Hall with a lithograph by Endicott. "The Ship on Fire"
was lithographed by Lewis & Brown of New York City in the first
American edition published by Atwill. Atwill also published the delightful "Not Married Yet!" (1841) with a tinted lithograph by G.
W. Lewis of New York City.

Evidence of Russell's popularity beyond the Alleghenies is indicated in a W. C. Peters & Co., Cincinnati publication of "The Spider
and the Fly" (1844), embellished with a pictorial title page by an
unidentified lithographer.

* * *

Russell's melodies use motives common to melodies all over the
world. The phrase of his "Rouse! Brothers, Rouse!" (Ex. 2) is similar to the first phrase of the German folk song "Wohlauf in Gottes
schöne Welt!" (Ex. 3).[23]

The Rossini-inspired "Woodman! Spare That Tree!" (Ex. 4)
melody runs parallel with the German folk-lullaby "Schlaf, Kindchen,
Schlaf" (Ex. 5).

Russell's "My Heart's in the Highlands" (Ex. 6) and "The Soldier
and His Bride" (Ex. 7) show the same melodic outline as the German song "Ich hab mich ergeben" (Ex. 8) of Brahms's *Academic
Overture* fame.

Russell's melodies use many simple motives that can be easily
remembered and associated. The same motives occur in many different

---

[23]All musical examples have been transposed to the key of C major.

### Ex. 2 "Rouse! Brothers, Rouse!"

### Ex. 3 "Wohlauf in Gottes schöne Welt!"

### Ex. 4 "Woodman! Spare That Tree!"

### Ex. 5. "Schlaf, Kindchen, Schlaf."

### Ex. 6 "My Heart's in the Highlands."

### Ex. 7 "The Soldier and His Bride."

### Ex. 8 "Ich hab mich ergeben."

Ex. 9 "The Heart That's True."

Ex. 10 "Oh Weep Not, Oh Weep Not."

Ex. 11 "The Old School House."

Ex. 12 "I'm Afloat, I'm Afloat."

Ex. 13 "To the West! To the West! To the Land of the Free!"

Ex. 14 "The Gambler's Wife."

Ex. 15 "The Old Arm Chair."

Ex. 16 "The Newfoundland Dog."

Ex. 17 "My Mother's Bible."

Ex. 18 "Resignation."

Ex. 19 "I Love to Dwell in the Bosom's Cell."

Ex. 20 "Cheer! Boys, Cheer!"

Ex. 21 "The Heart That's True."

Ex. 22 "I Love, I Love the Free."

Ex. 23 "The Chieftain's Daughter."

Ex. 24 "I'm Afloat, I'm Afloat."

Ex. 25 "Some Love to Roam o'er the Dark Sea Foam."

Ex. 26 "Rockaway."

Ex. 27 "Our Way across the Mountain, Ho!"

Ex. 28 "The Emigrant's Farewell."

Ex. 29 "The Minstrel of Tyrol."

Ex. 30 "The Sea King's Burial."

Ex. 31 "We Have Been Friends Together."

Ex. 32 "Not Married Yet."

Ex. 33 "The Fisher Boy Merrily Lives."

songs. One discovers a motive that descends by step in "The Heart That's True" (Ex. 9), "Oh Weep Not, Oh Weep Not" (Ex. 10), and "The Old School House" (Ex. 11).

The simple motive of descending thirds ignited reactions of audiences. It occurs in "I'm Afloat, I'm Afloat" (Ex. 12), "To the West! To the West! To the Land of the Free!" (Ex. 13), and "The Gambler's Wife" (Ex. 14).

The simplest of any possible melodic elaborations, a repeated tone pattern occurs in "The Old Arm Chair" (Ex. 15), "The Newfoundland Dog" (Ex. 16), and "My Mother's Bible" (Ex. 17).

Like the German nineteenth-century composers of popular music, Russell gives preference to the intervals of the sixth and seventh.[24] The sixth is reached (1) through the third of the subdominant chord in "Resignation" (Ex. 18), "I Love to Dwell in the Bosom's Cell" (Ex. 19), and "Cheer! Boys, Cheer!" (Ex. 20); (2) through a sus-

[24]Hermann Rauhe, "Zum volkstümlichen Lied des 19. Jahrhunderts," in *Studien zur Trivialmusik des 19. Jahrhunderts*, pp. 159-98.

pension before the fifth of the tonic (6-5 cadences) in "The Heart That's True" (Ex. 21), "I Love, I Love the Free" (Ex. 22), and "The Chieftain's Daughter" (Ex. 23); (3) through a melodic climax-tone in "I'm Afloat, I'm Afloat" (Ex. 24); (4) through a melodic anti-climax tone in "Some Love to Roam o'er the Dark Sea Foam" (Ex. 25); (5) through a nonaccentuated skip in "Rockaway" (Ex. 26); (6) through an accentuated skip in "Our Way across the Mountain, Ho!" (Ex. 27) and "The Emigrant's Farewell" (Ex. 28); and (7) as a part of a triadic chord in "The Minstrel of Tyrol" (Ex. 29). Russell treats the seventh (1) as an accentuated leading tone in "The Sea King's Burial" (Ex. 30); and (2) as a tritone in "We Have Been Friends Together" (Ex. 31).

The interval of the ninth is reached (1) through a succession of thirds in "Not Married Yet" (Ex. 32); and (2) as a dotted yodler interval in "The Fisher Boy Merrily Lives" (Ex. 33).

*  *  *

It is important to note that Russell's commemorative songs of reminiscence and nostalgia are escapist songs.[25] They do not glorify a past social or cultural period, but rather one of natural beauty and simplicity in the lost days of youth. In only one category might some of the songs be thought of as cultural primitivism: those which glorify the life of the Indian and his harmony with nature. The Indian that

---

[25]Russell exploited the public tendency to indulge in poetic and musical nostalgia. He seemed to revel in productions that had the scent of the old about them. He was very effective with songs such as "The Fine Old English Gentleman," "The Old Clock," "The Old Farm Gate," "The Old Night-Cap," "The Old Schoolhouse," "The Old Watermill," "The Old Armchair," "The Old Bell," "The Old Sexton," etc.

But music critics pitched their standards of taste too high when they criticized some of Russell's "old whatever" settings! Two stanzas from a poem entitled "The Old Pipe" read:

> How RUSSELL got thee, thereby "hangs a tale;"
> Conjecture whispers, but conjecture lies.
> He purchased thee in Venice—at a sale—
> From an old gypsy, on "the bridge of sighs."
> He puff'd away and moralizing thought,
> If this pipe's worth a sous, MY PIPE'S worth more;
> From this old gypsy I have wisdom bought—
> I'll tune MY PIPE upon another shore,
>                                Poor old Pipe!
>
> He quit the land of poesy and song,
> Without a sigh to heave or tear to wipe;
> How many a FREE-BORN maiden's ear hath hung
> Resistless on the music from his pipe!
> Thou'rt useless now—the tube is out of tune,
> Like an old harpsichord, or chordless harp—
> Therefore I'll give thee, as a friendly boon,
> (And let him smoke it, if he can) to Sharpe,
>                                Poor old pipe!

appears in Russell's "The Indian Hunter" is genteel, like the praying heroic "Chieftain's Daughter." The Indians are really a paradigm evocation of Rousseau's noble savage and the basis, to some extent, for the hero that later emerged as "The American Adam" figure in literature. In his "Cheer! Boys, Cheer!" Russell describes the Indian in his natural habitat in the forest in the best Fenimore Cooper fashion.[26] In "The Soldier and His Bride," Russell and Morris, however, cannot hide their debt to white frontier society by cursing the red man for having slain the soldier McRea and his bride.

The presence of this yearning for bygone days may account, too, for moralizing intentions that often accompany Russell's songs. Some are concerned with the abolition of social sores in England and America. He claimed to have helped abolish slavery through the medium of some of his songs. Yet in his *Panorama of Negro Life, in Freedom and in Slavery*, Russell incorporated blatant racist elements; the Negro is described as a "merry and light hearted people; little given to thinking . . . and with a strong disposition for making the best out of a bad job. Thus the dread of the whip tomorrow will never prevent them from being merry tonight, and the strong sense of humor, or perhaps rather of a certain peculiar drollery which they possess— bursts out at all times and places, quite regardless of external depressing circumstances."[27]

The question we finally face is what was the structure of social perception that sustained and mediated the vast array of Russell's musical communication? Is it possible to ask, joining Leo Löwenthal,[28] if insight and entertainment were joined in Russell's work and conversely if they were related in the musical-social public sphere of that very time? Did Russell just entertain a mass audience, playing on their sentimentality and trivializing their experience, or did he communicate to so-called elites as well as a multitude of listeners significant insights that illuminated their present lives and their recollection of times past?

Through his descriptive songs we can give a tentative answer to those questions.[29] Through a song such as "The Maniac," Russell created an aesthetic form that communicated equally an emotional reality and a cognitive insight that had a significant truth value in

---

[26]Russell, *Cheer!*, p. 159.

[27]See introduction to Henry Russell's vocal and pictorial entertainment entitled *Negro Life, in Freedom and in Slavery* (London, [185–]).

[28]See Leo Löwenthal, *Literature, Popular Culture and Society* (Englewood Cliffs, N.J., 1961), p. xix.

[29]Russell's descriptive songs include "The Maniac," "The Gambler's Wife," "The Newfoundland Dog," "The Ship on Fire," "Wind of the Winter Night," and "Whence Comest Thou?"

the ear of the listener. This ability then to aesthetically "form" social and human truths through music does provide a basis for evaluating the *oeuvre* of Henry Russell. His autobiography gives an additional subjective cue in that he states that "music is never employed better than when it is made the medium of thought and ideas which are elevating to humanity at large."[30] It seems that this message is one for the "many" as well as for the sophisticated few. It tells something basic about the human conditions of that time; this could perhaps happen only in America in the 1830s, and it helps to explain Russell's lifelong enthusiasm toward his American experience.

Johannes Riedel

---

[30]Russell, *Cheer!*, pp. 251-52.

# Dreams of Death and Life: A Study of Two Songs by Johannes Brahms

In his essay "Brahms the Progressive" Arnold Schoenberg[1] draws attention to the style elements of Brahms's music that point to the future. Not only the richness of his harmonic vocabulary but his "direction toward an unrestricted musical language" are significant. Schoenberg specifies this by quoting asymmetry, combination of phrases of different length, rhythmic shifts, and fusion of diversified musical ideas. However, inventiveness and inspiration are only briefly mentioned and hardly anything is said about the emotional element in Brahms's music. Emotion and Romanticism are prevalent in the songs, though balanced by intellectual processes. The spectrum of Brahms's lyric expression is very wide, from folklike simplicity, playfulness, and humor to deep seriousness, resignation, and melancholy. In the later years of his life sombre moods prevailed, culminating in his last vocal work, the *Vier ernste Gesänge,* op. 121.

Two songs in which the text deals with man's ultimate destiny—death—are the subject of this study: "Der Tod, das ist die kühle Nacht" (Death is the cool night) and "Immer leiser wird mein Schlummer" (My slumber becomes lighter).

\* \* \*

In the summer of 1884 Brahms completed his opus 96, a group of four songs that were published by N. Simrock, Berlin, two years later. Three texts are by Heinrich Heine, the great poet, and one by G. F. Daumer. Brahms composed fifty-four songs to the verses of this Bavarian clergyman, who has no standing in German literature and would be entirely forgotten were it not for Brahms's music. The poem of the first song, "Der Tod, das ist die kühle Nacht," is taken from Heine's cycle *Heimkehr* (Return to home), published in 1823. Two short stanzas consist of four lines each, varying in metrical

---

[1] *Style and Idea* (New York, 1950), p. 52.

structure. Rhymes occur only between the first and last lines of each strophe.

In the beginning of the poem the contrast between death as cool night and life as oppressive day is stated in general. The personal application of this antithesis follows. Darkness approaches, the poet becomes tired of the day (life), and he falls asleep. In his dream he experiences the vision of a tree in which a young nightingale sings of pure love. The song seems to be audible in the dream, but in the music the return to despondency is expressed.

The song consists of two approximately equal parts (13 versus 14 bars) with an added postlude of 4 measures. Strophic construction is absent. Two main elements comprise the melodic material. The first, associated with night (death), stresses the rhythm ♪ ♩ in the piano and the ascending line e' f#' a' c''.[2] It is two bars long and is complemented by a more contoured second phrase of the same length, representing the day. After a short initial upward trend, it descends in diatonic intervals to c'. The entire day-motive is played by the piano, consisting of two segments, the initial neighbor note (*a*) and the cadential ending (*b*).

Ex. 1  Johannes Brahms, "Der Tod, das ist die kühle Nacht," mm. 4-6.

Here the sonority is dense (oppressive), since the melodic line, reinforced by thirds, is doubled in both hands of the piano. The range is one octave c'-c''. Chromatically ascending piano chords in the "night" rhythm from c' to g' open the second segment of the first part (bars 6 to 11). This chromaticism was foreshadowed by the diminished seventh chord in bar 2. The voice line is interrupted by rests punctuating the text (drowsiness) and giving it a declamatory character. More contoured is the last part of the first stanza where the day-motive returns, this time in minor, ending on the dominant key G major. Remarkable is the difference between the static harmony in the first part and the increasing harmonic rhythm and variety of chords in the second, where melody and bass move in contrary directions.

The dream vision of the second stanza is ingeniously characterized. The piano accompaniment moves abruptly into a very high range. The dynamic level increases gradually from *p* to *f*. In the right hand the night rhythm is combined with the chromatic chord pro-

---

[2]The Edition Peters, *Brahms Album*, Band 1, for high voice has been used here.

gressions, this time descending. The three last chords outline the initial neighbor notes of the day motive (*a*) in chords and augmented rhythm (bars 18, 19). The left hand plays arpeggiated chords in sixteenth notes over pedalpoints (on G, later C), indicating the unreality of the apparition. In the voice line, the intervals of the beginning of the night-motive, now transposed to g' a' c'' d'', are combined with the jubilant cadential section of the day-motive (*b*), which is sequenced and soars to a'', the climax of the whole song. Bars 18 and 19 again outline the intervals of the beginning e'' f#'' a''. The piano twice intones alone the cadential *b* as it appeared in the melody four bars earlier, now scalewise descending. Words and music of bars 18, 19, and 20 are repeated a third lower in condensed form, asserting the importance of the dream. Then the dynamic level drops suddenly and the tessitura becomes low again; the sixteenth notes in the bass disappear. The accentuated words "Ich hör' es" (I hear it) in the voice (bar 23) refer to bar 10 (mich schläfert).

For the last line of the poem the day-motive is chosen. The piano has it twice in its entirety, first above a dominant ninth chord on G, then after a short halt on the tonic ⁶₄ chord, in the subdominant region. The harmonization shows seventh chords instead of triads, and the setting is different. The reinforcements of the melody in doubled thirds are thinned out, first to a single doubling at the tenth, second to octaves. The pedalpoints on G, later on C, continue to the end. The voice first states the second part of the day-motive, then after a rest, only the cadential ending (*b*) a fourth higher in ethereal softness to the last words "sogar im Traum."

In the four bars of the postlude the motion dies down. We hear twice the head-motive (*a*) of the "opressive day" supported once by the harmonies of a plagal cadence—identical with those of the prolongations in bars 18-19—then by the dominant ninth chord. The rhythm of the night-motive is intermittently used in the bass. Quiet, sonorous major triads on C may indicate the redeeming peace of sleep or death.

* * *

Dreams and thoughts of death also dominate the second song of this study: "Immer leiser wird mein Schlummer." It is the second in a group of five comprising Brahms's op. 105. Written in September 1886, it was printed in 1889 by Simrock along with the four others. Hermann v. Lingg, the author of the text, was a Bavarian army surgeon who published a book of verses in 1855. This poem is the only one by Lingg that Brahms set to music. Each of the two stanzas consists of seven trochaic verses. Four metrical feet are the rule; however, the

third and last lines are shorter (3), the concluding verse of the first
stanza longer (5). The shorter lines necessitate word repetitions in the
music. These appear also at the end of each strophe for greater emphasis. Three rhymes in seven verses show the following scheme:
*aabcbbc.*

Premonition of death and longing for the beloved are the core of
the poem. Again dream is involved as the grieved maiden imagines
she hears the voice of her lover. She awakes and weeps bitterly as her
hope remains futile. The certainty of her impending death before
spring and the thought that she will be forgotten and betrayed by her
lover leads to an impassioned plea that he may soon come to see her
once more. This imploration, perhaps in vain, ends the poem. Brahms
uses the varied strophic form, but the parts that literally return are ingeniously shifted. Every stanza consists of three parts—different in
organization—and piano accompaniment. The first segment (bars
1-9) may be subdivided into two equal phrases of 2½ measures plus
a smaller phrase for the third line that is partly repeated in prolongation. Here the piano doubles the voice part, adding lower sixths to
the unison. The bass fills in the space between the dotted notes of
the melody with broken octaves resulting in continuous eighth-note
motion, similar to the complementary rhythms of Baroque style. In
the second section (bars 10-14) two shorter melodic phrases (two
bars each) are accompanied by a repeated independent counter motive
in the piano, beginning with arpeggios. In bars 15-24, the melody
is dissolved in small fragments, interrupted by rests. Only the last
verse, partially repeated in prolongation, shows more continuity. Syncopated chords in the right hand and arpeggios in the bass form the accompaniment without doubling the melody.

The organization of the varied strophic form is intricate and best
shown by the diagram on pages 232 and 233.

The first phrase is used three times in the second strophe (bars
24-33) compared with only two appearances in the first. It is first
played by the piano alone, then exactly repeated as in the first stanza,
and the third time modified. Also the closing of the segment shows
melodic and harmonic differences though the partial repetition of the
words is retained (bars 34-36). Segment 2 literally returns (bars
37-41) along with the first two bars of the closing part. The harmony
then changes and the last line is more prolongated than in the first
strophe.

The melodic phrases in this song are mostly descending, reflecting
the sombre mood. The first opens with a cambiata figure and then
proceeds downward scalewise for a fifth. The rhythm of dotted-

quarter-notes-plus-eighths is sustained. The accents fall on nonharmonic tones (appoggiaturas). As often in Brahms's songs, the musical thought is primary and does not always coincide with the prosodic accent. So the last word of this phrase, *Schlummĕr*, sounds *Schlummēr* as the end syllable is stressed for musical reasons. Max Friedlaender has pointed out the similarity of this and the cello theme in the middle movement of the second piano concerto.[3] However, character and content are different.

Rhythmic prolongation at the repeated words has already been mentioned. So the end of the first phrase appears later augmented and interrupted.

Ex. 2 Johannes Brahms, "Immer leiser wird mein Schlummer," mm. 2-3, 7-10.

The scalewise descending of the main phrase is widened to a triadic fall when it closes the stanzas. Fragmentation of the melody in the penultimate verse consists of three sequences of ascending thirds interrupted by rests. In the first strophe the sequences are descending (on c'', b♭' and a'), in the second ascending (on c'', e♭'' and f#'') to reach the melodic climax of the whole song.

Treatment of harmony varies throughout. Slow harmonic rhythm prevails at first. The first segment does not leave the key (F minor) and cadences on the tonic. Modulation to the relative major (A♭) by diatonic progression occurs in the next section. Brahms reserved the most remarkable chord progressions for the last parts of the stanzas. There are three plagal cadences in sequence beginning on $\frac{6}{4}$ chords. They lead in the first strophe to G♭, F♭, and E♭ major, from where the harmony returns to the tonic F minor. In the second stanza, only non-cadential $\frac{6}{4}$ chords arranged in mediant relationship on C♭, D, and F are followed by extended cadences in the main key. Here the chords are not only used functionally but also in equal intervallic distances, a very progressive device. No wonder that Elisabeth von Herzogenberg, to whom Brahms sent the song (first performed by Hermine Spies), complained about the "cruel" *Quartsextakkords* in her letter of 2 December 1886 to the composer.[4] Even today they sound very daring.

Two remarks about the performance practice of this song may be added. Brahms prescribed *Langsam und Leise* (slowly and softly). There is no difference of opinion about the dynamic level. It is very

[3]Max Friedlaender, *Brahms's Lieder*, trans. C. Leonard Leese (London, 1928), p. 176.
[4]Johannes Brahms, *Briefwechsel*, ed. Max Kalbeck, (Berlin, 1912), 2: 130-34.

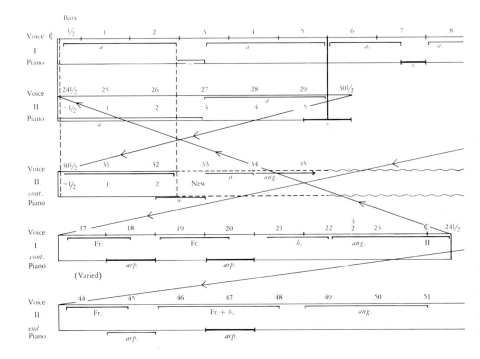

The exactly repeated bars match horizontally and vertically.

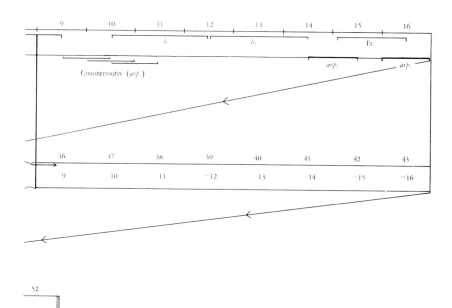

low throughout, mostly *pp* even with diminuendos, except for one dramatic outburst (one forte bar), which immediately recedes, at the climax of the stanza. The slow tempo, however, is modified by the *alla breve* notation ¢ . Dr. Eusebius Mandyczewski, Brahms's personal friend and *adlatus*, stated[5] that the composer complained about the custom, even generally practiced today, of taking the tempo too slow. The lilting rhythm of the melody does not permit dragging.

Economy of the thematic material and its adaptation by only slight changes to a great variety of nuances show the composer's mastery. Subtle relations between motives and complete integration of melody, harmony, and setting provide unity. All intellectual devices, however, are only means to achieve perfect musical expression of the emotional and spiritual content of the poems. Hence the indelible impression of Brahms's songs. Max Reger eloquently formulated his thoughts about the composer's greatness, writing in 1907: "What guarantees immortality to Brahms . . . is the fact that he was able to produce new undreamed of spiritual moods on the basis of his own individual spirit."[6]

Paul A. Pisk

---

[5]In a personal conversation with me.
[6]Quoted in Karl Hasse, *Max Reger,* Die Musik, Sammlung illustrierter Einzeldarstellungen, 42-44 (Leipzig, [1921]), p. 211.

# PART V

# The Habitat of Homing Melody

Homing melody is the most un-European contribution of the blues to the music of this country. Until recently any music produced here, whether by white musicians or black, has been put down as crumbs from the groaning board of Western, that is to say European, Civilization. The question of how the blues stands out is a real one.

Much has been made of the fact that the typical blues melody consists of three phrases of four measures each. But so does "Silent Night," as Western a tune as there ever was. Conceived on Christmas eve, 1818, for performance with guitar,[1] Franz Grüber's carol spread from the Austrian Tyrol throughout Christendom. It was acceptable and unexceptionable, an example of the "dreiteilige Periode," included by Hugo Leichtentritt under regular phrase structures.[2] The chief distinction of the blues is not its phraseology.

The form embodied in the twelve-measure period, *a a b,* is often underlined. Yet this was the mainstay of the trouvères in their ballades and of the minnesingers in their lovesongs. In fact the German passion for the *a a b* "Bar form" sets an entire scene of *Die Meistersinger* rolling with Wagnerian laughter.[3] The chief distinction of the blues is not its form.

Admittedly the harmonic progression usual in the blues is of the purest European derivation. As a matter of fact I-IV-I-V-I is identical with the first five chords of the *passamezzo moderno,*[4] part of the small change of Western harmony since the sixteenth century. It is because this ubiquitous formula is fundamental that such common airs as "Way down upon the Swanee River" and Dvořák's "Humoreske" combine mellifluously. The chief distinction of the blues is not its harmony.

From the point of view of the major scale, which dominated early Tin Pan Alley, certain scale degrees appeared to be strangely flattened in the practice of blues musicians. But these "blue" notes have always

---

[1] *The Hymnal 1940 Companion,* 3rd ed. rev. (New York, 1951), p. 27.
[2] Hugo Leichtentritt, *Musikalische Formenlehre,* 3rd ed. enl. (Leipzig, 1927), p. 15.
[3] Richard Wagner, *Die Meistersinger von Nürnberg,* Act III, sc. 1.
[4] Lawrence H. Moe, "Passamezzo, pass'e mezzo," *Harvard Dictionary of Music,* 2d ed. rev. and enl. by Willi Apel (Cambridge, Mass., 1969), pp. 646-47.

been welcome in the world of English folk song. Maud Karpeles's figures show that approximately half the tunes published by Cecil Sharp flat the seventh degree, and forty percent of them the third degree as well.[5] The charm of the old favorite, "Gently, Johnny, my Jingalo," lies precisely in its "flatted" seventh degree.[6] And the most widely diffused tune of fifteenth-century Europe, "L'homme armé," flats both seventh and third,[7] if one is allowed to project major-mode terminology on the chief scale of the Middle Ages, the Dorian mode. To the extent that the true blue seventh and the true blue third are not an exact half-step below their well-tempered major equivalents, they invest the music with a special flavor. Still, the chief distinction of the blues is not its scale degrees.

The chief distinction of the blues, above all else, is homing melody. In the most characteristic blues every phrase comes to rest on the same note, and not always from the same direction. This is homing melody. In other words all the cadences are closed, unrelieved by any open cadences on the way. This is one of the rarest phenomena in the musics of the world.

Countless melodies are in the *a a b* form—before and after "Ja nuns hons pris," the prison song of Richard the Lion-Hearted (1157-1199).[8] But they usually pause on half cadences along the way. In this ballade, for example, although each of the three sections ends on the same note, each pauses in the middle on a neighbor of that note.

True homing melody is different. All the stops are full stops—no commas, just periods. The best-known example of its genre, W. C. Handy's "St. Louis Blues," contains two homing melodies. The introduction and the middle strain are not in a blues vein at all, concentrating rather on powerful dominant-seventh cadences, eight-measure phraseology, and the rhythmic pattern of the habanera or tango. But the first strain, "I hate to see," is the very essence of the blues.[9]

Not only a homing melody, it is also a tethered melody, a melody that comes back to the principal note several times within a single phrase. Unlike the rather heavy tethered melodies of César Franck, this one is beautifully balanced. Within the span of ten notes the principal note appears three times, each time approached from a different degree of the scale.

---

[5] Maud Karpeles, "Folk Music: English," *Grove's Dictionary of Music and Musicians,* 5th ed., 3 (1954): 231.
[6] Beatrice Landeck, comp., *Songs My True Love Sings* (New York, 1946), pp. 16-17. In this version "The parson's near at hand."
[7] Willi Apel, "L'Homme armé," *Harvard Dictionary of Music,* p. 467.
[8] A. T. Davison and Willi Apel, *Historical Anthology of Music* (Cambridge, Mass., 1946), 1:16.
[9] W. C. Handy, ed., *A Treasury of the Blues* (New York, 1949), pp. 71-72.

It is impossible to provide a recipe for beautiful melody, but some of the loveliest, in very disparate cultures, employ this multiple approach to the tone that tethers. A classic example is William Byrd's "Non vos relinquam orphanos" (I will not leave you comfortless) (Ex. 1).

Ex. 1 William Byrd, "Non vos relinquam orphanos."[10]

Non   vos   re - lin - quam   or - pha - nos   al - le - lu - - - - -ia.

Like the first, the final strain of "St. Louis Blues," "Got de St. Louis Blues," is both homing and tethered, but there is ragtime as well as blues in its ancestry.[11] A formula of a few notes (three in this case) is repeated in such a way as to wrench its rhythm, making the tethered effect a restless one.

Handy's "Beale Street Blues" and "Memphis Blues" (called the first written blues) are among others that display homing melody.[12] On this street and in this city lies perhaps the only public park dedicated to a native American musician. Surely Handy was a city man, but his "Friendless Blues" shows his indebtedness to the folk-blues of the countryside.[13] In his anthology he precedes this with its original, the quartet version of "Got no mo' home dan a dog," which he knew as a teenager back in his native town of Florence, Alabama, about 1890.[14] The framework is clearly that from which the blues developed. As in all the homing melodies discussed so far, the home note arrives at the midpoint of the phrase on the downbeat of the third measure. This note, if nothing is done to it, lasts full two measures. Therefore, from the earliest examples of the blues, a break of some kind is added, either a shout, a snatch of singing, or an instrumental flourish. Thus although each phrase comes home, the effect is not just what Abbe Niles calls "three short hops."[15] The break fills in the space between hops, bringing it closer at least to "one sustained flight." "Got no mo' home dan a dog" is content with the simplest of breaks, just the word "Lawd" on one or two additional chords.

Turning to strict country blues, among those from the Mississippi delta presented by Samuel Charters in the first volume of *The Blues-*

[10]Davidson and Apel, 1: 164.
[11]Handy, p. 74.
[12]Ibid., pp. 102-5, 60-63.
[13]Ibid., pp. 55-57.
[14]Ibid., p. 52.
[15]Abbe Niles quoted in Handy, p. 12.

*men* are some impressive homing melodies, including Charley Patton's "Down the Dirt Road Blues," Son House's "Depot Blues," and Sam Collins's "Signifying Blues."[16] In the first of these (Ex. 2) not only all the phrases of the melody proper but also the exclamatory breaks are homing.

Ex. 2 Charley Patton, "Down the Dirt Road Blues."[17]

The classical paradigm of the blues and of homing melody is "Joe Turner."[18] Discussing this "grandfather" of the genre, Abbe Niles writes, "All early blues may have been merely conscientious renditions of *Joe Turner*."[19] This old black American tune was long a favorite throughout the South. Its balance of unity and variety is unexcelled. Since it is a homing melody, the last note is the same in each of the three phrases. On the other hand this final note is approached in three different ways. First it completes a falling triad (G-E-C), then a cadence characteristic of the blues (D#-E-C), and lastly a cadence falling by steps (E-D-C).

"Joe Turner" served as the tune for every imaginable kind of text before it appeared in print. It provided the basis for W. C. Handy's "Joe Turner Blues" (1915) and for many arrangements including one by Elie Siegmeister in *A Treasury of American Song*.[20]

But surely the birth of homing melody did not take place along with the birth of the blues. It must have antecedents trailing back into the distant past. Unless something in the special lifestyle of our own

---

[16]Samuel Charters, *The Bluesmen* (New York, 1967), 1:51-52, 67-68, 124-25.

[17]Ibid., p. 52. Copyright 1967 by Oak Publications, A Division of Embassy Music Corporation. All rights reserved. Used by permission.

[18]The melody is given in Eileen Southern, *The Music of Black Americans: A History* (New York, 1971), p. 335.

[19]Abbe Niles quoted in Handy, p. 15.

[20]Olin Downes and Elie Siegmeister, *A Treasury of American Song,* 2d ed. rev. and enl. (New York, 1943), p. 374.

Afro-Americans led them to invent it, they must have got it some-where, and it seems eminently non-European. One provocative exhibit points back to Africa, "Do bana coba" (Ex. 3), the only African mel-ody quoted by W. E. B. DuBois in *The Souls of Black Folk*. Dr. Eileen Southern reproduces this tune in connection with the three-line sorrow song, "probably the prototype for the blues of a later time."[21]

Ex. 3 "Do bana coba."[22]

"Do bana coba" is not only a perfect example of *a a b* form, it is also a perfect homing melody. DuBois calls it a "heathen melody" crooned by his grandfather's grandmother who was "seized by an evil Dutch trader two centuries ago."[23]

So suggestive a clue invites further research. It remains to be dis-covered if homing melody is as remote from European traditions as it appears and whether it is widespread in any music of Africa. What-ever its provenance, homing melody stands out as the chief distinction of America's most distinct contribution to world music.

Henry Leland Clarke

---

[21]Southern, pp. 191-92.

[22]W. E. B. DuBois, *The Souls of Black Folk,* 16th ed. (Chicago, 1929), p. 254; ibid., 26th ed., with introduction by Saunders Redding (New York, 1961), p. 191. All the early editions assign the melody a time signature of four-four, although the first and third measures take up the time of only seven eighth notes in each case. The alterations of the 1961 edition (indicated here beneath the staff) present the entire melody as in the meter of seven eighth notes. The latter interpretation seems preferable. While impossible in American blues melody, it is convincing in a melody from Africa.

[23]Ibid., p. 254.

# This Ae Nighte:
# Theme and Variations on the
# Lyke-Wake Dirge

The poetry of the ancient *Lyke-Wake Dirge* caught the musical imaginations of two eminent twentieth-century composers: Benjamin Britten and Igor Stravinsky. Britten's *Serenade* (1943), in which the poem was used, was one of that composer's earliest works to receive wide acclaim. Stravinsky used the poem as part of his notable *Cantata* (1952), one of several studies in the setting of English texts to which the composer devoted himself at that time.

The origin of such an anonymous folk lyric often seems impossible to trace. This stems from the fact that it comes mostly from an oral tradition, usually centuries old, and refers to a mixture of ancient beliefs that obscure its exact beginnings.

While the *Lyke-Wake Dirge* is not strictly a ballad, early references to it and versions of it are found in ballad collections and discussions assembled largely during the nineteenth century. During the seventeenth century, however, John Aubrey (1626-1697) mentions the poem in conjunction with his surveys of funeral customs in the Yorkshire county of England. Aubrey's antiquarian surveys, begun in 1671, lasted into the 1680s and were left recorded in his manuscript entitled *The Remaines of Gentilisme and Judaisme* (1686-87).[1] Aubrey was apparently the first to write down the lyrics of the *Lyke-Wake Dirge*. Although he does not attempt to capture the music of the original, he does go into much detail in translating the lyrics and relating the poem to customs of the past:

> From Mr. Mawtese, in whose father's youth, sc. about 60 yeares since now (1686), at country vulgar Funerals, was sung this song.
> At the Funeralls in Yorkeshire, to this day, they continue the custome of watching & sitting up all night till the body is

---

[1] John Aubrey, *Remaines of Gentilisme and Judaisme* (1686-1687), ed. James Britten (London, 1881).

inhersed. In the interim some kneel down and pray (by the corps) some play at cards some drink & take Tobacco: they have also Mimicall playes & sports, e.g. they choose a simple young fellow to be a Judge, then the suppliants (having first blacked their hands by rubbing it under the bottom of the Pott) beseech his Lop: [Lordship] and smutt all his face.

This beliefe in Yorkshire was amongst the vulgar (phaps is in part still), that after the person's death, the Soule went over Whinny moor and till about 1616-1624 at the Funerall a woman came (like a Praefica) and sang the following Song:

1 This ean night, this ean night,
    eve[r]y night and awle:
Fire and Fleet and Candle-light
    and Christ recieve [*sic*] thy Sawle.

2 When thou from hence doest pass away
    every night and awle
To Whinny-moor thou comest at last
            thy silly poor
and Christ recieve thy Sawle.

3 If ever thou gave either hosen or shun
    every night and awle
Sitt thee downe and putt them on
    and Christ recieve thy Sawle.

4 But if hosen nor shoon thou never gave nean
    every night &c:
The Whinnes shall prick thee to the bare beane
    and Christ recieve thy Sawle.

5 From Whinny-moor that thou mayst pass
    every night &c:
To Brig o'Dread thou comest at last
    and Christ &c:

                no brader than a thread
6 From Brig of Dread that thou mayst pass
    every night &c:
To Purgatory fire thou com'st at last
    and Christ &c:

7 If ever thou gave either Milk or drinke
    every night &c:

The fire shall never make thee shrink
and Christ &c:

8 But if milk nor drink thou never gave nean
every night &c:
The fire shall burn thee to the bare bane
and Christ recive thy Sawle.[2]

Frank Sidgwick, in his book *Popular Ballads of Olden Times,* quotes Aubrey's marginal notes and adds comments of his own regarding the manuscript that help to clarify the meaning of most of the words of the poem:

$1^1$ 'ean,' one
$1^3$ 'Fleet,' water. - Aubrey's marginal note.
$2^3$ Whin is a Furze. - Aubrey.
$2^4$ This line stands in the ms. as here printed.
$3^1$ Job cap. xxxi. 19. If I have seen any perish for want of cloathing, or any poor without covering: 20. If his loyns have not blessed me, and if he were not warmed with the fleece of my sheep, &c. - Aubrey.
$3^3$ There will be hosen and shoon for them. - Aubrey.
$4^3$ 'beane.' The 'a' was inserted by Aubrey after writing 'bene.'
$6^1$ 'no brader than a thread.' Written by Aubrey as here printed over the second half of the line. Probably it indicates a lost stanza. . . .
$8^3$ 'bane' might be read 'bene.'[3]

The term *whin,* identified by Aubrey as *furze,* is perhaps better known to some as *gorse,* the thorny evergreen shrub with yellow flowers found on heathlands all over Europe. Sidgwick also lists other sources where Aubrey's version of the poem appears.[4]

A Scottish version of the poem was recorded by Sir Walter Scott in his *Minstrelsy of the Scottish Border* in 1821.[5] Scottish customs of

---

[2]Ibid., pp. 30-32.
[3]Frank Sidgwick, *Popular Ballads of Olden Times,* Ballads of Mystery and Miracle and Fyttes of Mirth, 2d series (London, 1904), pp. 90-91.
[4]Ibid., p. 238: "1. John Brand. *Observations on Popular Antiquities,* ed. Ellis (1813), ii, 180-81. (Not in the first edition of Brand.)
2. W. J. Thoms. *Anecdotes and Traditions.* Camden Society, 1839, pp. 88-90, and notes pp. 90-91, which are reprinted by Britten (see below).
3. W. K. Kelly. *Curiosities of Indo-European Tradition and Folklore,* 1863, pp. 116-7.
4. Edward Peacock. In notes, pp. 90-92, to John Myrc's *Instructions to Parish Priests,* E.E.T.S., 1868. (Re-edited by F. J. Furnival for the E.E.T.S., 1902, where the notes are on pp. 92-94.)
5. James Britten. *Aubrey's Remains of Gentilisme and Judaisme*: the whole ms. edited for the Folklore Society, 1881, pp. 30-32."
[5]Sir Walter Scott, *Minstrelsy of the Scottish Border,* 3 vols. (London, 1821).

burial may have dictated some of the imagery in the poem, for Scott uses *sleet* (1³) instead of *fleet* in his rendering. This he translated as *salt* which was laid upon the breast of a corpse in the following manner, according to John Brand's *Observations on Popular Antiquities*:

> On the death of a Highlander, the corpse being stretched on a board, and covered with a course linen wrapper, the friends lay on the breast of the deceased a wooden platter, containing a small quantity of salt and earth, separate and unmixed; the earth, an emblem of the corruptible body; the salt, an emblem of the immortal spirit. All fire is extinguished where a corpse is kept; and it is reckoned so ominous, for a dog or cat to pass over it, that the poor animal is killed without mercy.[6]

Sidgwick suggests, however, that Scott may have miscopied the old f (=f) as ſ (=s).[7]

The evidence becomes even more confusing when one considers the definitions of the Reverend J. C. Atkinson and *The New Oxford English Dictionary*. Rev. Atkinson states in his excellent discussion on the *Lyke-Wake Dirge* in *A Glossary of the Cleveland Dialect* (1868):

> I cannot but think the fire, the fleet, and the candle-light are all connected with the Lyke-wake customs, and that *fleet* itself is either the same as Clevel. Flet, live embers, or a near connection of it. The usage, hardly extinct even yet in the district, was on no account to suffer the fire in the house to go out during the entire time the corpse lay in it, and throughout the same time a candle was (or is yet) invariably kept burning in the same room with the corpse. The efficacy of burning embers, as against the same dangers or casualties supposed to be averted by the fire and the candle-light, is not, at the least, less than that of either of them.[8]

However, *The New Oxford English Dictionary* identifies *flet* as Anglo-Saxon for house room or our *flat*. Atkinson's definition seems the more convincing because the poem's oldest extant version comes from Yorkshire.

Other differences found in Scott's version of the poem are not so controversial. For example, he uses *meate* instead of *Milke* (7¹; 8¹). He also repeats the first verse at the end of the poem, and, of course, writes the whole thing in Scottish dialect. Scott omits "no brader than

[6]John Brand, *Observations on Popular Antiquities* (London, 1841), pp. 143-44.
[7]Frank Sidgwick, *Popular Ballads*, p. 238.
[8]J. C. Atkinson, *A Glossary of the Cleveland Dialect* (London, 1868), p. 596.

a thread" and "thy silly poor," but he does point out that there was likely a verse missing where "no brader . . ." had appeared.

Finally, Scott describes the tune as "doleful and monotonous,"[9] but he does not say where he heard it, nor does he mention his poetic source.

More modern renditions of the poem seem to favor Scott's poetry, although "fleet" is retained from Aubrey's version. As found in *The Oxford Book of Ballads*, for example, it reads:

### I

This ae nighte, this ae nighte,
 —*Every nighte and alle,*
Fire and fleet and candle-lighte,
 *And Christe Receive thy saule.*

### II

When thou from hence away art past,
 —*Every nighte and alle,*
To Whinny-muir thou com'st at last:
 *And Christe receive thy saule.*

### III

If ever thou gavest hosen and shoon,
 —*Every nighte and alle,*
Sit thee down and put them on:
 *And Christe receive thy saule.*

### IV

If hosen and shoon thou ne'er gav'st nane,
 —*Every nighte and alle,*
The whinnes sall prick thee to the bare bane;
 *And Christe receive thy saule.*

### V

From whinny-muir when thou may'st pass,
 —*Every nighte and alle,*
To Brig o'Dread thou com'st at last;
 *And Christe receive thy saule.*

### VI

From Brig O' Dread when thou may'st pass,
 —*Every nighte and alle,*
To Purgatory fire thou com'st at last;
 *And Christe receive thy saule.*

---

[9] Sir Walter Scott, *Minstrelsy*, 2: 361-66.

### VII

If ever thou gavest meat or drink,
    —*Every nighte and alle,*
The fire sall never make thee shrink;
    *And Christe receive thy saule.*

### VIII

If meat or drink thou ne'er gav'st nane,
    —*Every nighte and alle,*
The fire will burn thee to the bare bane;
    *And Christe receive thy saule.*

### IX

This ae nighte, this ae nighte,
    —*Every nighte and alle,*
Fire and fleet and candle-lighte,
    *And Christe receive thy saule.*[10]

Sir Arthur Quiller-Couch explained how such a "combination" ballad comes about in his preface to *The Oxford Book of Ballads.*[11] He said that readers did not want comparative versions of a ballad, but rather one that was as "authentic" as possible. In order to create such a work, the editor has to acquaint himself with all extant versions of a ballad, then through their perusal, gain as much insight as to its character and origin as he can. He must also be able to detect errors and corruptions that the reciters may have made and, at the same time, decide which are the earlier versions. Having done all of this, the editor then turns to the work of former editors using from them what he deems fitting until he indeed does recreate one form of the poem.

If one wishes to see a presentation of comparative versions of many of the English and Scottish ballads, he must, of course, refer to the most eminent work in this field, Francis James Child's *English and Scottish Popular Ballads.* Unfortunately, Child did not include the *Lyke-Wake Dirge* in his work, no doubt because it is not strictly a ballad, although certain ballad characteristics are present in it. Its form, with the recurrent refrains and the repeated final stanza, resembles the ballad form and is related also to that of the fifteenth-century carol. Following the definition of ballad in *The Concise Cambridge History of English Literature* (1970), although not strictly a narrative, the imagery of the *Lyke-Wake Dirge* is "strong, bare, objective and free from general sentiments and reflections." It would certainly seem to be meant for singing and has been submitted to oral

---

[10]Arthur Quiller-Couch, ed., *The Oxford Book of Ballads* (London, 1927), pp. 138-40.
[11]Ibid., p. x.

tradition. Finally, although it does not deal with any of the usual ballad subjects of battle, domestic complications, deeds of heroes or outlaws, or riddles, its subject matter is starkly tragic, its rising grimness being equaled in few other poems in all of literature.

Most previous discussions of the *Lyke-Wake Dirge* link it with beliefs from other mythologies and religions. We need now to present a synthesis of these discussions as they apply to the imagery in this poem.

First, the idea of performing a dirge comes from the Roman Catholic ceremony of the Office for the Dead. In fact, the term itself is derived from the Latin antiphon, *Dirige Domine* (*Liber Usualis*, p. 1782), a part of the Office for the Dead. A dirge has become simply a musical composition designed to be performed at funeral or at memorial rites.[12] Secondly, the term *lyke* refers to the Anglo-Saxon *lic* or *lice,* meaning body or corpse, while *wake* means watch, hence, a lyke-wake is a "corpse watch."

Sir Walter Scott gives a description that refers to the performance of the *Lyke-Wake Dirge*:

> The late Mr. Ritson found an illustration of this dirge in a MS. of the Cotton Library, containing an account of Cleveland, in Yorkshire, in the reign of Queen Elizabeth. It was kindly communicated to the editor [Scott] by Mr. Frank Ritson's executor, and runs thus:—
> "When any dieth, certaine women sing a song to the dead bodie, recyting the journey that the partye deceased must goe; and they are of beliefe (such is their fondnesse) that once in their lives, it is good to give a pair of new shoes to a poor man, for as much, as after this life, they are to pass barefoote through a great launde, full of thornes and furzen, except by the meryte of the almes aforesaid they have redemed the forfeyte; for, at the edge of the launde, an oulde man shall meet them with the same shoes that were given by the partie when he was lyving; and, after he hath shodde them, dismisseth them to go through thick and thin, without scratch or scalle."—Julius, F VI. 459.[13]

With slight variations, this same journey from life to death, as described in the *Lyke-Wake Dirge,* is found in Mohammedan, Jewish, Nordic, and Teutonic beliefs. Perhaps the closest parallel travels may be found in the Nordic journey to Hela's kingdom of Nifl-heim. This

---

[12] Willi Apel, "Dirge," *Harvard Dictionary of Music,* 2d ed. rev. and enl. (Cambridge, Mass., 1969), pp. 235-36.
[13] Scott, *Minstrelsy,* 2: 361-62.

region, which was found under the earth, was reached over the rough, cold, dark roads of the extreme North, and even the gods took nine days to reach its gate. It was bounded by the river Giöll over which a crystal bridge hung by a single hair. The bridge was guarded by a skeleton named Mödgud who would not allow any to pass without a toll of blood. The dead were buried with an especially strong pair of shoes, Hel shoes, to protect them from the rough roads over which they had to pass. After passing over the crystal bridge, the dead reached the Ironwood through which they must go to reach Hel-gate. Hel-gate was guarded by the dog Garm whose rage could only be appeased by an offering of a Hel-cake, "which never failed those who had given bread to the needy."[14]

Walter Kelly points out that Christianity transformed the Norse goddess of death, Hela, into a place and "in like manner . . . transformed the goddess Ostara into a season—Easter."[15]

The next closest parallel description of the soul's journey after death may be read in Sale's preface to the *Koran,* as quoted by James Britten in his edition of Aubrey's manuscript and by W. J. Thoms in his *Anecdotes and Traditions*:

> The trials being over, and the assembly dissolved, the Mohammedans hold that those who are to be admitted into Paradise will take the righthand way, and those who are destined to hell-fire will take the left; but both of them must first pass the bridge, called in Arabic, al Sirat, which they say is laid over the midst of hell, and describe to be finer than a hair and sharper than the edge of a sword, so that it seems very difficult to conceive how anyone shall be able to stand upon it; for which reason most of the sect of the Motazalites reject it as a fable; though the orthodox think it a sufficient proof of the truth of this article, that it was seriously affirmed by him, who never asserted a falsehood, meaning their Prophet; who, to add to the difficulty of the passage, has likewise declared this bridge is beset on each side with *briars and hooked thorns,* which will, however, be no impediments to the good, for they shall pass with wonderful ease and swiftness like lightning or the wind, Mohammed and his moslems leading the way; whereas the wicked, what with the slipperiness and extreme narrowness of the path, the entangling of the thorns, and the extinction of the

---

[14]H. A. Guerber, *Myths of the Norsemen from the Eddas and Sagas* (London, 1909), pp. 180-81.

[15]Walter K. Kelly, *Curiosities of Indo-European Traditions and Folklore* (London, 1863), p. 112.

light, which directed the former to Paradise, will soon miss their footing, and fall down headlong into hell, which is gaping beneath them.[16]

Thoms further points out that the Jews speak of the Bridge of Hell as being "no broader than a thread" from which the idolators fall into perdition.

It is interesting to note here the Elf Queen's description of the "Path of Righteousness" in the ballad of *Thomas Rhymer*:

> O see ye not yon narrow road,
> So thick beset wi' thorns and briers?
> That is the Path of Righteousness,
> Though after it but few inquires.

As a matter of fact, *Thomas Rhymer* is another parallel to the *Lyke-Wake Dirge,* for Thomas also crosses into an "Otherworld" although it is not the realm of the dead. His journey takes him across a wide desert to three paths that the Elf Queen describes as the "Path of Righteousness," the "Path of Wickedness," and the "Road to Elf-land," where she is taking Thomas. Before the two reach their goal, they cross "Rivers abune the knee" and hear the "roaring of the sea." Crossing water as a means of entering the spirit world is a commonplace in literature. The means for crossing these barriers is usually by boat; however, as in Thomas, it may be by wading, or it may be over a bridge. The bridge may pass over some sort of chasm or fire, instead of water, but all barriers of this nature imply, symbolically, the great gulf which exists between life and what is beyond.[17]

Yet a third parallel route exists in the real-life way to St. Patrick's Purgatory on Lake Dearg in Ireland. Sir Shane Leslie discussed this religious shrine in his booklet, *Saint Patrick's Purgatory.*[18] His description of the way to this place, which was shown on medieval maps of Ireland, seems to read like another *Lyke-Wake Dirge,* as the soul travels over rough country and ends up at the cave known as St. Patrick's Purgatory:

> The medaeval [*sic*] journey without roads was severe: from Dublin to Armagh by horse through pathless forest and bog, or

---

[16]William J. Thoms, ed., *Anecdotes and Traditions* (London, 1839), p. 91.
[17]Lowry Charles Wimberly, *Folklore in the English and Scottish Ballads* (Chicago, 1928), p. 108.
[18]In addition to Leslie's discussion of this strange place, the reader may find the following informative: George Philip Krapp, *The Legend of Saint Patrick's Purgatory: its later literary history,* a published dissertation (Baltimore, 1900); and Thomas Wright, *St. Patrick's Purgatory: an essay on the legends of Purgatory, Hell, and Paradise current during the Middle Ages* (London, 1844).

by boats hewn out of immense trees with which to traverse lochs like Loch Eirne, which brought pilgrims within six miles of Loch Dearg. The Lake could also be approached by path over the mountains from the north. The fourteenth and fifteenth centuries bristle with travellers' tales. These stories may be placed between the fantastic Lives of the early Irish Saints and the vogue for imaginative Voyages printed in later centuries, of which Gulliver's Travels offer an abiding parody. . . .

The Visions of Tundal and Owen[19] described the adventures of *Miles Hibernensis,* who passed through a horrible valley [Tyrone and Donegal mountains] over a narrow bridge [the stone causeway from the mainland to Saints' Island] and reached an infernal pit [this was the Cave or *Puteus* which certainly existed until closed by an order of Pope Alexander VI in 1497]. The Papal Order, recorded in the Annals of Ulster for that year, stated that it was understood from old books, including the History of the Knight[20] [*Stair an Ridire*], that this was not the Purgatory Patrick got from God, although everyone was visiting it as such.[21]

It may be that the *Lyke-Wake Dirge* reflects, if not a real journey, at least the countryside of its origin. Certainly the North Yorkshire moors with their wild land, on which nothing but heather and gorse and broom grow, would be enough to conjure the image of the thorny "Whinny-moor." As far as the bridge is concerned, there seem to be a number of natural stone bridges in that area that are attributed to the Devil. For, as the Dalesman explains, "whenever our ancestors were puzzled over the origin of any artificial river crossing, they promptly blamed the Devil. One of the finest examples of his handiwork is just outside the county at Kirkby Lonsdale, in Westmorland, but the Devil's Bridge spanning the Lune on the old road from Kendal into Yorkshire is a fine introduction to a stretch of England where the Satanic stone mason has been unusually busy."[22] Keeping this information in mind, might it not be that the "Brig o'Dread" was just that—a bridge of dread, built by Satan himself, and across

---

[19]The Vision of Owen was one of the first recorded journeys to purgatory and was written down by Henry of Saltery in the twelfth century. The Vision of Tundale is a somewhat later and more elaborate description belonging between the twelfth and fifteenth century. See *Medieval Visions of Heaven and Hell* by Ernest J. Becker, a published dissertation from Johns Hopkins University (Baltimore, 1899). Leslie is somewhat mistaken when he includes Tundale with *Miles Hibernensis,* as the latter usually refers to Sir Owen. Tundale is described as a wealthy landowner. See Becker, pp. 81-82.
[20]History of the Knight is another name for the Vision of Owen.
[21]Sir Shane Leslie, *Saint Patrick's Purgatory* (Private publisher, n.d.), p. 7.
[22]"The Dalesman," compiler, *Yorkshire Facts and Records* (Clapham via Lancaster, 1968).

which lay the fires of purgatory. Of course, in the poem it is also
the Bridge of Death, but we may guess that its poetic title was no slip
of the tongue.

History tells us why the *Lyke-Wake Dirge* reflects such a mixture
of beliefs. The evidence of a large Scandinavian population is found
in the Domesday Survey of 1086, which shows the blending over the
Yorkshire area of Anglian, Danish, and Norse names. We also know
that Christianity had by then become the religion of these people. So,
we find the dead traveling in their Norse Hel shoes, which they have
gained through Christian charity, to the flames of purgatory rather
than to icy Nifl-heim.

Medieval symbolism in the poem leads to a possible Christian interpretation of this dirge. The way across "Whinny-muir" represented
the sacrifice of blood made by Christ as symbolized by the thorns.
Sinners must be purified by blood before continuing. The "Brig
o'Dread" may pass over a river into which the sinful fall in order to
be purified through water. This is also found in the sacrament of
baptism. Unfortunately, the verses concerning this passage seem to
be missing from the dirge, but Atkinson obligingly made up two in
Wardour Street Scottish:

> If ever thou gave either awmous or dole,
> Every night and alle;
> At Brigg o'Dread nae ill thou sal thole,
> And Christe receive thy saule.
> But if awmous or dole thou never gave neean,
> Every night and alle;
> Thou s'fall* an' be brusten to the bare beean,
> And Christe receive thy saule.[23]

Finally, the fires of purgatory represent the last rite of purification
a soul must go through before being allowed to enter paradise. So it
can be seen that purification by blood, water, and fire are all represented in this dirge.

After this somewhat detailed overview of the poetry of the *Lyke-
Wake Dirge* and its mythological, religious, and ethnological associations, we now turn to some of the music used to represent it.

The original tune of this dirge is virtually unknown, the music
of ballads being even more difficult to trace than the poetry. Betrand

---

[23]Atkinson, *Glossary,* pp. 603-604. *"It will have been remarked that, in every case,
the soul of the wicked, or unrighteous, or worthless man, on coming to the Bridge of
the Dead, is represented as doomed to fall and abide the consequences of falling
thousands of feet, or in whatever other way the terrors of the fall are enhanced" (Atkinson's note, p. 604).

Harris Bronson says in the introduction to his book on *The Traditional Tunes of the Child Ballads* that "relatively few of the tunes sung to those [Child's] texts were transmitted to posterity, at least in identifiable form. The great bulk of our records of the music for the Child ballads has been gathered in the half-century since Child's death from oral sources he was unable to reach." Bronson continues by saying that ballad tunes were often transcribed into dance tunes in the seventeenth century, adapted into ballad-opera texts in the eighteenth, and turned into parlor versions with major-minor accompaniment in the nineteenth.[24]

In spite of all this, it may be that the most recent musical rendition of the poem is based on a version of the ancient tune. A group of present-day folk singers, known as The Young Tradition, were given their tune by Hans Fried, "who heard it long ago from an old Scots lady, Peggy Richards," according to the notes on the 1966 recording of their arrangement. This version was published in *Sing Out Folk Song Magazine,* vol. 18, nos. 2 and 3, in New York. The harmony is that of the group, in the style of the Cooper brothers of Sussex. The words are basically those of Scott, although the spelling is different and the word *fleet* is used instead of *sleet.*

Although the rhythm of the music is $\frac{2}{4}$ in this case and is most often $\frac{4}{4}$ in the other settings to be discussed, the metre of the poem is basically iambic tetrameter and hence, might indicate a possible $\frac{6}{8}$ rhythm in the original tune since it is likely that the music would follow the rhythm of the words very closely:

This ae nighte, this ae nighte,

Every nighte and alle,

Fire and fleet and candle-lighte,

And Christe receive thy saule.

At any rate, the ancient tune does not seem to have been recorded by any of the seventeenth, eighteenth, or nineteenth-century song collectors and so would appear lost today.

Be that as it may, the poem has inspired musical settings by composers of many styles. One version, composed around 1900 by Harold

---

[24]Betrand Harris Bronson, *The Traditional Tunes of the Child Ballads,* 4 vols. (Princeton, N.J., 1959-72), 1: xix-xx.

Boulton for the collection *Songs of the North*,[25] sounds more like a nineteenth-century hymn than anything else. However, it is arranged for soloist and chorus in much the same manner as some of the old Latin chants, with the soloist singing the verses while the chorus joins in on the refrains in diatonic harmony instead of organum. In true nineteenth-century drawing-room style, the whole is accompanied by the piano in C major and does not seem very dirgelike except for the fact that it is marked "Solemn and slow" in tempo. The words used are those of Scott but skip from the first stanza to stanza seven, excluding the verses on "Whinny-moor" and the "Brig o' Dread." After a two-bar introduction the voices enter:

A more sophisticated setting was composed by Sir Donald F. Tovey in 1931 for six-part chorus (S A A T B B). The entire work appears

[25]A. C. Macleod and Harold Boulton, eds., *Songs of the North* (London, n.d.), 5:62-63.

in the form of a rondo under the descriptive tempo marking, Largo, con ritmo d'una Marcia funebre. The rondo form of *A B A' B' A"* has varied returns that allow for musical description of the stanzas involved. Although highly chromatic, the *A* sections are all in A minor while the *B*'s are in F major. The A minor sections include stanzas one and two, five and six, and nine. These are the stanzas that speak of the actual journey of the soul, while the other four sections in F tell how the soul is to pass each barrier. Tovey used word-painting in every section of the work, and he concludes the piece with a coda based on a repetition of the words of the first stanza. The poetry used was that of Scott.

Finally, we come to the two settings by Igor Stravinsky and Benjamin Britten. Both Stravinsky and Britten use the *Lyke-Wake Dirge* as a part of a larger work, and in each case, the composer has used the poem to emphasize a central theme of death.

Stravinsky described his composition as secular since three of the poems were semi-sacred while the fourth was secular. He also described its complicated overall form, which can be seen in outline in the chart following this discussion.

From Stravinsky's description, we are made to understand that form is a very important factor in this work. In truth, the work is like a Chinese puzzle-box, containing form within form. The *Lyke-Wake Dirge* functions, as Stravinsky said, as the prelude, postlude, and two interludes of the *Cantata,* thus creating a unified structure through a ritornello effect: *R A R B R C R. R* represents the sections of the *Lyke-Wake Dirge* while the other letters represent the three other poems used.

The sections of the *Cantata* are balanced in a number of ways as can be seen by the chart on the following page.

The seven sections of the work show contrast by alternating chorus and solo parts. Although Stravinsky terms his work "secular," it is interesting to note that the predominant section, Ricercar II, is sacred, and, with the two sections of the semi-sacred *Lyke-Wake Dirge* surrounding it, it becomes the main part of this large arch form: *R A R B R C R.* Sections *A* and *C* balance each other by number of measures and by being primarily secular in their poetry.

Finally, the puzzles within the puzzle are found in the canonic sections of the *Cantata.* These pieces are each canonic and sectional, their sections alternating in much the same fashion as the overall form of the work. Last, but not least, Stravinsky treats the canonic melodies in the two Ricercars serially, thus making the *Cantata* one of the

CANTATA

| Section | Number of bars | Function | Texture | Number of parts | Literary mood |
|---|---|---|---|---|---|
| R Lyke-Wake Dirge | 24 | Prelude | chordal | 3-part chorus | sacred |
| A Ricercar I The maidens came . . . | 70 | Contrast | canonic | soprano solo | secular (sacred symbols in the lily and the rose) |
| R Lyke-Wake Dirge | 24 | Interlude I | chordal | 3-part chorus | sacred |
| B Ricercar II Tomorrow shall be . . . | 165 | Contrast | canonic | tenor solo | sacred (secular symbols in dance and true love) |
| R Lyke-Wake Dirge | 24 | Interlude II | chordal | 3-part chorus | sacred |
| C Westron Wind | 68 | Contrast | canonic | soprano & tenor duet | secular |
| R Lyke-Wake Dirge | 24+17 | Postlude+Coda | chordal | 3-part chorus | sacred |

transition works from his neoclassical style to his later dodecaphonic works.

Stravinsky's setting of the *Lyke-Wake Dirge* generally ignores the poetic rhythm of the words and imposes its own musical rhythm on the poem, emphasizing the words "Fire and sleete and candlelighte/ And Christ receive thy saule," by syllabic treatment. The text is from Scott's version. The melody varies slightly from verse to verse to comply with the syllabification.

Stravinsky seems to rely on understatement to emphasize the grim tale that is told in this poem. He makes no distinction between the verses as did Tovey, but rather proceeds as if the chanted funeral dirge were ever present among the living and the loving. This impression is made because the Dirge is split into four sections and seems to be the constant reality against which birth, religious love, and secular love play their parts:

A Lyke-Wake Dirge: a song of death and the afterlife to which we all must come.

Ricercar I, "And the maidens came . . .": a song of birth or childhood with religious undertones.

Ricercar II, "Tomorrow shall be my dancing day": a song of the love of Christ, his death and promise of life after death.

Westron Wind: a song of secular love.

Stravinsky's death march leaves one haunted by the thought that all must die sooner or later, believers or not.

It is quite likely that Stravinsky knew Benjamin Britten's setting of the Dirge. Britten's *Serenade* of 1943, scored for tenor, horn, and strings, is a careful selection of poems that describe various aspects of night—the term *serenade* coming from the Italian *serenata,* meaning an evening song. After the prologue horn call, the "Pastoral" lullaby describes the coming of night as shadows play tricks on the eyes and "Phoebus" sinks in the west. The following "Nocturne" describes the setting of the sun and the twilight that follows, with Elflandish horns blowing in the distance, their echoes dying as night falls. The word *dying* leads to the thought of death as a sleep and hence to the "Elegy." In this poem, death strikes as "the invisible worm," and the consequent funeral and journey of the dead is portrayed in the following poem, "Dirge." The moon in all her silver glory is praised in "Hymn," and finally, sleep itself, with deathlike imagery, is invoked in "Sonnet." The entire *Serenade* is closed by the "Epilogue" horn call that echoes that of the "Prologue."

This work is related through mirror images; that is, the first half is reflected by the last primarily through musical mood and literary ideas. To illustrate:

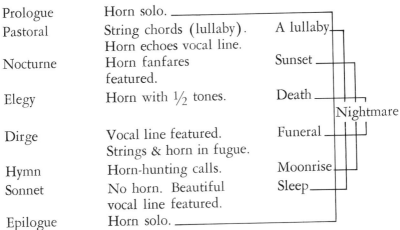

| Prologue | Horn solo. | |
| Pastoral | String chords (lullaby). Horn echoes vocal line. | A lullaby |
| Nocturne | Horn fanfares featured. | Sunset |
| Elegy | Horn with ½ tones. | Death |
| | | Nightmare |
| Dirge | Vocal line featured. Strings & horn in fugue. | Funeral |
| Hymn | Horn-hunting calls. | Moonrise |
| Sonnet | No horn. Beautiful vocal line featured. | Sleep |
| Epilogue | Horn solo. | |

Since the "Elegy" and "Dirge" form the nightmarish center of the work, it should be noted that they are more closely related musically than any of the other pairs of "images." Compare, for example, the horn solo of the "Elegy" with the vocal line of the "Dirge." The descending semitone motive of the horn and its sadness in the "Elegy" is turned into a mournful wail in the "Dirge" by the use of upper and lower neighboring tones.

In the "Dirge" the tenor begins alone on G natural, one semitone below the last note of the horn in the previous "Elegy," and sings the melody of the lament, which is repeated without change throughout the piece. In the last bar of this solo the strings enter with an eerie fugal accompaniment. The fugue's subject is only four-and-a-half bars in length and thus constantly changes its relationship to the repeated six-bar melody of the tenor. This relationship is changed at times through extensions within the fugue as in the third entrance of the fugue subject in bars 16 and 17 of the score. The fourth entry retains this extension in bars 22 and 23. After the fourth voice has completed its statement of the subject, there follows a six-bar episode that is simply a "treading of water" and dynamic building until it is time for the dramatic entrance of the horn, bar 31, emphasizing the "Brig o'Dread" and "Purgatory fire," the climax of the song.

Although the key signature is two flats, the tenor's melody is basically in Phrygian mode transposed to G, while the instrumental fugue is in Dorian mode transposed to E♭. It is this bimodality, along with the jagged fugue subject, that creates the impression of the wail of a lost soul over the flames of hell. Fear and fire burst out musically with the entrance of the horn, as mentioned above. It should be noted at this point that the whole accompaniment changes to E minor, while the voice remains in its transposed Phrygian mode. This produces some very harsh dissonances that further emphasize the dread fires and bridge. The horn part stops at figure 19 in the score, leaving voice and strings to finish the dirge with a serene warning to the marcher "who ne'er gave nane" of meat or drink during his lifetime.

It should be said that Britten does not use the Scott version but rather that given by *The Oxford Book of Ballads*. Like Stravinsky, Britten imposed his own rhythm on the lyrics for expressive purposes.

Britten has most successfully created the impression of a funeral dirge being sung over a corpse. We are made aware of the terror of facing the journey toward death by the imagery created by the fugue, while, at the same time, we are given a very clear picture of mournful lament. Britten's use of the octave glissando into each new stanza creates a continuous chant, as if the chanter, oblivious to all around him, with eyes closed, were singing over the dead body. The feeling of a procession is also made clear, first by the steady marching rhythm and second by the overall crescendo to the Brig o'Dread and subsequent decrescendo to the end, as it passes by the listener on its way to the graveyard.

Could it be said that Stravinsky finds meaning in form, while Britten finds form in meaning? Britten uses form to emphasize the words, whereas Stravinsky often subjects words to his own forms. These two composers represent divergent approaches to art. Stravinsky represents the severe classical, external approach, while Britten, on the other hand, must be considered subjective, almost romantic in his approach.

The *Lyke-Wake Dirge* has fired the imaginations of many. Its imagery, so strangely connected with distant times and places, has been a challenge to antiquarians, folksong collectors, poets, and musicians. Its mysteries have not yet been solved, and so it shall remain a challenge. Its origin and missing verses have not been found and may never be, nor has its original tune been discovered.[26]

Joan Milliman

---

[26]The Young Tradition group may have come close to it. For anyone interested, the BBC Music Library contains several renditions not discussed here.

# The Baroque and Composers
# of the Twentieth Century

The catchword "Back to Bach" was not long ago applied indiscriminately to composers who employed certain practices of the late Baroque in their writing. This was a convenient but inaccurate label. Few composers are interested in reconstructing the music of a bygone age; but music that is forward-looking may now and then profitably cast a backward glance. Long after the ecclesiastical modes had been superseded by the major and minor scales, they were found suggestive by such composers as Debussy, Ravel, Bartók, Stravinsky, Vaughan Williams, and many others, who found that the free use of modal scales provided a fresh flavor for their melodies, their harmonies, and they wrote modally colored works that moved freely from one mode to another, unhampered by a traditional modal theory.

The development of tonality was, of course, one of the great contributions of the Baroque, providing both harmonic foundation and melodic design for polyphony, and making possible the establishing of harmonic frameworks upon which the larger forms could be stretched. A major problem confronting the New Viennese School when they abandoned tonality was that of the construction of large forms. Someone has observed that the chief function of the development section of the Classical sonata is that of return to the tonic; without a tonic to return to, the form has lost its meaning. This is perhaps an oversimplificaion of the function of development: it has the equally important function of showing the musical materials in different lights, a dynamic function as opposed to the merely static one of repetition—and this is still possible even if tonality is dispensed with. Schoenberg discovered this presently; such a work as the Fourth String Quartet, entirely serial, nevertheless has the outward shape of the sonata, with its dependence upon motivic development of an almost Beethovenian kind. But the earlier works of Schoenberg and his disciples were miniatures, and those of Webern remained so.

One of the recurrent miracles of music is its ability constantly to renew itself. Offhand one may wonder why the possible permutations of available sounds have not long since been exhausted. Occasionally a new work that is tiresomely familiar before it ends may convince one that they *have* been, and that it is no longer possible to write pertinent and meaningful music without inventing a whole new aesthetic.

This is the point of view that has led to electronic music, to measured silences, to "total" organization, and to all the various schools of music-by-chance, in which the conjunctions and successions of sounds are left to coincidence or the whim of the performer. But many practitioners of these various crafts deliberately ignore or deny any relationship of their procedures to those of their predecessors. One is, obviously, free to prune one's own roots at will, and the process may be beneficial; but one severs them all at the risk of losing contact with the world about one.

A consideration of the influences of the Baroque upon musical composition in the twentieth century might begin by examining the term *baroque* itself. There is little agreement as to the derivation of the word or its application. I have seen a dictionary, published in 1911, that defines *baroque* as "in bad taste; grotesque." It is true that in times past it had a pejorative air about it, whether relating to the irregularity of a pearl or the bizarrerie of a mannered architectural style. Émile Mâle describes Baroque painting and sculpture as seeming "to express the springtime of the Church Triumphant, translated into exuberance of forms, ecstasy, and an invincible need of the infinite."[1] The principal distinction between classicism and the Baroque, according to Eugenio d'Ors, is that classicism arises from intellectuality, Baroque from vitality and instinct.[2]

Suzanne Clercx considers the Baroque "an art of movement, that is, an art in which dynamism appears as a permanent characteristic."[3] The transitional period between the Renaissance and the Baroque saw music torn between the chordal and the linear, between the resilient horizontality of polyphony and the somewhat less flexible verticality of harmonic writing that eventuated in the principle of the basso continuo.

That struggle has gone on ever since, with varying decisions. Through the Classic and Romantic periods, with few exceptions, polyphony assumed a secondary importance; save for isolated movements such as the finale of the "Jupiter" Symphony and the Grosse Fuge, the main emphases were homophonic. The superius had dissociated

---

[1] Émile Mâle. *L'Art religieux après le Concile de Trente* (Paris, 1932), quoted by Suzanne Clercx in *Le Baroque et la musique: essai d'esthétique musicale* (Brussels, 1948), p. 8.
[2] Eugenio d'Ors, *Du baroque* (Paris, 1935), quoted by Clercx, p. 13.
[3] Clercx, p. 17.

itself from the lower parts, whether by reason of contour or of pitch, and these others played the role of accompaniment. It is only within the present century that the pendulum has swung noticeably in the other direction.

The dissonantal treatment of the Baroque differed from that of the Renaissance. During the earlier period, permissible dissonances were those used in passing on weak beats, and suspensions of strong to weak beats.

Manfred Bukofzer writes that

the harmonic result of the combination of voices was conceived as a conjunction of intervals rather than as the unfolding of one chord. This intervallic harmony of the renaissance was di-ametrically opposed to the chordal harmony of the baroque. If harmony was chordally conceived, it became possible to intro-duce a dissonant note against the chord at any time, provided that the chord as such was clearly outlined. The bass, which in baroque music supplied the chords, thus enabled the upper voices to form dissonances more freely than before. The resolu-tion . . . could be effected by leading the dissonant voice to the next chord tone by either downward or upward motion.[4]

Bukofzer further points out the effect of dissonance treatment upon harmonic rhythm, or "the change of harmony per unit of time":

In a fast harmonic rhythm the renaissance composer could hardly use any dissonances, and for this reason all fast sec-tions in triple time stood out for the sparseness of dissonances. The dissonance treatment of baroque music not only permitted a fast harmonic rhythm, but supplied the main technical means for the affective style of the recitative.[5]

Emphasis upon the bass as the voice that produced chords was a natural consequence of Baroque dissonance treatment. The relation between bass and superius, which now appeared in "harmonic polar-ity,"[6] colored every aspect of melody, harmony, and counterpoint. This relation has maintained its importance almost to the present time. Brahms preferred to judge a composition by considering the relation-ship between bass and principal upper line, believing that everything else could be adjusted if these two were convincing in conjunction.

---

[4]Manfred Bukofzer, *Music in the Baroque Era, from Monteverdi to Bach* (New York, 1947), p. 10.

[5]Ibid.

[6]Ibid., p. 11.

Hindemith, too, laid stress upon what he called the "two-voice frame-work," upon which the rest of the musical texture depends. Only re-cently, and especially among the serial (or freely atonal) composers, has there been any considerable reaction against this principle.

The new concept of harmony in the early Baroque led to the use of new melodic intervals, including chromatic, augmented, and dimin-ished intervals. The rhythm of the Baroque drew away from the tactus of the Renaissance—the regular flow of beats that controlled it—in two directions: the recitative style, where the rhythms were speech-rhythms with little beat-emphasis, and the mechanically recurrent pulsations of dance music and stylized instrumental music. Between these two poles, Baroque music used all the intermediate stages of rhythm.

If, despite the basso continuo practice, Baroque textures were still mainly polyphonic, Baroque forms—at least those of instrumental mu-sic—were mainly additive. Keyboard and lute music made use of rhapsodic, somewhat improvisatory forms: prelude, toccata, fantasia, intonazione, while concerted music developed in the direction of the concerto grosso, and eventually of the solo concerto, animated by the great laws of antithesis and contrast.

And of all Baroque music, it is undoubtedly the concerto grosso that has had the greatest influence upon the music of our own time. It is to the example of Corelli and his successors, who transferred to the concerto da chiesa and the concerto da camera the respective tra-ditional sonata types, that we owe such works as the *Dumbarton Oaks* Concerto of Stravinsky and the Music for String Instruments, Percus-sion, and Celesta of Bartók.

The early or primitive Baroque was characterized by the appear-ance of purely instrumental music, especially the sonata, though this was still of uncertain form. It was this period that saw the first at-tention given to the idiomatic capabilities of voices and instruments, a subject that has played an important part in musical composition ever since. From the interchangeable parts of the Renaissance, any of which could be played or sung by whatever instrument or voice had the necessary compass, it is a long step to the development of specific styles and the conception of music in specific instrumental sonorities.

Having discovered and exploited the differences in idiomatic capa-bilities, the Baroque composer later came to discover the subleties that could be attained by deliberately exchanging idioms—transferring string ornaments to the keyboard, imitating string figurations in the winds, and so on. The richness of instrumental writing in the late Baroque owes much to this discovery.

In the seventeenth century, side by side with the efflorescence of vocal forms—opera, oratorio, and cantata—came the development of instrumental music and the rise of the concerto. By the late Baroque, which may be considered to have ended in Mannheim, Paris, and Vienna between 1740 and 1765, reciprocal influences of all these forms were operative. The fusion of sacred and secular had taken place, and in instrumental music the sonata and the concerto were its legatees, and well on the way to assuming the Classic fast-slow-fast succession in place of the conservative form of five or more movements. In these latter, the adagios had often been small in scope, serving mainly as transitions between the principal movements. It may be profitable to examine the Stravinsky work mentioned above to see what it owes to Baroque predecessors.

Stravinsky's autobiography closes too early to include any reference to the *Dumbarton Oaks* Concerto, written in 1938. Roman Vlad quotes the composer as "admitting" that the work "is based on Bach's Brandenburg Concertos."[7] To call this an "admission" raises an interesting point: it implies a feeling of discomfort or embarrassment on the part of the composer. It is more likely, of course, that Stravinsky merely pointed out what is at any rate obvious: the strong Bachian flavor of the opening movement, whose structure and contour have much in common with several of the Brandenburg Concertos: the same lithe rhythms, the same chord- and scale-derived lines, with the recurrent pedal note, the same diatonicism. Key relationships are a bit more static: such excursions from E-flat major as occur in the first pages are only tentative, not affecting the polarity of the key.

There is no clear-cut separation of concertino and ripieno in the work, though the winds and strings seldom exchange thematic materials. Even when all are participating, motives are treated more or less antiphonally. There is, to be sure, one extended episode (nos. 7-11) in which the strings do little more than accompany, while the bassoons and horns are entrusted with the thematic work. In recompense, a later episode (nos. 13-20), a fugato with many changes of meter, is given almost entirely to the strings. There is no recapitulation, though the motives of the beginning are brought back in modified form to provide a coda.

The structure of the movement is thus entirely additive, with enough reuse of thematic motives to maintain continuity. This is quite in keeping with the tradition of Bach, though he would ordinarily not use as many distinct thematic ideas in the course of a movement as Stravinsky has done here.

---

[7]Roman Vlad, *Stravinsky,* trans. Frederick and Ann Fuller (London, 1960), p. 119.

Béla Bartók's Divertimento for string orchestra, written a year after *Dumbarton Oaks,* also looks to the concerto grosso for its inspiration. Neither work represents its composer's first excursion into the forms and styles of the Baroque, but these offer perhaps the clearest demonstration of that interest.

The Divertimento, unlike *Dumbarton Oaks,* does divide its performers into concertino (in this case the string quartet) and ripieno (the string orchestra), thus coming closer to eighteenth-century practice. On the other hand, its form is clearly sonatalike, and in that respect shows the influence of a later period of schematic development. It is somewhat less contrapuntal than the Stravinsky work, though not by any means devoid of polyphonic manipulation. Bartók's ability to juxtapose textures of the greatest simplicity with those of considerable intricacy—without conveying an impression of heterogeneity—is well known.

The first thematic group, like that of the Stravinsky, has a kind of springiness in its step that betrays its Baroque ancestry. Bartók's is a syncopated theme, in a meter—unusual for him—that uses signatures of ⅜ and ⅝. The syncopations place short notes on accented beats, long notes on unaccented beats, thus imparting a Hungarian air though the meters are not at all Hungarian. But the extension of the line through variation of its rhythmico-melodic motives is accomplished by means that are clearly Baroque.

The first section is given over almost entirely to the tutti; the second presents the solo instruments antiphonally with the tutti, a measure at a time, with new thematic materials (no. 25). From this point on, the procedures are mainly developmental, unlike those in the Stravinsky work, and even though there is no clear-cut recapitulation, there is ample reemphasis on first- and second-group motives toward the close of the movement to justify its assignment to the sonata category.

Here, then, is a work that derives its spirit from the concerto grosso of the late Baroque, while its form is dependent upon later models. This can be said, too, for many works of the period; the rhythms particularly—with a good deal of stress upon recurrent pulsation—have been influential in the shaping of relatively recent musical expression.

These Baroque-type rhythms may turn up in places least expected: the melodic line that furnishes the basis of the canon in "Der Mondfleck" (no. 18) of Schoenberg's *Pierrot Lunaire* is characteristic; rhythmically it might almost have come from a Baroque concerto.

Antiphonal treatment (to some extent made necessary by differences in instrumental capabilities of the period) was, as we have seen, characteristic of the Baroque. The composer may have divided his playing forces into larger and smaller groups—concertino and ripieno —for purposes of sonorous contrast. On the other hand, he may have been led to this solution by the disparities in the idiomatic possibilities of his instruments; this is especially true when the music modulates, and those instruments incapable of following have to be left behind. We are familiar with the so-called "terrace dynamics" still a part of the Classic literature: while the strings explore the remoter keys, the winds are silent because they cannot play in those keys, and the return to the principal tonality is marked by the joyful reunion of all the participants in a fortissimo tutti.

Taking as a point of departure the idea of antiphonality for sonorous contrast rather than necessity, Bartók divides his strings into equal groups in the Music for Strings, Percussion, and Celesta, pitting them against each other in exact balance, and augmenting their sonorous resources with the other instruments. The opening fugue is not antiphonal, but the effect of the remaining movements is dependent upon the placement of the instruments: the two bodies of strings on opposite sides of the stage, with the other instruments clustered between them. The directional sense is an important factor; this work, more than any other nondramatic score of Bartók, is essentially three-dimensional.

Certain works of Stravinsky earlier than the *Dumbarton Oaks* Concerto show him in debt to the Baroque in several ways. The Capriccio (1929) for piano and orchestra is one of these. The title, Stravinsky wrote, seemed "to indicate best the character of the music."

> I had in mind the definition of a *capriccio* given by Praetorius, the celebrated musical authority of the eighteenth [*sic!*[8]] century. He regarded it as a synonym of the *fantasia*, which was a free form made up of *fugato* instrumental passages. This form enabled me to develop my music by the juxtaposition of episodes of various kinds which follow one another and by their very nature give the piece that aspect of caprice from which it takes its name.[9]

The title (Capriccio) fits Stravinsky's work only loosely; he himself says that while he was working at the composition he found his thoughts "dominated by that prince of music, Carl Maria von Weber,

---

[8]Praetorius d. 1621.
[9]Igor Stravinsky, *Autobiography* (New York, 1936), p. 159.

whose genius admirably lent itself to this manner."[10] This being the case, it would be a mistake to seek Baroque characteristics in the work thus inspired.

The Concerto in D for violin and orchestra is, however, somewhat closer to the Baroque idea. The titles of the four movements provide a clue: Toccata, Aria I, Aria II, Capriccio. Here, however, it is not merely a matter of taking old titles and disregarding their implications: three of the four movements are animated with the spirit of the late Baroque. The second Aria, for example, with its luxuriantly ornamented melody draped loosely upon a walking bass, owes allegiance to such pieces as the Chromatic Fantasy and the second movement of the Italian Concerto of Bach. While the Toccata does not really conform to the character of the Baroque solo work of the same name, which was:

> characterized by rhapsodic sections with sustained chords, rambling scale passages, and broken figurations over powerful pedal points which abruptly alternated with fugal sections,[11]

it nevertheless resembles in its mood and textures many keyboard works of Bach, and its structure, though outwardly somewhat like that of the sonata, is much freer as section follows section; there is no real development in its course. The Capriccio which serves as finale is full of Bachian melodic figurations, broken chords, rapid scales, and other devices that point clearly to its ancestry.

This is the Baroque of the basso continuo period, with little contrapuntal interest save the relationship between melody and bass; much the greater part of the work is entirely homophonic. Its models are apparently the keyboard solo works of Bach rather than the concerted works. It is altogether natural that Stravinsky, as a keyboard composer (working exclusively at the piano), should be influenced by the mechanism of the pianist's hand in the spacing of his textures, and it was to be expected that he would be more familiar with the keyboard music of the Baroque than its ensemble music, little played in the early 1930s.

Roman Vlad says of this work:

> Although there is no suggestion of actual borrowings, it would be fair to say that any . . . allusions there may be to works of the past are not used for grotesque parody effects. On the contrary, they seem to be rather a vehicle for the expression of wistful longing for the full expressiveness that

---

[10]Ibid.
[11]Bukofzer, p. 47.

music had once possessed. It can truly be said here that . . .
Stravinsky drops his attitude of revolt against romanticism and
abandons himself to the nostalgic "rechercher du temps
perdu."[12]

One is privileged, of course, to read into any music whatever one
wishes in the way of subjective interpretation. The "wistful longing
for the full expressiveness that music had once possessed" may or
may not have moved Stravinsky to the composition of the Violin
Concerto, though it is more than likely that it did not. To one listener, at least, this is less a demonstration of nostalgia for things as
they were than a calculated and deliberate exercise in the application
of old forms to new expressive purposes.

The Duo Concertant for violin and piano shares many of the
characteristics of the concerto; there are strong similarities of structure,
mood, and style. In place of the Toccata there is a Cantilena; two
Eclogues replace the two Arias; a Gigue replaces the Capriccio; and
there is a final Dithyramb which has no parallel in the Concerto, but
in its character is much like the second Aria.

Baroque characteristics continue for some time to play an important part in Stravinsky's work, but it is Paul Hindemith who, perhaps
more than any other recent composer of the first rank, turned the
procedures of the late Baroque to his advantage. His earliest available
scores show him armed with a fluent contrapuntal technique, firmly
grounded in fugue and other imitative polyphony, as well as in the
techniques of variation. His thematic material, even in the works of
his youth, tends to the "motoriness" of the concerto grosso—a "motoriness" that was indeed characteristic of much of the music of the
1920s and 1930s.

Hindemith is seen in 1922, at the outset of his career, producing
works as diverse in their techniques and points of view as the String
Quartet No. 3, with its fugal opening and its touches of bitonality (a
principle he later eschewed); the Wind Quintet, freely chromatic and
tonally contradictory; the somewhat Brahmsian Viola Sonata No. 1;
and the Piano Suite "1922," with its heavy-handed teutonic jazz. By
1925, with the String Quartet No. 4, most of these elements had been
fused in the "Hindemith style," after which, despite modifications,
there were no further stylistic incongruities.

The first movement of the Fourth Quartet is characteristic of the
"Hindemith style." It is a kind of triple fugue, the first section of
which exposes and develops a vigorous, motoric subject at considerable

---
[12]Vlad, pp. 115-16.

length. Hindemith's fugues seldom employ the conventional intervals of imitation; here the four entries of the exposition are successively on C#, E, G#, and A. There is no countersubject, though motives of the associative material recur irregularly during the working-out process.

The middle section of the movement represents a complete change of mood. It exposes simultaneously and develops two new subjects, gradually resuming the pace and character of the first section, when, after several preliminary statements of the head-motive only, the first subject returns and is combined with the other two. The coda is devoted to the first subject only.

Here in microcosm is the point of view that was to be retained in Hindemith's writing from this time on. If further evidence of Baroque influence were needed, one may cite the finale, a Passacaglia with a closing fugato, in which the melodic luxuriance, the exuberance of the writing, the urgency of the rhythms, all testify to a Baroque source.

Almost twenty years elapsed before Hindemith wrote another string quartet. One might expect to find in it sweeping changes: in 1925 the composer was but thirty years old, while in 1943 he was not far from fifty. Yet in his progress from youth to maturity he appears only to have intensified his attitudes and consolidated his techniques. Where he was content, in the Fourth Quartet, to set side by side a series of movements contrasted in mood but sharing no materials, he concerns himself in the Fifth Quartet with an over-all organization, leaving things unsaid in the earlier movements in order to close the argument in the finale.

Like the Third Quartet, the Fifth begins with a slow fugato on a chromatic subject, five statements (on D, A, G#, C, and D) with a cadential extension constituting the exposition. There are only five more complete statements in the remainder of the movement, and it stands, therefore, less as a complete movement than as an extended introduction to the lively sonatalike piece that follows. Here, too, the form is truncated: a full-fledged exposition of two thematic complexes is followed by an extended development group, but no real recapitulation takes place though there is a full close on an Eb major triad.

The third movement is a set of variations on a 61-measure theme. Four variations follow, widely differing in character. This is the only movement so far that can in any sense be considered complete—though from another point of view a set of variations is an open form and may continue indefinitely without establishing the necessity of close.

It is in the last movement, however, that Hindemith's command of the intricacies of Baroque polyphony reaches its zenith. He begins as if intending another sonatalike structure, the opening theme somewhat resembling in contour the subject of the first-movement fugato. This is only the first suggestion of reuse of materials, and the composer delays for some pages any confirmation of his intention. He sets before us other materials, two small motives,[13] and then, taking the first of these, begins what has been called a "super-fugue" as the main body of the movement. This begins simply enough with four entries (on E, B, F#, and E) and a short episode. Then follows an elaborate stretto on the fugue subject, after which all the preceding materials of the entire work are drawn, one by one, into the fabric: the first fugue subject, both themes of the second movement, the theme of the variations, and at last the opening theme of the finale, building to a broad climax and quasi-cadence. The mood changes abruptly for the coda, which is based largely upon the second of the small motives previously mentioned, with quotation of the other thematic materials.

The fugue plays a relatively unimportant part in post-Baroque music until the twentieth century, and the revival of interest in it suggests interest in the Baroque. The fugue on a single subject, as distinct from the earlier polythematic ricercari, seems to have been developed by such composers as Pasquini, Casini, and Bencini in the late seventeenth and early eighteenth centuries. After this, the fugue declined in Italy, and Domenico Scarlatti, who might have continued the tradition, displayed little interest in it; his fugues lack independence of contrapuntal writing, and his keyboard sonatas clearly anticipate the homophony of the Classic period.

Much twentieth-century fugue writing is, as might be expected, founded upon the fugal technique of Bach. It is again, perhaps, a matter of propinquity: Bach's are the well-known fugues and in many ways the culmination of fugal practice. It is natural, then, that they should be taken as models.

The fugues of Hindemith, of which two have been cited, are not necessarily Bachian in their details. *Ludus Tonalis,* for example, explores various types of fugal construction, but without countersubjects, without tonal answers, and, in a number of instances, with emphasis upon combinations of subjects, contrapuntal devices such as inversion and augmentation, and in one fugue the complete retrograde of the first half in the last.

Bartók's fugues are relatively few, though fugato passages may

---

[13]P. 46, 3rd system; p. 47, 3rd system.

be found in a substantial number of works. The only complete movement cast in the form of a fugue is the opening Andante of the Music for String Instruments, Percussion, and Celesta. This is based upon a single sinuous chromatic subject in four distinct motives that are destined to play important roles in the movements that follow. In the fugue itself, the imitations are at alternately higher and lower fifths: A, E, D, B, G, F#, etc., culminating on E♭, at which point it turns back to the beginning, the subject itself being inverted.

The movement is remarkably economical, using no materials beyond the subject itself. Lacking countersubject, episodes, and "free" voices, the texture is one of remarkable concentration. As was his custom, Bartók did modify the shape of his subject, especially intervallically, but created the entire fabric from a mere handful of notes. This kind of unanimity is almost unique in recent music; Bartók himself approached it only in the Fourth String Quartet.

Of the other devices of Baroque polyphony—canon, inversion, augmentation, diminution, retrograde, etc.—most have been incorporated into contemporary practice in one way or another, and it would be almost impossible to discover any recent score in which none of them played a part. The devices of inversion and retrogression have contributed substantially to the development of the "method of composition with twelve tones," making it possible to present the basic materials of a serial composition in four distinct forms without transposition or other manipulation.

Stravinsky's one-page Double Canon for string quartet, in memory of Raoul Dufy (1959), seems to have an air of ingenuity. The layout on the page, with noncoincident barlines, and the staves for the two lower parts beginning after and ending before the others make it appear somewhat "advanced." Upon examination, however, the work turns out to be a barren, mechanical juxtaposition of a twelve-tone row, imitated in retrograde and inverted forms at varying intervals, the phrases all of the same length, with unfortunate coincidences of sound (e.g., second system: first violin, viola, and violoncello play A#, second violin E-C#). By comparison with Schoenberg's double canon cancrizans in "Der Mondfleck" (no. 18 of *Pierrot Lunaire*), this is a rather pedantic exercise.

The Schoenberg, however, is technically much more demanding. The clarinet, imitated canonically three beats later by the piccolo, and the violin, imitated four beats later by the violoncello, play a double canon that from the middle of the tenth measure reverses direction and plays back to the beginning. At the same time, the piano plays a version of the clarinet-piccolo canon in augmentation, with added imitative contrapuntal parts, in such a way that by the time it reaches the point at which the others turned back, they have already returned to the starting point. Coupled with this is the Sprechstimme, half-sung, half-spoken, quasi-imitative, that progresses without returning upon itself. Such exercises as these, of course, can hardly be expected to make themselves clear to the listener. Retrograde forms, except in the rarest of instances, are seldom aurally identifiable, since their rhythms—the most distinguishable element—are reversed. Dotted rhythms, anacruses, and similar unequal figures change their entire character in retrograde.

It is therefore optimistic to expect the listener to know what is really going on in "Der Mondfleck" from the technical standpoint. Most of the rhythms are far too complicated to identify themselves when played backwards. Whether this matters is a moot point; the composer need not be concerned about the listener's ability to decipher his methods, so long as he finds the music in some way meaningful.

*Pierrot Lunaire* is, of course, a pre-twelve-tone work, but one prophetic of things to come. One might go in detail into processes that relate Baroque polyphony to twelve-tone composition. In one respect the composers who have recently been following Webern have provided us with a coincidence, if not an anomaly. Around 1590, as is well known, the Florentine Camerata (whom one writer calls "a noisy group of literati"[14]), under the leadership of the Counts Bardi and Corsi, attacked Renaissance music and established theories in accordance with which music was to be written. The theorizing of the Camerata is generally taken as the beginning of the Baroque era.

Since that time the sequence has been reversed: composers have written their music and left it to the analysts to deduce their theories from the works themselves. In the past few years, however, composers of the most "advanced" tendencies are once more promulgating theories before the music. In this sense perhaps we have come full circle and are on the threshold of a new Baroque.

Halsey Stevens

---

[14]Bukofzer, p. 5.

# The Musicologist in the
# Research Library

Although great libraries of music have flourished in Europe for centuries, their establishment in the United States and Canada has been a comparatively recent phenomenon. More than three decades ago, when the Music Library Association (MLA) was founded, there were few significant music collections, and for the most part they were located in such major cities as Washington, New York, Boston, Philadelphia, Pittsburgh, St. Louis, Cincinnati, Detroit, Minneapolis, Los Angeles, and San Francisco. A handful of libraries of music specializing in research materials were serving scholars at such universities as Yale, Harvard, and Rochester.

Following World War II, and particularly during the late 1950s and throughout the 1960s, a dramatic change took place. With the growing prominence given to music in the public schools, the expansion of fine arts curricula in colleges, and the extensive programs of graduate work in theory and musicology in universities, a demand arose for libraries to implement such studies. New collections of music seemed suddenly to mushroom. Simultaneously, in response to a growing general interest in all styles of music, many community libraries were developed with significant stocks of phonorecords and supporting books and scores. At present the membership of MLA includes hundreds of libraries representing collections of all sizes, located in all parts of the nation. MLA's recently established sister organization, the Canadian Music Library Association, has shown parallel growth. Within the past decade librarians from both the United States and Canada have taken an active part in the many commissions and projects of the International Association of Music Libraries (IAML).

During the 1970s the number of new music libraries has admittedly decreased, but the existing collections have continued to grow, not only in size but in the scope of their holdings and their services. As their patrons have become at once diverse in their interests and numerous in their respective demands, library objectives have likewise become varied. The term *music library* (which in former times was easily defined as a collection of musicalia) may now mean many different things: a score collection, a book collection, a record collection. Such collections may be a division of a public library, a department of a college library, or a branch of a university library. They may serve as a browsing place for the general populace, a listening-post for young and old, a performance resource for a conservatory, a reading-room for the research scholar, or a combination of several of the above. A collection of popular recordings is every bit as much a music library as is a collection of first editions and incunabula, albeit of a different kind and function. Diversity and specialization, though seemingly contradictory, exist side by side.

When a library is young, the development of its collection may appear dramatic, even spectacular. New items are acquired as rapidly as possible to fulfill the expectations of its patrons, and the library becomes a repository for many different kinds of musicalia. But as the library matures, it must inevitably reach that point at which some specialization becomes desirable—if not necessary—in order to render the sort of service demanded by its clientele. Thereafter, while containing a variety of resources, the collection is recognized for the areas of its greatest effectiveness. Thus a public library may become known primarily for its phonorecords despite the presence of scores and books, a conservatory library may become notable for its scores while containing recordings and books, and a university library may be recognized for its scholarly editions and resources for research.

The profession of music librarianship has kept pace with the development of collections. Both the variety of music library holdings and the specialized services pertaining to their use are recognized by national and international library associations. The very existence in IAML of separate commissions on public libraries of music, on conservatory libraries, on research libraries, and on *phonothèques* attests to this. Moreover, the several technical commissions (e.g., on cataloguing and classification, on bibliographical projects, and iconography) suggest the variety of knowledge expected of a music librarian. The IAML commission on education for music librarianship is currently studying the staff organization of libraries as it affects training programs for the prospective professional personnel working with musicalia. In the meanwhile, MLA has evolved a set of guidelines for studies recommended for the "complete music librarian," indicating the need for a broad background of music in its many aspects as well as an understanding of technical processes of general librarianship.

In the case of the librarian in a research library the subject training required to fill a professional position runs parallel to that of the musicologist and the theorist. At the same time, the strong graduate programs in musicology and theory in our major universities have given unprecedented impetus not only to the amassing of music resources but also to music librarianship as a profession. For a musicologist interested in musicalia (and what musicologist is not?) the research library may be the best of all possible worlds. Where else can he deal first-hand with the sources of music-making and of scholarly studies? Where else can he participate in the acquisition of new materials (an exciting adventure akin to amassing a collection of one's own), and where else can he share his knowledge with others on a one-to-one basis?

Perhaps this is why the heads of such libraries as the Music Division of the Research Library of the Performing Arts at Lincoln Center and the music research collections at such institutions as Yale University, the University of North Carolina, the University of Iowa, the University of California at Berkeley, and the University of Rochester are musicologists, most of them with scholarly publications to their credit.

Musicologists and music librarians alike have contributed generously to scholarship through their bibliographical tools. Fred Blum's *Music Monographs in Series* (New York, 1964), Sydney Robinson Charles's *A Handbook of Music and Music Literature in Sets and Series* (New York, 1972), Vincent Duckles's *Music Reference and Research Materials,* 3rd ed. (New York, 1974), Walter Gerboth's *An Index to Musical Festschriften and Similar Publications* (New York, 1969), and Anna Harriet Heyer's *Historical Sets, Collected Editions, and Monuments of Music,* 2d ed. (Chicago, 1969) are examples taken at random.

These tools and many others like them have been valuable to the researcher. A host of other projects may be undertaken. Judging from the number and nature of inquiries received by librarians in music research collections, scholars need as many indexes, checklists, descriptive catalogues, and bibliographies as can be supplied by a musicologically inclined librarian or a library-minded musicologist.

Rita Benton's *Directory of Music Research Libraries* in three parts: *Canada and the United States* (Iowa City, 1967), *Thirteen European Countries* (Iowa City, 1970), and *Spain, France, Italy, Portugal* (Iowa City, 1972), compiled for the Commission on Research Libraries of IAML, gives the location and principal areas of specialization of hundreds of research collections. Taken together, the resources of these libraries represent a formidable array of both primary and secondary sources. Now it is clear that a sort of *Répertoire International des Sources Musicales* (RISM) for nineteenth-century holdings would be a most welcome addition to our existing bibliographical tools. Although a project to undertake such a compilation has been discussed by a subcommission of IAML under the chairmanship of Donald Krummel, it is obviously too unwieldy a task to attempt on an international or even a national scale. In 1973 the consensus of the subcommission showed that an index to the holdings of individual libraries may at least seem more feasible.

To propose a catalogue or an index is one thing, but to prepare it is quite another. The cataloguer of a scholarly collection must be a scholar himself, with sufficient knowledge of sources to identify the items at hand and to describe them accurately. Because a faulty catalogue may be worse than none at all, the cataloguer is obliged to check and recheck, to make comparisons between variant editions and different printings of the same edition, and to note significant details. In a research library, therefore, there is no such thing as an over-qualified professional staff, especially in the cataloguing department and in reference.

Barry Brooks's *Thematic Catalogues in Music* (Hillsdale, New York, 1972) accounts for nearly 1,450 separate thematic indexes. But thematic catalogues do not exist for a large number of composers or for many manuscript collections. Moreover, it is not only the compositions of early writers that must be treated, for indexes of nineteenth- and twentieth-century music are also needed to implement research.

Much remains to be done in the area of American music. Most obviously, such distinctively American products as early songsters and Sunday School music books, cinema music, cafe music, musical comedy, and musicales need cataloguing and indexing. Nineteenth-century sheet music, often with beautifully lithographed title pages or engraved vignettes, represents a vast resource for American studies. The large range of jazz and pop music, heretofore considered by "serious" scholars to be merely ephemera, must be accounted for before it is too late. The possibilities seem almost endless.

Although the *Répertoire International de Littérature Musicale* (*RILM Abstracts*), the *Music Index,* and *Bibliographie des Musikschrifttums* are invaluable bibliographic aids in dealing with mid-century sources, there is a need for retrospective periodical indexing, especially for journals of the eighteenth and nineteenth centuries, as well as for those of the early decades of the twentieth.

The preparation of such bibliographical tools, while seemingly tedious, can be rewarding for the scholar-librarian who, in doing spade-work for other researchers, often makes interesting discoveries for himself. The same search for music that motivates the historical musicologist also motivates the research librarian. As a musicologist-turned-librarian, I do not advocate librarianship for all scholars of music but I do suggest that there may be such a discipline as bibliographical musicology.

Ruth Watanabe